ARTISTS & CRAFTSMEN OF THE 19th CENTURY DERBY CHINA FACTORY

David Manchip

Dedicated to my wife Gill

ARTISTS & CRAFTSMEN
OF THE 19th CENTURY
DERBY CHINA FACTORY

David Manchip

Landmark Publishing

Published by

Ashbourne Hall, Cokayne Ave
Ashbourne, Derbyshire DE6 1EJ England
Tel: (01335) 347349 Fax: (01335) 347303
e-mail: landmark@clara.net
web site: www.landmarkpublishing.co.uk

ISBN 1 84306 139 2

Print: Bath Press, Bath
Design: Mark Titterton

Front cover: Self-Portrait of William Dexter.

Back cover: Derby porcelain model of Palemon and Lavinia c.1820.
Gilded by Samuel Keys Senior.

CONTENTS

PREFACE

I think the author should be commended for taking on the investigation of the porcelain workers at the Derby Factory during the first half of the 19th century. The fact that it took him six years to do so shows how complex a task it was.

He has already proved his ability as a serious researcher by his article on the Brampton Manufactory in the catalogue, *Not just a bed of roses*, which accompanied the exhibition on William Billingsley at the Usher Gallery, Lincoln, in 1996.

Although he does not collect Derby Porcelain specifically he admits to being seriously interested in porcelain with particular reference to its social history implications.

I consider he has, once and for all, lain to rest arguments regarding the inferiority of Bloor productions. He gives compelling reasons for the presence of sub-standard wares, but shows how the workers could produce, given suitable conditions, complex pieces and services the equal of their 18th century colleagues. Indeed I had not realised that many of the Derby workers who moved to the Potteries or Yorkshire (Rockingham) proved that their Derby training had been of the highest quality, by becoming supervisors, in their particular speciality, at their new locations

Fundamental to this work is how he has unearthed and documented sources, many of them new, applicable to each individual. From the facts and statements obtained he has been able to prove some wrong, to confirm the truth of others and, by making reasonable assumptions, has been able to build up a more accurate profile of that person, than has ever been achieved previously. He has also been able to record the progress of their careers often when they moved from Derby. What, I believe, has not been done before, is to extend the research to other members of the family, even if they moved beyond the Derby orbit.

The photographs have been chosen carefully to back up the research. It is nice to be able to record that the willingness of the Derby collectors to allow their prized possessions to be illustrated continues! The freshness of the photographs adds to the appeal and effectiveness of the book.

The bar charts make it easy to compare the various workers and the times they were at different locations.

As a long-standing collector of Derby Porcelain, I believe that this entertaining and scholarly book, significantly adds to our knowledge of the period under investigation. I trust that the author will have the courage and tenacity to produce a further work on a different period. If not, his investigative powers are such that I would certainly recommend him for a job as a forensic scientist!

DR. JOHN FREEMAN

ACKNOWLEDGEMENTS

To be able to publish a book such as this requires the co-operation of many people. The gathering of information needed the help of professionals in record and register offices throughout the country. This help was always forthcoming in a courteous and cheerful way and I would like to thank them all for their endeavours on my behalf. I would particularly like to mention the staff of several of these offices for 'going the extra mile', in retrieving information which I suspected was lurking in their records.

Bridgnorth Register Office: Stoke-on-Trent Register Office; Derby Register Office; Derby Records Office, Matlock; Derby Local Studies Library, Matlock; Worcestershire Library and History Centre; Shropshire Records and Research Centre; Teeside Archives, Middlesbrough; Burton upon Trent Library; City of Westminster Archive Centre; Birmingham Record Office; Chelsea Local Studies Library; Tyne and Wear Archives Service.

Many individuals, including collectors, dealers, auctioneers, and descendants of workmen at the Derby china factory, have helped in various ways, such as the gathering of information, the location of relevant items for photographs and in many interesting discussions on aspects of the research. In this respect I would like to thank the following persons: Harry and Valerie Cordwent; Geoffrey and Valerie Peacock; Geoffrey Collins; Nicholas Gent; Rowena Edlin-White – descendant of the family of William Dexter; Michael Watson – descendant of the family of Henry Lark Pratt; Pam Hendrickson – descendant of the family of Richard Ablott; Ernest and Christine Rouse – descendants of the family of James Rouse; Vega Wilkinson; Bruce and Sue Fearn; Joan Shaw; Bryan Bowden; Ronald Moore; Malcolm and Shirley Savage; Philip Heath; Robin French; Harry Frost.

The illustrations in this book are a testament to the generosity of collectors and also to the two Derby museums in making their collections available. Without their co-operation, this book would not have been possible. Whenever I visited a collection I received a great deal of hospitality, a willingness of the person concerned to place their collection at my disposal, and a keen interest in what I was hoping to achieve. I have given credit, with the relevant photograph, to those who allowed me to do so. To those who wished to remain anonymous, I say a hearty thank you and hope that the appearance of their prized possessions in this book will give them some pleasure.

Museums are a very important part of the conservation of historical items and the dissemination of information concerning them. In order to achieve these goals they have to be both authoritative and accessible. We are fortunate to have two museums that fit this description, viz. The Derby Museums and Art Gallery and The Royal Crown Derby Museum. The numbers of photographs from these two museums that appear in this book bear witness to their support. We are also fortunate to have curators in these museums whose patience and forbearance, whilst dealing with a long, demanding list of enquiries, goes beyond the bounds of duty. In this respect, and many others, my grateful thanks go to Anneke Bambury of The Derby Museums and Art Gallery, and to Jacqueline Banks of The Royal Crown Derby Museum.

John Everett, who not only went that extra mile in his desire to help, but several hundred, took most of the wonderful photography in this book!

A research-based book is always an expensive one to produce, and I would like to thank my sponsors, Geoffrey Bond, Peter Jackson, and my brother, Peter Manchip, for their generous help.

I would also like to thank my wife Gill, for reading my manuscript and for correcting my penchant for introducing too many commas, and for her other meaningful observations.

Thanks go to Dr. John Freeman for reading the manuscript and for his valued opinions as to its content.

Finally, I would like to give a special thank you to my friend, Peter Jackson. His enthusiasm for the project was matched only by his help and support. His knowledge, concerning the products of the Derby China factory, is second to none, and his ability to pinpoint the whereabouts of items relevant to the story of particular artists was invaluable. The time he made available to me from his incredibly busy schedule was much appreciated, and the many discussions and debates we had concerning artists and their work meant that I learned a great deal from his fifty years of experience in this field.

INTRODUCTION

For far too long the products of the Derby Porcelain Factory in the nineteenth century have played second fiddle to those of the eighteenth century. Collectors clamour for pieces from the 'Golden Period' i.e. from 1785 to 1800. Not without justification, it must be said, with artists such as William Billingsley, John Brewer, Zacharia Boreman, William 'Quaker' Pegg, Thomas 'Jockey' Hill, George Complin, James Banford etc and gilders such as Thomas Soare, Joseph Stables and William Cooper.

It must be remembered, however, that some of these artists were still working well into the 19th century. Their palettes changed to reflect both changing tastes and, importantly, changing bodies and glazes. As explained by Haslem, the painters of the nineteenth century used more local colour than their predecessors, and he goes on to say, 'the glazes which were used before the beginning of the present [19th] century were so soft and fusible as to permit the colours to sink into and incorporate with them. On the contrary, the colours do not sink into the harder glazes which were afterwards introduced, but lie on the surface'. In another part of his book he says, 'a marked change is observable in the articles which were produced after 1811. Large quantities of Japan patterns were executed, rich in gilding and gay in colours, and the general style of the patterns gradually assumed a more showy character. The manufactory was, however, never without talented workmen, and numerous beautiful ornaments, and many rich services were produced which, although they differed in taste from those of the Duesbury period, possessed much artistic excellence; and at no time did the reputation of the Derby works stand higher for the production of its celebrated biscuit figures.'

Commercial pressures were on Derby as never before, firstly because Robert Bloor needed to repay the money for the purchase of the factory, and generally because of the growing number of porcelain manufactories that were to compete with Derby in the coming years. It would be fair to say that the quality of the wares between 1805 and 1848 was variable but that their top productions were the equal of any factory at this time. If they had not been so, Derby could not have survived for the length of time that it did. Haslem, when talking about some work, by Corden and an unnamed gilder, says, 'Not only were the paintings on these plates excellent, but the gilding and chasing of the different borders were of the highest class; and the manner in which all this was imitated proved that talented artists were at the time employed at the works'. Throughout this publication are the names of some of those talented artists and craftsmen.

To a large extent the names of the workers at the factory, especially the potters, kilnsmen, modellers, figure makers etc have been forgotten. The painters and gilders have fared better but there are still a large number that need to be given the credit for their work.

The research used in retrieving and compiling these lost names has utilised much anecdotal evidence from sources such as Haslem, Jewitt and various others. In fact, I have drawn heavily upon John Haslem, as we will never again have the chance to be so close to the people involved and to know some of the day to day details of their lives. However, memories are not always entirely accurate, and when workmen were asked to recall events, sometimes between 20 and 60 years in their past, they weren't always reliable. Some of the more elderly workmen, it turns out, did not accurately know their age, nor sometimes the year that they either arrived at, or left, the Derby factory. Haslem's information has therefore been used as a starting point. Various evidence has been found both supporting and disproving much of the biographies currently in the public domain. Sadly there also remains a body of this work where proof either way could not be obtained. Most of the research, however, is original and naturally varies in both quantity and quality (by which I mean in terms of human interest) from person to person. In fact, some of the lesser known amongst them, especially the potters and kilnsmen, have only the bare facts of their time at Derby, and nothing is known about the individual articles they produced. That they contributed to those beautiful objects that now stand on our shelves is beyond question and that their names should be remembered is only just.

I have tried, wherever possible, to give a rounded view of their careers and not to concentrate solely on their period at Derby. Some of the workmen were apprenticed at other factories, came to Derby, worked there for a while and left for pastures new. Some of the painters worked in oils or watercolour before they ever painted on china. Some, trained as china painters, went on to be drawing masters or artists and to have even longer careers in these fields. Some of the gilders found that they were even more talented as painters, and were called upon for this type of work. There was even a workman, trained as a gilder, who was later to earn a living as a figure modeller. The variations are endless, but however they arrived at Derby, one thing seems clear; that the inherent talent at Derby affected them. This gave rise to the saying in the Potteries that 'a Derby man has an extra wheel' and the fact that many other factories had foremen and overlookers who had previously been trained, or who had worked at the Derby factory.

I have deliberated for a long while over the timing of the publication of this book, wondering if I should continue with more research before its production. However, I have come to the conclusion that it will accomplish more by being published, so that further research will be stimulated, and even more information will come to light, and at the least I hope that this book will be a directory from which this future research can be facilitated, but naturally I hope for more!

The attributions in this book have been made as carefully as possible but in a minefield such as this Derby period I await with bated breath to be corrected.

REFERENCES

The information contained in this book is such that, by its very nature, it needs to be closely referenced. However, if every time an event is mentioned in the text, it were also given a reference, then the book, I believe, would be unreadable. To overcome this, every event from parish registers, mentioned in the text, will be explicit; i.e. it will have the name, date and place. The record office where this event can be traced will be found in Appendix B.

Where a birth date is not known, from parish register entries, efforts have been made to trace the year of birth from multiple other sources, such as census returns, death certificates, etc. Census returns for 1841, however, are only accurate to within four years, due to the method used by enumerators at this time, e.g. an entry '50' can mean an age of between 50 and 54 years. The 1851 and subsequent census returns were supposed to state the actual age, but it should be remembered that these were not always accurately recorded.

When an event has been taken from the civil register, that event will be referenced and the G.R.O. volume and page number (where known) given. The address of the relevant Register Office will then be found in Appendix B.

Any other source, from which events have been gleaned, will be made explicit in the text.

I hope that this method will enable the book to be more readable without sacrificing the ability of the sources to be found and checked.

There are many entries in parish records, in my own database, that I have not found necessary to include in this book, but if any researcher would like to have access to these, I would be willing to help.

Queries can be made by email to:
dave_manchip@lineone.net

RESEARCH AIDS

When viewing and analysing the vast quantities of documents and parish registers used in this book, I have found a number of terms which are used to describe the occupation of the person being investigated. Sometimes these are confusing, but when taken in conjunction with a term used before or after the particular event, or when used in conjunction with information from other sources, can be clarified. I have therefore given a list of these terms and their meaning in the hope that it will facilitate speedier research.

I have also made certain assumptions. These have been used to approximate the time when a particular artist or craftsman would have been producing items for the Derby factory, as a fully-fledged journeyman (i.e. having finished a recognised apprenticeship), and also the total time that this particular workman was at the factory. These assumptions, and the method by which they were arrived at, will be documented at the appropriate paragraph.

Terms used in Documents

China Painter – Term used to describe either a Painter (Landscape, Fruit or Flowers) or Gilder, normally working at the factory, but sometimes as an independent decorator.

Painter – Used mainly to describe a 'House Painter', but also to describe an Artist (painting in oils or watercolour). Has also been used when an individual has later been described as a China Painter.

Artist – Used to describe a Painter in either oils or watercolours.

Drawing Master – Teacher of either drawing or painting.

China Manufacturer – Used in two different ways. (a) Used to describe an owner or manager of an establishment manufacturing porcelain. (b) Used to describe an individual manufacturing china i.e. a 'Potter' or a 'Turner'. This has also been seen as **'China Facturer'**.

China man – Another confusing term. Normally describes an individual selling or dealing in porcelain or earthenware, but has been used to describe a workman at the factory. N.B. William Billingsley was described as a 'China man' on his marriage licence documents!

Carver and Gilder – Normally applied to carvers and gilders with wood.

Potter – Used to describe a potter working in a porcelain or earthenware factory, or as an independent manufacturer. Sometimes used (especially in Stoke-on-Trent documents) to describe anyone working in a pottery or china manufactory, with their speciality added. E.g. Potter, China Painter, or Potter, Warehouse worker. Etc.

Apprentices

As stated earlier, certain assumptions have been made in order to arrive at an approximate date when individuals reached the status of journeymen.

Very few dates of commencement or indentures have been found, but those that have indicate ages of between 10 and 14 years as those for the commencement of an apprenticeship, with the greater preponderance being between 12 and 14 years. The term of apprenticeship was normally for 7 years. There are, of course, exceptions. William Billingsley, for example, was apprenticed at the age of 16 years and his apprenticeship was shortened to 5 years, possibly in order to end before he reached his majority, i.e. 21 years. There is also the complication that sometimes children were taken on at the factory and their aptitude for a particular branch of the work was tested. If it was found that they were likely to succeed, they were indentured as apprentices. Another interesting fact is that many of the workmen tended to marry within two or three years of the end of their apprenticeship.

With all this in mind, where an individual's apprenticeship starting date is not known, but his date of birth is known[1], I have assumed an age of 12 years to be the date for the start of his time. Adding 7 years to this gives the approximate date of the start of his adult working life and the time he would be producing items at the factory, which may at some time be identified. I am not therefore claiming absolute accuracy, but these calculations enable us to be very much nearer the apprenticeship dates than is currently the case. I estimate that in the worst case any finish date should be accurate to within plus or minus two years.

[1] Since the time between birth and baptism is so variable, where no birth date is given, efforts have been made to ascertain dates of birth from later documents, e.g. census returns etc.

BIOGRAPHIES

Richard Ablott

Richard Ablott was born in Canada, in about 1815[1], and was the son of a soldier serving at Fort Garry, Manitoba. He would normally have been apprenticed at the Derby factory around 1827, and would have finished his time by about 1834. However, he appears in the list of workpeople at the factory in 1832, where he is recorded as a painter, although Haslem spells his name with an 'e', he must either have been one of the four 'boys' (probably apprentices) mentioned in this list, or have been apprenticed at a very early age, to have finished his time by the age of 17.

He was married to Sarah Rice at St. Werburgh's, Derby, on 5th May 1835, and continued to work at the factory. On 12th November 1837, a daughter, Sarah, was christened at St. Peter's, Derby, at which time he is described as a 'China Painter', living in St. Peter's Street. A further daughter, Jane, was christened at St. Peter's, on 26th June 1840, at which time he is described as a 'Landscape Painter', and was still living at the same address.

He appears to have left Derby shortly after this time, as he is not found in the 1841 Derby census returns. Haslem, in his book *The Old Derby China Factory*, says that, 'After leaving Derby, Ablott was employed by different manufacturers, chiefly in the Staffordshire Potteries, and for a time at Coalport'. Evidence to support the first part of this statement comes from the civil register of Stoke-on-Trent. The birth of a son Thomas, in 1842, at Stoke[2], was followed by the birth of a daughter, Ann, registered on 23rd November 1846[3]. At this time he was described as a 'China Painter', and the family were living at Upper Cliff Bank in Stoke-on-Trent. Another daughter, Eliza, was registered in June 1849[4], again in Stoke-on-Trent.

He then moved to Burton upon Trent, where he went into business for himself as a china dealer. It is possible that at this time he bought china in the white to decorate, which could help explain the number of porcelain plaques that are currently to be found painted by him. In the 1851 census for Burton upon Trent[5] he is described as a 'Dealer in China', living with his wife, a son, Thomas, and three daughters, Sarah, Ann, and Eliza, in Bridge Street. He was still residing there on 8th August 1855, when the birth of a daughter, Mary, was registered[6]. At this time he is described as a 'Dealer in Earthenware'. He is next found in the 1861 census returns, still living at number 25 Bridge Street, with his wife Sarah, their son, Thomas, and their now four daughters. At this time he is described as a 'China Painter', and his wife as a 'Store Keeper'. An entry in *Wright's Midland Directory of Leicester & Loughborough, With Burton on Trent 1864,* under a section entitled 'China and Glass Dealers', reads, 'Ablott Richard 27 Bridge Street'. This seems to extend his stay in Burton upon Trent for at least a further three years.

His next known move was to Shropshire to work at the Coalport factory, and Haslem, in his book *The Old Derby China Factory*, says, 'In the Derby Exhibition of 1870, Mr. Carter, of Derby, showed a dessert-service which was made at Coalport, and painted with views in Derbyshire by Ablott, and he has since had services, numerous plates, and other pieces painted with rich and highly finished landscapes by the same artist'. Confirmation of his residence in the area comes from the Madeley census returns for 1871, where he is described as a 'Landscape Painter on China' and was living with his wife, Sarah, and four daughters at Russell Terrace, Madeley. It is not known precisely when he arrived at Coalport, but it must have been some time after 1864.

He seems to have left Coalport within a few years of the 1871 census, as Haslem, writing in the present tense in 1876, says that Ablott was currently working for the Davenport factory. However, he cannot have worked there for very much longer after this date, as Michael Messenger, in his book *Coalport 1795 to 1926*, referring to Ablott, states that, 'a signed landscape has been observed on a Powell and Bishop tray manufactured between 1876 and 1878, and apparently manufactured at the factory' (Powell and Bishop seem to have been in business in Hanley, between 1867 and 1878, when they then joined with a man called Stonier who supplied crockery to shipping companies). Some support for this statement comes from the 1881 census returns for Burslem[7], where he is described as an 'Artist', born in Canada, and was living at Newcastle Street, Burslem, with his wife Sarah and three unmarried daughters, Ann, Eliza and Kate.

He died on 10th September 1895[8], at which time he was described as a 'Retired Potters Artist', and

Colour Plate 1. Landscape painted in 1832 by Richard Ablott aged 17 years, whilst still an apprentice at the Derby factory. His palette at this time shows the influence of Daniel Lucas who, during Richard Ablott's apprenticeship, would have been the main landscape painter at the factory. *Private Collection.*

Colour Plate 1a. The reverse of the plaque showing Richard Ablott's signature and the date.

Colour Plate 2. Porcelain Plaque painted and signed on reverse by Richard Ablott. Inscription 'Summer on the Thames'. Dimensions: 10 in X 7¼ in. Palette and level of sophistication suggest an early date, probably at Derby.
Sam Collins Collection.

Colour Plate 3. Porcelain plaque with a view of 'The Lower and Turk Lakes Killarney'. Painted by Richard Ablott and signed on the reverse. *Private Collection.*

Colour Plate 4. Porcelain plaque with a view of 'Innisfaller Lakes of Killarney'. Painted by Richard Ablott and signed on reverse. *Nadine Okker Collection.*

Colour Plate 5. Porcelain plaque with a view of 'Upper Lake Killarney'. Painted by Richard Ablott and signed on reverse. *Nadine Okker Collection.*

Colour Plate 6. Porcelain plaque with a view of 'The Baths at St Gervas'. Painted by Richard Ablott and signed on the reverse. *Nadine Okker Collection.*

Colour plates 3, 4, and 5 seem to be part of a series.

Colour Plate 7. Porcelain plaque painted with a riverscape by Richard Ablott. Signed lower right. *Private Collection.*

Colour Plate 8. Porcelain plaque. Rare floral painting set in a landscape in the French style by Richard Ablott. Framed size 11⅞ in X 10 in. *Descendants of Richard Ablott, Canada.*

was living at 5 Newport Street, Wolstanton, Staffordshire.

1. His age is inferred from various census returns and from his death certificate.
2. Inferred from the 1851 census for Burton upon Trent.
3. Civil Register, Births, December Quarter 1846, Stoke on Trent, Volume 17 Page 193.
4. Civil Register, Births, June Quarter 1849, Stoke-on-Trent, Volume 17 Page 222.
5. 1851 census, Burton upon Trent, Burton upon Trent Library. Listed under Indexes as Richard Abbott sic.
6. Civil Register, Births, September Quarter 1855, Burton upon Trent.
7. 1881 census for Great Britain RG11 2712/52 Page 4.
8. Civil Register, Deaths, September Quarter 1895, Wolstanton, Volume 6b Page 89.

Thomas Bagley

The origins of this workman are not known. His surname is spelt in a variety of ways in the parish registers, (e.g. Bagley, Baguley, Baggaley, Bagguley) making it difficult to be certain that it is the same person. However, there are a few other clues which help in this respect. His wife's name was Jane and there are children registered to a 'Thomas Bagley' and Jane, spelt in these various ways, in the parish registers at Derby. The first of these, George, was baptised at St. Werburgh's on 11th August 1828. In the register 'Thomas Bagguley' is described as a 'China Manufacturer', living at Ford Street, Derby.

At All Saints church, on 5th April 1830, a daughter was baptised to 'Thomas Baggaley' and Jane. This time the register records him as a 'Labourer' and he was now living at Willow Row. He is next found in the list of workpeople at the factory in 1832, where he is described as 'Thomas Bagguley' and was a 'Biscuit Fireman'. He continued to work at the factory and a son, another George, was baptised at All Saints on 5th April 1835, at which time he was described as a 'China Worker', living at Chester Place. When his daughter, Mary Anne, was baptised on 28th April 1839, he was described as 'Biscuit Fireman at the China Works'. He is finally found in the 1841 census returns for Derby under the name Thomas Bagley. In these returns he was described as a 'Potter', and was living with his wife, Jane, and three of his children at Chester Place.

It is probable that he continued until the closure of the factory in 1848, and it is possible that he transferred to the King Street works afterwards. In the recent book *Old Crown Derby China Works*, by Robin Blackwood and Cherryl Head, the authors say that according to Fred Williamson[1], a fireman named 'Baddeley' went to the King Street establishment on the closure of the Nottingham Road works. Considering the aforementioned corruption of this workman's surname, it would be no surprise to find that this is Thomas Bagley.

1. *Old Crown Derby China Works*, page 59.

Isaac Baguley

Isaac Baguley was born in Shropshire in c.1794[1], and was almost certainly apprenticed at the Coalport factory as a painter or gilder. He would have started his apprenticeship about 1806, finishing his time in 1813. His name, in the records, is constantly misspelt, and appears in different registers as Baggurley, Bagley and Baguley. The last spelling is, I believe, the correct one, as this is the spelling used on later ware of his own manufacture.

He was married to Winifred Haston at Shifnal in Shropshire, on 31st December 1815, and the couple's first child, John, was christened at Madeley on 24th March 1816. At this time he was described as a 'China Painter', and his address was given as Coalport. He continued to work at the Coalport manufactory until at least 1817 as a daughter, Phoebe, was christened at Madeley on 23rd March 1817.

He moved to Derby sometime between this date and 1819, as a daughter, Prudence, was christened at St. Alkmund's, Derby on 7th April of that year. At this time he was described as a 'China Painter' and was living at Nottingham Road. Three other children were christened at St. Alkmund's: Joseph, who was baptised on 1st March 1821; Alfred, baptised on 5th August 1822; and the last being Edwin, on 30th November 1823. Both Alfred and Edwin were later to follow in their father's footsteps and become china painters.

He left Derby, probably sometime in 1826, when there was a 'turnout'[2] of the gilders, (as described by Haslem), to go to the Rockingham factory. His daughter Emma was born in Swinton in August 1826, and she and her sister, Harriet, who was born in August 1828, were both christened at Swinton by Sheffield on 21st September of 1828.

He continued to work at Rockingham and, on 10th May 1835, three more children, Anne, Frederick and Louisa, were christened at Swinton by Sheffield.

Jewitt, quoting from a document dated 1829, states that, 'Mr. Baguley had charge of all the painting and gilding department in china and enamel earthenware'. He also says, 'At the close of the Rockingham Works in 1842, the stock, &c., was sold off and dispersed, and the manufactory which had produced so large a quantity of elegant services, &c., was entirely discontinued. A small portion of the building was taken by an old and experienced workman, Isaac Baguley (formerly employed at the famous Derby China Works), who was one of Messrs. Bramelds best painters and gilders. Here he commenced business in a small way on his own account, and continued to do some little business until his death. Mr. Baguley did not manufacture the wares himself, but purchased what he required in the biscuit and white state, from other makers, and then painted, gilt, and otherwise ornamented them for sale. At his death, his son, Alfred Baguley, succeeded him, and, for a few years, carried on this decorative branch of the business on the old premises. His mark was the same as that of the old works – the crest of Earl Fitzwilliam with the name Baguley added.'

Evidence to support Jewitt's statement is found in the 1851 census returns for Swinton, where Isaac Baguley was living with his wife, Winifred, and his son, Alfred, at the Rockingham Works. In these returns both he and his wife are described as aged 57 years and born in Madeley, Shropshire. Both he and his son are described as 'China Painters' and, as his wife is described as a 'Gold Burnisher on China', it is surmised that at some time she worked at the Rockingham factory in this capacity.

An entry in the *Gazetteer and General Directory of Sheffield 1852,* under Swinton, reads 'Isaac Baguley, china painter and gilder, and china &c., dealer'. Another, in the *General Directory of Sheffield, Rotherham, 1856*, again under Swinton, reads 'Baguley Isaac, china painter and dlr'.

Isaac Baguley died at the Rockingham Works on 28th February 1859, at which time he was described as a 'Porcelain Manufacturer'[3].

The information from Jewitt is also confirmed in a recent book, '*Rockingham 1745-1842*' by Alwyn and Angela Cox, and they add that his sons, Alfred and Edwin, were apprentice china painters at the works. They also say that in 1865, Alfred transferred the business to nearby Mexborough and remained there until his death in 1891. They comment that most of this post-1842 work is of good, but not outstanding, quality and conveys little idea of Isaac's talents as an artist. Evidence, which vali-

dates much of the foregoing, is contained in the 1881 census for Mexborough[4]. In it, Alfred Baguley is described as a 'China And Earthn Dealer' living with his wife Elizabeth and his daughter Annie, at High Street, Mexborough, Yorkshire. It is interesting to note that Annie was 24 years old and was born in Mexborough, which indicates that Alfred's family was living in Mexborough in 1857 or earlier.

[1] Inferred from 1851 census returns for Swinton.
[2] This refers to a reduction in the workforce in this department.
[3] Civil Register, Deaths, March Quarter 1859, Rotherham, Volume 9b Page 305
[4] 1881 census for Great Britain RG11 4687/138 Page 28.

Joseph Bancroft

Joseph Bancroft was born in 1796 and christened on 23rd March 1797 at Spondon, Derbyshire. He was apprenticed at Derby around 1806, as a child apprentice, and would have finished his time by 1813. His apprenticeship was as a flower painter, and according to Haslem he also learnt to paint shells.

He was one of the signatories, in 1806, to a document, agreeing to purchase the volume *The Cabinet of Arts* as a source book for their work at Derby. This agreement seems very strange as it was between a mature, established painter, John Brewer, aged 41, a painter just out of his apprenticeship, John Stanesby, aged 20, and the 10 year old apprentice, Joseph Bancroft.

Haslem says that he left soon after his apprenticeship to go to London, and shortly afterwards to the Potteries. No information has been found which either confirms or denies the first part of this information, concerning his stay in London. However, according to Godden, he was working at Mintons in October 1831, and probably earlier as his name appears in the first available wages book. Again, in his book, *Ridgway Porcelains*, he says that it appears that Bancroft was employed by John & William Ridgway for an unknown period in the mid-1820s before he joined Mintons. The reason for this statement is that the notation 'Bancroft's sprigs' appears in the Ridgway pattern book against dessert service design 937 of about 1825.

He is found in the 1851 census at Stoke where he is described as a 'Painter, Potter' (*sic*), aged 55, lodging at Penkhull. He was for many years Mintons' leading painter and continued as such until his death in about 1857.

The turn of the 19th century is a difficult period for attribution to certain painters at the factory. The work of Joseph Bancroft, John Stanesby and Philip Clavey is still to be documented. The items in Colour Plates 10 and 11 are tentatively put forward as the work of Joseph Bancroft for several reasons. Haslem makes the statement that Bancroft learned to paint flowers and shells, and in the Bemrose collection is a watercolour of shells and seaweed attributed to Bancroft by Bemrose*. Later at Mintons, Bancroft painted many items with feather groups. Although these are more sophisticated than the item shown, it must be remembered that in 1810 Joseph Bancroft was only 14 years old. Both items shown were manufactured within the period of his stay at Derby.

* See *Painters and the Derby China Works*, page 101, item 51.

Colour Plate 9. Watercolour of a hollyhock.
Said by Bemrose to be by Joseph Bancroft.
Derby Museums and Art Gallery.

Colour Plate 10. Derby Vase painted with shells possibly by Joseph Bancroft c.1810-1815. Marks: Crown, crossed batons, dots and D in red. 36 in red for gilder. Height 7 in, Width 5 ½ in.
Harry and Valerie Cordwent Collection.

Colour Plate 11. Cabinet Cup and Saucer painted with feathers possibly by Joseph Bancroft. Marks: Crown, crossed batons, dots and D in red. 25 on cup and 14 on saucer in red for gilder. Height of cup 3 ¼ in.
Harry and Valerie Cordwent Collection.

James Barlow (senior)

James Barlow was born in 1798 in Burslem, Staffordshire. He was apprenticed in about 1810, as a potter, and would have finished his time by about 1817.

He was married to Sarah Hickling at All Saints, Derby, on 28th September 1818, and at the christening of the couple's first child, James, which took place at St. Alkmund's, Derby, on 14th February 1819, he is described as a 'China man', living at Nottingham Road. The couple had a further five children christened in Derby, at which he is described variously as a 'Potter' or 'China Potter'.

He is in the list of workpeople at the factory, in 1832, in the Potting department, and subsequently, in the 1841 census returns for Derby, where he is described as a 'China Potter', living at 42 Erasmus Street. According to information given to Haslem by John Whitaker*, in 1837, on the death of James Fairbanks senior, James Barlow took over as foreman of the potters and continued as such until his own death in 1842.

Two of his sons were to follow their father into the industry. **James** was to become a china painter (see next biography) and **Richard** was to become a potter. His daughter, **Harriet**, also worked at the factory as a 'China Burnisher'.

Richard was baptised at St. Alkmund's, Derby, on 5th October 1823. He was probably apprenticed at Derby at a fairly early age, considering his father's position at the factory. In the Derby census returns of 1841 he is described as a 'China Potter', in the age group 15 to 19, living with his parents at Erasmus Street. He probably remained at the factory until its closure in 1848. He is next found in the 1851 census returns for Stoke-on-Trent where he is described as a 'Potter (Ornamental Repairer)', aged 27, living with his wife, Harriet, and their two children, James, aged two, and Harriet, aged 4 months, both born in Stoke-on-Trent.

* John Whitaker, potter, employed at Derby 1818-1848. See Biography.

James Barlow (junior)

James Barlow was the son of James Barlow senior, the foreman of the potting department from 1837 to 1842, and was baptised at St. Alkmund's, Derby on 14th February 1819. He was apprenticed to the Derby factory as a gilder in about 1830, and would have finished his time around 1837. Haslem states that as well as gilding, he also painted birds and butterflies.

He was married to Catharine Sarah Sant at Duffield, Derbyshire, on 28th August 1837 and his daughter, Sarah Ann, was baptised at St. Peter's, Derby, on 3rd September 1838, at which time he was described as a 'China Painter', and was living at Leonard Street.

He continued to work at the factory and is found in the 1841 Derby census returns, where he is again described as a 'China Painter', and was still living at Leonard Street. He continued working at the factory until near the close, in 1848.

Haslem says that after the closure of the factory, he went into the Potteries and, writing in 1876, says that Barlow had for some years been foreman for Messrs. Allerton and sons, Longton, Staffordshire. This sequence of events is not entirely correct, as there is evidence that he left Derby to work at the Coalport factory. Proof of this is found in the 1851 census returns for Madeley, Shropshire, where at this time he is described as a 'China Painter', living there with his wife and five children. His arrival at Coalport can be fairly accurately assessed as the last child to be born in Derby was James, who was born in 1845, and the first to be born in Madeley was Dorothea (registered at birth as Dorothy Harriot), who was born there in the September quarter of 1847.

The length of his stay at Coalport is not precisely known, but he was certainly in the Potteries by 1858, as a son, George, was born on 1st February at Commerce Street, Longton, in that year, at which time he was described as a 'China Painter'. This evidence supports Haslem's statement concerning the Potteries along with another birth, which is found in the Stoke-on-Trent civil register. At the birth of a daughter, Alice Catharine, on 14th September 1861[1], he was again described as a 'China Painter', living with his wife, Catharine Sarah, at Gower Street, Longton.

In the recent book *Old Crown Derby China Works, The King Street Factory 1849-1935*, the authors state that there are documents showing two small orders placed with James Barlow. In a letter sent to Sampson Hancock in 1878, he requests secrecy regarding their transactions. This letter, taken from the book, is transcribed below:

> 55 Carlisle St. Dresden
> March 5 1878
>
> Sir,
> I shall forward your ware tomorrow – Monday. I have sent you 2 comb trays, 1 taper 1 Ring Stand. I had to make 2 packages. I think with the additions and Box and hamper you must send me £2-0-0 make it payable at Dresden post office. To Catherine Barlow as I am not at home in post hours. Let this little transaction be strictly private as I am not in business now and I hold a good situation.
> Hoping you and your family are well,
> I remain
> Yours respectfully
> James Barlow.

That this concerns the subject of this biography is beyond doubt. The name Catherine refers to his wife, Catharine Sarah (Sant) and the situation he refers to is Foreman of Messrs Allerton and sons of Longton.

[1] Civil Register Births, September Quarter 1861, Stoke-on-Trent, Volume 6b Page 213.

John Beard

John Beard was born in Derbyshire in 1787, and was apprenticed as a gilder at the Derby factory. The most probable date of his apprenticeship is 1799, which means he would have finished his time by about 1806.

He was married to Harriet Porter at Duffield, Derbyshire in 1808. The couple's first child, William, was baptised at St. Peter's, Derby on 6th March 1811. At the baptism of their second son, John, at St. Peter's on 15th June 1815, he was described as a 'China Painter', and was living at Osmaston Street. A further three children were born between the years 1817 and 1824 and were christened at St. Peter's, Derby. On these occasions he was described as a 'China Painter'. Initially the family lived at Osmaston Street, but by 1821 they had moved to Eagle Street.

He continued to work at Derby until at least 1824 and most probably until 1826, when there was a 'turnout' of the gilders. During this time he was using the gilder's number 8, which he had taken over from William Longdon senior.

By the autumn of 1826 the family had moved to the Potteries where at Shelton, on 5th November 1826, their daughter Emma was christened at Bethesda Chapel. Their last child, a son, Alfred, was christened at Burslem on 26th June 1831.

Geoffrey Godden, in his book *Minton Pottery and Porcelain of the First Period*, states that John Beard's name is included under Painters and Gilders in the only available Minton wages book, covering payments from October 1831 to November 1836, and that the 1831-42 estimate book shows him to be a landscape painter. Godden thought that there was an element of confusion concerning the identity of the person listed in the wages book, as both father and son are in the Staffordshire census returns for 1841, 1851 and 1861. However, considering the early date, i.e. 1831, of the entry in the wages book, when John junior would be only 16 years old, and the fact that John senior is known to have been in the district in 1826, I think it fairly certain that it is John senior who is referred to in this document.

The entry in the 1851 Stoke census returns describes him as a ' Painter and Gilder', aged 64, born in Derby and living with his wife, Harriet, and his son Alfred, at John Street. In view of the evidence of John senior being a landscape painter at Minton, it would be wise to consider if any of the landscape work at Derby between 1806 and 1824 should be attributed to him.

His son, John, who was also to become a china painter, was almost certainly apprenticed in the Potteries. The 1851 Stoke census entry for John describes him as a 'China Painter', aged 35, and living with his wife, Anne, and their daughter Adeline. John junior died on 18th September 1872 at the age of 57 years at 11 Lansdown Street, Shelton.

Robert Blore

Robert Blore was born in 1812 but was baptised at St. Alkmund's, Derby, on 1st April 1816. By the usual calculation he would have been apprenticed at Derby, as a modeller and repairer, in about 1824 and would have finished his time by 1831. He then appears in the list of workpeople at the factory in 1832, in the Figure Makers department.

He was married to Mary Ann Fox at St. Werburgh's, Derby, on 25th December of the same year, and at the time of his wedding he was described as a 'China Potter'. The couple's first child, Joseph, was baptised on 1st December 1833, followed by another, Mary Ann, baptised on 28th February 1836, both at King Street New Jerusalemites, Derby.

Haslem, in his book *The Old Derby China Factory*, states 'Blore served his apprenticeship at the Derby factory, but left soon afterwards, and worked at Messrs. Minton's'. He then goes on to say that 'he returned to Derby in about 1830 and for a short time manufactured small articles in china at Bridge Gate. These were animals and articles of an ornamental character such as vases, ewers, &c., were mostly so small as to be little more than toys, and they resemble those made by Cocker'.

It appears however, that Haslem may have incorrect information concerning this workman. From the evidence above, it is clear that Robert Blore would almost certainly still be an apprentice in 1830, and that he was employed as an adult at the factory in 1832. It therefore seems very unlikely that he was employed at Mintons during his early career. However, he may very well have left the factory sometime after 1832, to start up in business for himself. Unfortunately, the records of the Church of the Jerusalemites do not give either occupations or addresses, so that it is not possible to detect a change of either. However, in support of Haslem's assertion that he was at some stage self employed, he was found to still be working at Derby in 1841, although not necessarily at the factory, where he is listed in the census returns for that year. In these he was described as a 'Model Repairer' and was living at Bridge Gate.

There is also a suggestion, by John Twitchett in his book *Derby Porcelain 1748-1848 An Illustrated Guide,* that Robert Blore went to work at his father's yard, although no evidence was put forward to support this possibility. In spite of this, it does seem feasible, as Robert's father, Joseph Blore, at the baptisms of his children between 1814 and 1824, was variously described as an 'Earthenware Dealer', 'Porcelain Manufacturer', and 'China Manufacturer', and during this time was living at Bridge Gate. There is also an entry in *Pigot's Commercial Directory of Derbyshire 1835,* under a section entitled 'Stone and Marble Masons' and another entitled 'Spar & Marble Ornament Manufacturers' which reads, 'Joseph Blore (and sculptor) 68 Bridge Gate'.

Haslem further states that Blore went to the Potteries to work for Mason's at Lane Delph and afterwards to Yorkshire to superintend a pottery in Middlesbrough. Although I have no evidence for Lane Delph, he was certainly in the Middlesbrough

area by 1844, as a daughter, Matilda, was baptised at the Parish Church, Middlesbrough, on 9th August 1844[1]. The register records him as 'Manager at the Pottery'.

Robert Blore arrived in the area to become the manager of The Middlesbrough Earthenware Company. Richard Otley, a Darlington man and town planner for Middlesbrough had started the company in 1834. At this time it was called The Middlesbrough Pottery Company and was managed by Joseph Warburton. By 1841, Joseph Warburton had resigned his position and bought a pub, the Queen's Head in nearby Dacre Street. The new owners, Isaac and John Wilson, took over in 1843, and it seems feasible that this is the time that Robert Blore also took over as manager. Several entries in various documents confirm his position as manager and that he is indeed the Robert Blore from the Derby factory. *Whites Directory for Middlesborough-on-Tees* for 1847 has an entry as follows: 'Blore Robt., ptry. mngr., Fvrshm. st.' At the birth of a daughter, Alice Esther, who was born on 4th April 1848[2], the family was living at Feversham Street, Middlesbrough. At this time his occupation was given as 'Potter'.

In the 1851 census for Middlesbrough, the family are found living in Graham Street. Robert is described as a 'Pottery Manager', and was living with his wife, five children and his nephew, Joseph Blore, who was described as a 'Potter'. By 1854, the family had moved back to Feversham Street, where on 30th July of that year their son, Robert William[3], was born.

Apparently, the Pottery took an active part in the life of the town, and had both a band and a cricket team. Robert Blore, who seems to have been a popular man, was a committee member of the Mechanics Institute, and many of his workforce were members. A fascinating snippet comes from a book *The Pottery That Began Middlesbrough* and is as follows: 'In 1851, when the Mechanics Institute took its Annual Whit-Sunday steamer trip (sometimes they went to Whitby, sometimes Newcastle) they had a bright idea for improving the day out. They invited the Pottery Band to come along and provide the music, paying them £1 for their trouble. The Band would appreciate a day in the fresh air. Conditions in the potteries were not what 20th century factory inspectors would tolerate. The dust from flint grinding, the lead, which formed a high proportion of the material used in glazes, all contributed to poor working conditions. But at least the factory would be warm. It must have had attractions in that respect because one night in May 1859 a Middlesbrough policeman found John Brown, a tramp, peacefully asleep on the premises – having got in "by an insecure window".'

He continued as manager and by 1857 the Blore family had moved to Wilson Street. In the 1861 census he and his family are still found at this address. At this time he was living with his wife and four children and was again described as a 'Pottery Manager'. In *Whites Directory* for 1867 he is shown as 'Bloore (*sic*) Robert, manager, 44 Albert Road'. He died at this address on 25th July 1868, aged 56 years[4], and was described as a 'Manufacturer of Pots'. So ended the career of the man who managed the very first industry in the place that was to become Middlesbrough.

Robert Blore's son, Herbert, had left Middlesbrough in his youth, but had returned with a new wife shortly before his father's death in 1868. He joined the company and eventually he also became the manager of the firm his father had managed for over 20 years. He was still the manager when the pottery eventually closed in 1887.

[1] Parish Registers at Middlesbrough Local Studies Library

[2] Civil Register Births, June Quarter 1848, Stockton, Volume 24 Page 501.

[3] Civil Register Births, September Quarter 1854, Stockton, Volume 16 Page 262.

[4] Civil Register Deaths, September Quarter 1868, Stockton, Volume 16 Page 422.

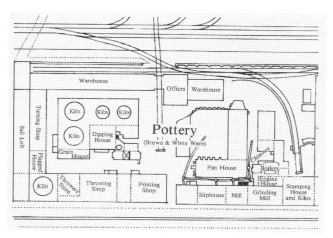

Figure 1. Plan of the Pottery in 1853. Ordnance Survey map of Middlesbrough 1854 edition. *Cleveland County Library, Middlesbrough Reference Library.*

Colour Plate 12a. Front view of 'Sleeping Endymion'.

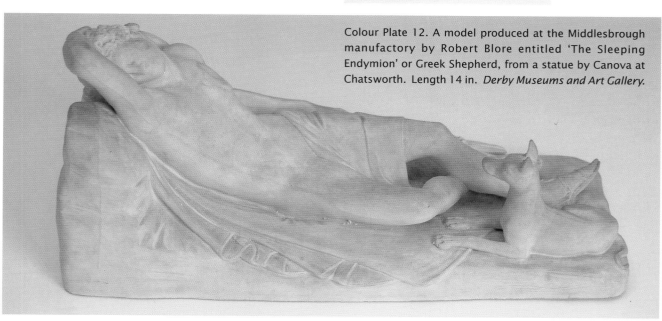

Colour Plate 12. A model produced at the Middlesbrough manufactory by Robert Blore entitled 'The Sleeping Endymion' or Greek Shepherd, from a statue by Canova at Chatsworth. Length 14 in. *Derby Museums and Art Gallery.*

John Booth

John Booth was baptised at St. Alkmund's, Derby on 20th June 1822, and was the son of Robert Booth and Letitia Sadler. He would probably have started his apprenticeship at the Derby factory about 1834 and finished his time around 1841. He is found in the 1841 census returns for Derby where he is described, along with his brother Robert, as working at the China Manufactory.

He was married to Mary Twigg at Duffield, on 26th February 1844[1]. The certificate records him as a 'Painter', living at Hazelwood, Derbyshire. His father's name was recorded as Robert Booth whose occupation was given as 'Joiner'.

At some time later, the family moved to Loughborough in Leicestershire, where on 18th May 1847, a daughter, Letitia, was born[2]. John Booth was described on the certificate as a 'Painter', and the family was living at High Street, Loughborough. However, shortly after he seems to have returned to Derby.

In the 1851 census returns for Derby he is described as a 'Journeyman/painter', aged 26, and was living with his widowed mother Letitia, his wife Mary, and his three children at Duke Street. It is possible that at this time he was working at the King Street factory, although the description concerning his occupation from 1844 onwards, and the addresses at which he was living earlier, which do not seem to associate with either pottery or china factories, leave room for doubt.

The family was still living at the same address in 1861, where in the census returns he was now described as a 'China Painter'. This indicates that he had taken up the occupation for which he was trained, and was now working at the King Street factory. The family had in the meantime increased in number with the birth of a son, John, in 1857.

He continued to work at the King Street factory and is found in both the 1871 and 1881[3] census returns where he is described as a 'Painter' and 'China Painter' respectively, and was still living in Duke Street. Since he was working at King Street for thirty years or more, and no identified work has been found, it is probable that he was a gilder.

---

[1] Civil Register, Marriages, March Quarter 1844, Derby.

[2] Civil Register, Births, June Quarter 1847, Loughborough, Volume 15 Page 145.

[3] 1881 British census returns RG11 3405/20 page 34.

Robert Booth

Robert Booth was baptised at St. Alkmund's, Derby, on 4th May 1820, and was the son of Robert Booth, a joiner, and Letitia Sadler. He would probably have been apprenticed at the factory in about 1832, and have finished his time by 1839.

He appears in the 1841 census returns for Derby, living with his brother, John, at Duke Street, where they are both recorded as working at the China Manufactory. On 28th December of the same year, he was married to Emma Simpson, at the Agard Street Chapel[1]. The marriage certificate records him as a 21-year-old bachelor, living at Bridge Street, Derby, and whose occupation was a 'China Enameler' *sic*. His father's name was given as Robert Booth.

He continued to work at the factory and when a daughter, Ann, was born on 23rd April 1845, at 7 Johns Street, Derby St Peter[2], he was described as a 'China Worker'. Later, at some time between the birth of his daughter, Ann, and the birth of a son, John, on 7th July 1847, at Coalport[3], he had moved to work at the Coalport China Factory. The birth certificate records him as a 'China man'.

For whatever reason his employment at the Coalport factory did not endure, and he returned to Derby. In the 1851 census returns for Derby, he is described as an 'Enamel Fireman' living with his wife and his three children, Robert, Ann and John, at 31 Bradshaw Street. This indicates that he had probably joined the King Street works shortly after his return from Coalport. However, on 20th July 1852, on the birth of a son, Joseph William, at Bradshaw Street, Derby[4], he is recorded on the certificate as a 'Plumber', which I believe was probably an error in recording, although all the other details concerning the family are correct.

By the year 1855 he had moved to work in Worcester. At the birth of a daughter, Letitia Frances, on 21st November 1855[5], he is recorded as 'Fireman at China Works', and was living with his wife Emma, at Park Place, St Martins, Worcester. Considering his address, and the description of his occupation, it is most likely that it was at the Grainger Factory where he gained employment.

He remained at the Worcester factory, and in the *Post Office Directory of Worcestershire, 1876*, is an entry that reads, 'Booth Robert, grocer, 69 London Road'. Later in 1879 in *Littlebury's Directory and Gazetteer of Worcester & District, 1879*, is another that reads, 'Booth Robert, shopkeeper, 69 London

Road', and 'Booth R. Jun, China Painter, London Road'. The explanation for these entries is found later in the 1881 census returns for Worcester[6]. In these returns, Robert Booth is described as 'Fireman (Enamel)', aged 61, and was living with his wife, Emma, who was described as a 'Shopkeeper, at 69 London Road Shop, Worcester St. Peter'. Also living at this address was his daughter, Letitia, who was described as a 'Painter on Porcelain', along with her sister Ann, a dressmaker.

It seems that after short stays at the Coalport and King Street factories, after his original training and employment at the Nottingham Road works, he became the enamel kiln fireman at Graingers, Worcester for at least 30 years. He died in 1886 at the age of 66 years.

[1] Civil Register, Marriages, December Quarter 1841, Derby, Volume 19 Page 479.

[2] Civil Register, Births, June Quarter 1845, Derby, Volume 19 Page 563.

[3] Civil Register, Births, September Quarter 1847, Madeley, Volume 18 Page 82.

[4] Civil Register, Births, September Quarter 1852, Derby, Volume 7b Page 347.

[5] Civil Register, Births, December Quarter 1855, Worcester, Volume 6c Page 264.

[6] 1881 British census returns, RG11 2918/16 Page 26.

Thomas Andrew Brentnall

Thomas Brentnall was christened at Horsley, Derbyshire on 4th September 1801. According to Haslem, he was apprenticed at Derby as a flower painter. He would have started his apprenticeship around 1813, and have finished his time about 1820. Again, according to Haslem, Thomas Brentnall was one of the five painters to be discharged by Robert Bloor in 1821 and who, with the others, joined the Coalport Factory. It can be seen, therefore, that as he was at the factory as a fully-fledged painter for only about one year, not much of his work will be found on Derby porcelain.

After he moved to Coalport, Godden, in his book *Coalport and Coalbrookdale Porcelain*, states that Brentnall decorated much of the ware bearing the 1820 Society of Arts mark. The length of his stay at Coalport can be partially traced by the parish registers and the later census returns.

He was married to Jane Hayward on 26th April 1825, at St. Leonard's, Bridgnorth. The couple's first child, John George, was baptised on 30th July 1826 at Broseley and his second son, William Henry, was baptised on 12th July 1829, again at Broseley.

By 1830, however, he was working at the Rockingham factory in Swinton, Yorkshire, where his name is found in the 1831 Militia List[1]. In an article in the *Yorkshire Gazette* of 14th April 1832,

Colour Plate 13. Coalport Ink-Stand c.1825, in Coalbrookdale style and marked (on the base and one of the pots) with script "Coalport" and "CD" in underglaze blue. All five pots are detachable, and flower painting is by Thomas Brentnall. *Shrewsbury Museum Services.*

Thomas Brentnall is named as one of the artists who were to work on the royal dessert service for William IV. He was still at the Rockingham factory in 1837, when a son, Alfred, was born in Swinton[2]. Exactly how much longer he was there is not known for certain, but by 1841 he was working in the Potteries, and is listed in the 1841 Shelton census returns. His son, Thomas Andrew, was born on 15th May 1846, at John Street, Shelton[3].

In his book *Old Times in the Potteries*, William Scarratt, quoting correspondence received from a former potter, lists artists that formerly worked for John Ridgway at Cauldon Place and includes 'Mr. Tom Brentnal *(sic)*, dainty landscape painter'. This information is reinforced by Haslem who states that Brentnall, 'on leaving Coalport, worked at several manufactories in Staffordshire, the latter part of his time for Messrs. Ridgway, of Cauldon Place. He died about 1869 aged 70'.

He actually died on 24th January 1871 at which time he was living at 59 John Street, Shelton, and was recorded as a 'China Painter'.

[1] Militia lists were compiled in the previous December. See *Rockingham 1745-1842* by Alwyn and Angela Cox.
[2] 1881 British census RG11 Piece 2727, Folio 29 Page 53.
[3] Civil Register, Births, June Quarter 1846, Stoke-on-Trent, Vol 17 Page 205.

Colour Plate 14. Flower-encrusted vase c.1825 painted by Thomas Brentnall. Marked with the script "CD" in underglaze blue.
Shrewsbury Museums Service.

John Brewer

John Brewer was the elder of two brothers who worked at the Derby Factory. According to Major Tapp, in an article in 1932[1], their parents were both artists and had studios in London at Rupert Street (1762-1767), Duke Street (1768-1778) and finally Mercers Street (1779-1786). This information, in fact, was gleaned from the *Dictionary of Artists*, published in 1805 by Algernon Graves, and gives details of artists exhibiting at several of the major societies, including the Royal Academy. Tapp also says that the family originally came from Madeley in Shropshire, although he gives no evidence for this statement other than quoting Haslem[2], who makes a statement to this effect in his book.

In fact, John came from a large family, all baptised in churches[3] in the area where their parents had artists' studios. Tapp states that the names of the parents were John Brewer and Ann Warburton, but this does not appear to be the case, as the children in the register were all registered to John Brewer and Rosamond, and the family was as follows:

John Brewer, born about 1760, St. Martin in the Fields, Westminster.
Penelope Brewer, christened 22nd April 1762, St James, Westminster.
George Brewer, christened 6th November 1766, St. Martin in the Fields.
Samuel Brewer, christened 29th November 1767, St. Martin in the Fields.
Penelope Brewer, christened 7th May 1769, St. Martin in the Fields.
Ann Brewer, christened 23rd September 1770, St. Martin in the Fields.
William Sheldrake Brewer, christened 5th January 1772, St. Martin in the Fields.
Sarah Ann Brewer, christened 28th February 1773, St. Martin in the Fields.
Robert Brewer, christened 28th January 1776, St. Martin in the Fields.
Nathaniel Sheldrake Brewer, christened 25th December 1779, St. Martin in the Fields.
It can be seen from the above that the first Penelope did not survive infancy.

That this is indeed the correct family can be ascertained by matching the dates of christening with the ages of both John and Robert at the time of their deaths, and by the names of their brothers, George and Nathaniel, who Major Tapp mentions in his article. Although the information in the register is not entirely readable concerning John's birth, it was in the mid 1760s. According to information on his age at the time of his death[4], his birth date was in 1765. Robert's is more accurate, and was in 1776[5]. In his article, Major Tapp mentions their brother George, who Haslem calls 'Poet George', and says that he was a personal friend of the 6th Duke of Devonshire, for whom he is said to have painted one of the ceilings in the eastern extension at Chatsworth. He published works such as *Pleasantries in Rhyme and Prose*, which was dedicated to John Hirst of Winchmore Hill. He was also said to have been a Lieutenant in the Swedish Marine.

Major Tapp, who had the benefit of contact with a descendant, also mentions Nathaniel, who he says was born in the parish of St. Paul, Middlesex, and whom he was able to trace by a medal in the possession of that descendant, Mrs. Hilda Brewer. He stated, however, that he could find no trace of him in the printed register at St Paul's, Middlesex. The reason for this of course is that the information was in the St. Martin in the Fields register, not St. Paul's.

Mrs. Brewer had 19 miniatures shown at 'The Society of Artists', between 1765 and 1773. Major Tapp, as indicated earlier, stated that her name was Ann, and in the appendix to his private publication in 1932 added this name when using the reference from *The Dictionary of Artists*. However, this Dictionary states only 'Mrs. Brewer'.

The date that John Brewer arrived at the Derby factory has, until recently, been unclear. Thorpe and Barrett quote a letter which they claim was dated 17th April 1793, from the proprietor William Duesbury II's brother-in-law Nicholas Edwards, stating that John Brewer was to take up painting on porcelain, 'tomorrow week'. In spite of this, they also said that he did not come to Derby until 1795. That letter is now known to have been dated 17th April 1795.

Further evidence for the year 1795 comes from research by Andrew Ledger, who quotes from several letters between Lygo and Nicholas Edwards, and Edwards and William Duesbury, concerning the arrival of John Brewer in Derby during April 1795. This evidence, taken together with the manuscript (undated) in the National Art Library concerning the accounts submitted by John Brewer, and which start from 29th April and continue until September of the same year, complete the case.

Supporting evidence comes from my own research and is as follows: John James Brewer was married to

Colour Plate 15. Landscape painted by John Brewer. Signed and dated 1797. *Charles Norman Collection.*

Colour Plate 16. Landscape painted by John Brewer. Signed and dated 1796. *Charles Norman Collection.*

Figure 2. Signature of John Brewer taken from his marriage certificate.

Colour Plate 17. Two Handled Chocolate Cup. Pattern 391.Painted with a bouquet of flowers similar to a Chocolate Cup and an arrangement in a signed watercolour by John Brewer, illustrated by Major Tapp in his article in 1932. Note: Pattern 391 is allocated in the 18th century Derby pattern books as 'Basket of flowers Brewer in colors'. *Private Collection.*

Colour Plate 18. A Derby 'Animal Service' Plate. Pattern 268. c.1795-1800. Diameter 9¼ in. Painted to the centre by John Brewer with two dogs in a wooded landscape. Crown, crossed batons, dots and D in blue, pattern 268 in blue. Note: This pattern is allocated to 'Brewer' in the 18th century pattern books. *The late Anthony Hoyte Collection. Photograph courtesy Neales Auctioneers Nottingham.*

Colour Plate 17a. The reverse of this cup is also illustrated and discussed in an article by Margaret Vivian in 'Antique Collecting', 1936. In this article she also illustrates a Christmas card, by John Brewer, from the collection of Mrs. Hilda Brewer, painted with a group of fruit and flowers. *Private Collection.*

Colour Plate 19. Derby porcelain Campana vase painted with a large panel of Venus Clipping the Wings of Cupid by John Brewer c.1810. Marks: Crown, crossed batons, dots and D in red. 6¾ in tall, 5½ in wide. *Peter Jackson Antiques.*

Colour Plate 20. Derby Bough pot painted with a seascape and flowers by John Brewer c.1795. Height 5½ in, width 9½ in. Marks: Crown, crossed batons, dots and D in puce. Gold X in footrim. *Private Collection.*

Colour Plate 21. Rare Derby coffee can with military scene by John Brewer c.1795. Height 3 in, Diameter 2³/₄ in. Marks: Crown, crossed batons, dots and D in puce.
Harry and Valerie Cordwent Collection.

Colour Plate 21a. Side view of coffee can.

Colour Plate 22. Derby teacup and saucer painted with military scenes by John Brewer c.1795. Cup Pattern 458, height 2¹/₂ in, diameter at rim 3 in. Saucer pattern 456, diameter 5¹/₂ in. Marks: Crown, crossed batons, dots and D in puce, with pattern numbers on each. Note: Although the pattern numbers are different, the patterns on each piece are the same and match the description in Tea Book 2, No 458. *Harry and Valerie Cordwent Collection.*

Colour Plate 23. Cabaret painted with birds by John Brewer c.1795. Marks: Crown, crossed batons, dots and D in puce. *William Allen Collection.*

Colour Plate 24. Cabaret Tray from above service showing close up of central painted panel. Tray: 15½ in X 11 in.

Mary Ann Thornton on 28[6] September 1786[6]. A witness at this wedding was George Brewer. The couple's first child, George Abbot, was baptised at St. Annes, Soho, Westminster, London, on 27th June 1794[7] which indicates that the family was not in Derby at this time.

The parents are described in the register as 'John James Brewer and Mary Ann.' Their next child, William Frederick, was christened at St. Alkmund's, Derby, on September 5th 1796. Again, in the register, the parents are described as 'John James Brewer and Mary Ann', making it almost certain that this is the same couple in each case. Charlotte, their last child, was baptised at St. Alkmund's, Derby, on 13th September 1800.

John Brewer was, therefore, working at the factory from April 1795 until he became a drawing Master in the district. Advertisements, inserted by John Brewer, in connection with his development of a practice as a 'Drawing Master', started to appear in the *Derby Mercury* in the year 1808 and continued until 1815, soliciting the favours of the 'Nobility, Gentry, and the Public of Derby'. However, the date that he left the factory is not accurately known, nor is the answer to the question of whether he painted special commissions for Kean or Bloor, during his time as a drawing master.

There are, however, several pointers which may indicate a possible date for his departure. The first of the advertisements on Thursday, February 11th 1808, states, 'Mr. Brewer returns his most grateful thanks to the Nobility, Gentry and the public of Derby and its Vicinity for support during the last two years and respectfully informs them that he continues to give instruction in the elegant Art of Drawing in Water Colours and solicits a continuance of favours. Terms may be known by application at his House, London Road, Derby.'

It can be inferred, I think, that John Brewer was still working at the factory in 1806, when he signed an agreement with John Stanesby and Joseph Bancroft[8] for the purchase of *The Cabinet of Arts* as a source book for their work at Derby. However, this advertisement suggests that he had been developing a drawing practice from about the year 1806, and that by advertising he had already, or was seriously contemplating, making it his full time occupation.

The nature of some of the following advertisements in the *Derby Mercury* were such as to indicate that his house was open from early morning until dark, for persons to view his work. He also indicated that he was prepared to travel to homes and schools to instruct pupils in the art of drawing and painting etc. Haslem states, when talking of John Brewer, 'He had a large practice as a teacher of drawing in Derby and the neighbourhood'. Not, I suggest, conducive to his continuing to work at the factory. The foregoing does not, of course, preclude him from accepting commissions, although it does suggest he would not have too much time for external obligations.

There are also certain events that took place previous to, and around this time which may have a bearing on the date of departure of John and the arrival of Robert. My researches lead me to believe that in the year 1808, there were about seven or eight major painters working at the factory. These were John Brewer, George Robertson, John Stanesby, Philip Clavey, Leonard Lead, William Wheeldon and perhaps John Wardle and Thomas Martin Randall[9] (the number may even be less, as the margin of uncertainty for their year of departure concerning both Clavey and Stanesby is 1807-1808, and nothing is known for Wardle after 1800).

If John Brewer had left the factory by 1808, along with Stanesby and Clavey, this would have left the factory very short of painters, and a replacement would normally have been quickly sought. John Brewer was very much respected at the factory, and had the confidence of his employers. So what more natural than on leaving, that his employers should act on his recommendation to employ his brother, Robert, as his replacement?

He died in 1816, and a notice to that effect was published in the *Derby Mercury* of April 16th 1816:
'On Sunday morning aged 51 of a fit of apoplexy, Mr John Brewer, landscape painter, many years resident in this town, of acknowledged abilities as an Artist, and remarkable for the modesty of his character in his own pretensions, and for his candour respecting the merits of others: He has left a family in the deepest affliction.'

The following illustrations show John Brewer's versatility by demonstrating his ability to paint a wide variety of subjects such as animals, figures, flowers, shipping, landscapes, and military scenes.

1 *The Early Derby Ceramic Artists* – The Brothers Brewer 1764-1820 by Major William Tapp, M.C. Private Circulation 1932.

2 *The Old Derby China Factory*, John Haslem, George Bell, 1876. Republished Wakefield, 1973.

3 Parish of St. Martin in the Fields and parish of St. James Westminster at Westminster City Archives, 10 St. Annes Street, London.

[4] Obituary in the *Derby Mercury* April 16th 1816.

[5] Civil register, Deaths, June quarter 1857, Birmingham Register Office, 300 Broad Street, Birmingham B1 2DE.

[6] Marriage of John James Brewer and Mary Ann Thornton 28th September 1786 at St. Martin in the Fields. Westminster City Archives, 10 St. Annes Street, London.

[7] Westminster City Archives.

[8] *Painters and the Derby China Works*, John Murdock & John Twitchett, Trefoil, 1987 & *Derby Porcelain Takes the Biscuit*, page 27, Peter Jackson, 1992.

[9] At the present time there is no solid documentary evidence of Thomas Martin Randall's dates at the Derby China Manufactory.

Robert Brewer

Robert Brewer was baptised on 28th January 1776 at St. Martin in the Fields, Middlesex (see previous biography).

Major Tapp, in his article[1], said that although Robert Brewer had two daughters, whom he names as Matilda and Emma, he had not been able to trace their birth registers. He also said that Robert had three sons: George Henry, baptised December 15th 1802; James, baptised June 14th, 1810; and Francis, baptised December 13th 1813, a well-known modeller at the Madeley factory, up to 1840. He added that this information could be found in the St. Alkmund's registers. Most, but crucially not all, of this information was correct! Robert Brewer actually had four sons, the second of whom was called John. The date and place of baptism of his first son, George Henry, was incorrect.

Haslem, in his book *The Old Derby China Factory,* says that Robert worked at both Coalport and Worcester for a short time. It appears that Robert probably did join Coalport at some stage, because he was married to Ann Hatton on 12th August 1800 at Madeley, Shropshire. He then appears to have moved, probably to an enamelling establishment in Birmingham, as their first child, Emma, who was born on 30th May 1801, was baptised there on 24th October 1805.

A further two children were born in Birmingham. George Henry was born on 12th December 1802, and John born on 5th October 1805. The children were all baptised on the same day (24th October 1805) at St. Phillip's, Birmingham. Robert then appears to have moved to Worcestershire, as another child, Matilda, was baptised at St. Peter's on 25th March 1808. Finally, sometime between 1808 and 1810 he moved to Derby, where his son James was baptised at St. Alkmund's Church on 14th June 1810. His last son Francis was also baptised at St. Alkmund's, on 13th September 1813.

Over the years, various writers have been of the opinion that Robert was the more versatile of the two brothers, but that it was hard to differentiate between them because only the surname appeared in the 18th century pattern books.

It is now clear that it is only John that is referred to in these pattern books, as Robert did not join the factory until after 1808. Therefore any item attributed to 'Brewer' via the pattern books can only refer to John Brewer. An important aspect of this information is that attributions, such as those made to pattern 268, by other researchers[2], which contain references such as "see Brewers Sett", can now be resolved.

On the death of his brother in 1816, Robert took over his position as a drawing master and Haslem says that on leaving the factory, he issued a card dated from 14, Exeter Row, Derby, on November 15th 1817. He is said to have styled himself a pupil of the 'celebrated Paul Sandby', expressed thanks for favours already received, and solicited future patronage. Haslem also says that for several years before his death he resided with a daughter near Birmingham, and died there in May 1857, in his 82nd year.

Confirmation of most of this statement is found in the 1851 Birmingham census returns, where Robert Brewer is described as a 'Landscape Painter', and was living in Bordsley Park, Aston, with his daughter, Emma, and his son-in-law, Henry Edwards, who was an Inland Revenue Officer. Curiously, the ages of all the residents are incorrect on the census form. Robert would have been 75[3] years old at this time and Emma, his daughter, 50 years old. However, that this is the correct Robert Brewer can be checked by an entry in *Aris's Birmingham Gazette* of 1st June 1857, in the 'Deaths' column, which states, 'On the 23rd, at Great Barr, Staffordshire, in his 81st year, Mr R Brewer, Landscape Painter, formerly of Derby'. His death certificate confirms this as it states that he died on 23rd May 1857 at Perry Barr, and that he was an 'Artist' of 80 years of age.

Major Tapp also mentions two of Robert's children in relation to a scrapbook, owned by descendants at the time (1932).

The scrapbook, amongst others, contains six paintings of figures, flowers and fruit by his daughter Matilda and thirteen of birds, flowers, shipping and landscapes by his son George Henry.

Colour Plate 25. Watercolour of a moonlight tavern scene painted by Robert Brewer. Framed size 20 in X 15 in. *Royal Crown Derby Museum.*

Figure 3. Signature of Robert Brewer, taken from his marriage document.

Colour Plate 26. This watercolour includes roses, ranunculi, anemones, stocks, etc. Painted and signed by Robert Brewer. *Private Collection.*

Colour Plate 27. Large Derby Campana vase painted by Robert Brewer c.1818. Marks: Crown, crossed batons, dots and D in red, gilder's numeral 33 for the gilder Thomas Till. Height 18½ in, Diameter 15 in. Late Anthony Hoyte Collection.
Photograph courtesy Neales Auctioneers of Nottingham.

Colour Plate 28. Derby porcelain Campana vase painted with a continuous rural landscape by Robert Brewer. No marks: No 1 in black. Height 16½ in, Diameter 13½ in. *Harry and Valerie Cordwent Collection.*

Colour Plate 28a. Reverse of campana vase in Colour Plate 24.

George Henry Brewer

George Henry Brewer was married to Jane Chandler on 1st June 1834 at St. Werburgh's, Derby. At the time of their marriage they were, according to information given to Major Tapp, presented with a powder box, the lid painted with a bird in landscape by Robert Brewer, and on the base the initials 'G.J.B.', which he says stands for George and Jane Brewer. The couple were in Derby until at least 1851, as in the Derby census returns at the time they had eight children – George, Matilda, Mary, Ann, Emma, John, Kate, and Harriet – baptised at St. Werburgh's, between the years 1835 to 1849. During this time he was described as a plumber, living in Agard Street, Derby.

Mrs. Mary Brewer

Major Tapp also states that a Mrs. Mary Brewer, who he says is the wife of Robert Brewer, was an exhibitor at the Royal Academy c.1850, from 4 John Street, Worcester. This is incorrect, however, as Robert's wife was Ann Hatton, and the Worcester census returns for 1851 reveal Mrs. Mary Brewer as a widow, aged 51, who was a miniature painter and photographer, born in Stroud, Gloucestershire.

[1] *The Early Derby Ceramic Artists-The Brothers Brewer 1764-1820* by Major William Tapp, M.C. Private Circulation 1932.
[2] *Sources of Animal Decoration on Derby Porcelain*, by J.C.Holdaway. Derby Porcelain International Society, Journal 3, pages 44-53.
[3] His age in these census returns is given as 71 and his place of birth as 'Kentish Town, Middlesex'. His daughter's age was given as 34 years and her birthplace as Dudley.

Francis Brewer

Robert's last son, Francis, was to become a well-known modeller at the Coalport manufactory. According to Jewitt, he started his career in Shropshire at the Madeley factory of Thomas Martin Randall, although he gives no source for this statement. Godden, in his book *Coalport and Coalbrookdale Porcelains[4]*, comments 'It has been recorded that he was a modeller at the nearby Madeley factory, which closed in 1840; but this was, in the main, a decorating establishment, giving little scope to a modeller. Brewer moved to the Coalport factory, probably in the late 1830s, as the first vase drawn in the traveller's pattern-book is called 'Brewer's vase'; and there is also a jug called

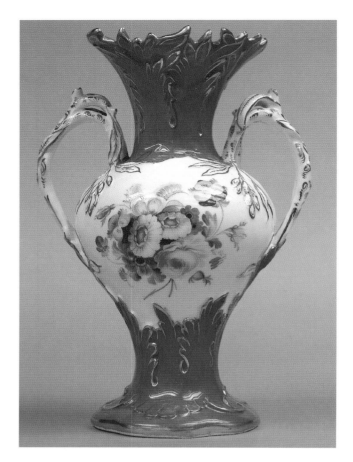

Colour Plate 29. An example of the Brewer Vase, modelled by Francis Brewer. *Courtesy of Shrewsbury Museums Service.*

'Brewer's jug', indicating that the design was the work of this modeller.'

Evidence supporting Godden's statement concerning the date of Francis Brewer's arrival at the Coalport manufactory is found in the parish marriage register on 16th August 1837, where he was married to Ann Molineux at Madeley, Shropshire. In the 1841 census returns he is described as a 'china modeller', aged in the band 25 to 29 (his age according to the Derby registers is 28), living with his wife, Ann, and his son, Herbert, who was born in Shropshire in 1840. His address at this time was given as Villa Terrace, Madeley. He continued to work at Coalport until at least 1851, when he is again found in the census returns for this area, although the enumerator had entered his name as 'James Brewer'. It is obvious from the description of the rest of the family that this is indeed Francis Brewer and his family.

[1] *Coalport and Coalbrookdale Porcelains*, G. Godden, Herbert Jenkins, London, 1970.

Joseph Brock

Joseph Brock was baptised in the parish of Saint Botolph Without Aldersgate, London, on 28th May 1786. He would probably have started his apprenticeship around 1798 and finished his time by 1805. On 28th May 1809, he was married to Sarah Furniss at All Saints, Derby.

Haslem, in a brief statement, while talking about Joseph's grandson, the sculptor Thomas Brock, states that Joseph worked at Derby for the first quarter of the 19th century, before going to Worcester, where he worked for a further 25 years.

Proof of the first part of the statement, concerning Derby, comes from the parish registers where his first child, a daughter, Jane Mary, was baptised at All Saints on 7th August 1811. When his second daughter, Jane Furness, was baptised at All Saints, on 3rd March 1813, he was described in the register as a 'China Painter', and was living at Searl Street. The last child baptised in Derby was William, who was baptised on 11th March 1824 at St. Werburgh's.

At this time he was again described as a 'China Painter' and was still living at Searl Street.

However, when he left the Derby factory, he did not go directly to Worcester as suggested by Haslem. Rather he went to Shelton, in Staffordshire, where it is possible that he worked for Ridgway. Evidence, which supports his move to the Potteries, is in the register of baptisms at the Bethesda Chapel, Shelton, where on 7th May 1826, a son, John, was christened.

He is next found in the 1841 census returns for Worcester, where he is described as a 'China Gilder', and was living with his wife, Sarah, and his four children, Ann, Thomas, William and John, at 24 Tallow Hill, in the parish of St. Martins. The census returns show that all of the children were born outside the county.

The entries, in the 1851 Worcester census returns, show that he had given up china painting by this time, as he is described as a 'Messinger (sic) in a solicitors office', aged 64, but was still living with his wife, Sarah, at the same address.

Colour Plate 30. Derby cup and saucer possibly gilded by Joseph Brock* c.1830. Cup height 2½ in, Saucer diameter 5½ in. Marks: Printed crown and D in red. Gilder's numeral 14 in red for Joseph Brock on saucer. *Royal Crown Derby Museum.*

* The items shown in Colour Plate 30 are attributed in the Royal Crown Derby collection to Joseph Brock and illustrate the difficulty in attributing work to a particular gilder in the period 1825-1848. Unfortunately there are a number of variables. (a) A particular gilder's numeral, where known, is from a list c.1820. (b) Porcelain type is not currently accurately dated. (c) The date of the introduction of particular factory marks is not precisely known. In the case of the items concerned, the gilder's numeral would indicate Joseph Brock. However, current information has the introduction of the mark "Gothic Crown over D" at 1830-1834. This would preclude Joseph Brock as the gilder of these items, as he left the factory between 1824 and 1826. However, more research needs to be undertaken to establish greater accuracy concerning factors (b) and (c).

Colour Plate 31. Derby shaped circular dessert plate painted by Thomas Steel. Marks: Crown, crossed batons, dots and D in red, gilder's numeral 14 in red for Joseph Brock. Diameter 8¾ in. *Late Anthony Hoyte Collection. Photograph Courtesy Neales Auctioneers of Nottingham.*

Joseph Broughton

Joseph Broughton was christened at All Saints on 6th September 1804, and according to Haslem was apprenticed at Derby in 1816 when he was eleven years old *(sic)* and served his apprenticeship to japan painting and gilding. He would, therefore, have finished his apprenticeship around 1823.

Haslem goes on to say, 'with the exception of an interval of a few weeks, he continued at the old works until they were closed, a period of thirty-two years. Afterwards, and until within some ten days of his death in July 1875, he was constantly employed at the small establishment in King Street.'

Evidence, which supports all of Haslem's statement, is as follows. He was married to Mary Cook on 6th October 1829 at St. Werburgh's. The couple's first child, a daughter, Sarah Ann, was baptised at St. Alkmund's, Derby, on 6th January 1832, at which time he was described as a 'China Painter'. He is also found in the list of workpeople at the Derby factory in 1832, where he is recorded as a gilder. A further seven children were born to the couple between 1834 and 1849, during which time the family lived firstly at Deans Row and then at Nottingham Road,

Derby. He is described as a 'China Painter', living at Deans Row with his wife, Mary, and five of their children in the 1841 Derby census returns.

After the close of the works he was employed at the King Street factory, and is found in the 1851 Derby census living with his wife, Mary, and their six children at Nottingham Road, at which time he was described as a 'China Painter'. Later at the marriage of his son, Alfred, at St. Alkmund's, Derby, on 27th September 1856, he was again described, on the marriage certificate, as a 'China Painter'. He is next found in the 1871 census for Derby, where he was then described as a 'China Gilder', living with his wife and family at 12 Bath Street. He then continued working at King Street until within ten days of his death, in July 1875.

In the 1820 list of gilders, which was compiled by Haslem from information supplied by Joseph Broughton, his number is stated to be 16. Since the workmen retained their numbers until they either died or left the factory, this number, when found on pieces from about 1820 until the close of the factory in 1848, will identify his work. From the above it can be seen that he had a career, between the two Derby factories, spanning fifty-nine years.

40

Colour Plate 32. Rare Derby teapot c.1812-1815 gilded by Joseph Broughton. Marks: Crown, crossed batons, dots and D in red. 16 in red for Joseph Broughton. *Derby Museums and Art Gallery.*

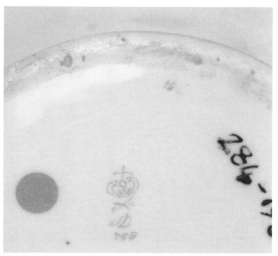

Colour Plate 32a. Base of teapot showing pattern number and gilder's numeral 16 for Joseph Broughton.

Thomas Broughton

Thomas Broughton, a gilder, was born in 1796. The place of his birth, however, is not known. He was married in Derby, at St. Werburgh's on 7th February 1820, to Maria Penton. Presumably he would therefore have been in Derby for some time previously.

The couple's first child, John Penton, was baptised at St. Werburgh's, Derby, on 7th April 1821, at which time he is described as a ' China Painter' and was living at Bold Lane. He remained at Derby until atleast August 1829, as the death of his son John Penton was recorded at St. Werburgh's on the 29th of that month. However, he appears to have left

Derby shortly after, as a daughter, Frances, was baptised at Madeley, Shropshire, on 18th April 1824. It can be surmised from this that he left to work at the Coalport China Manufactory.

Two more children were born in Madeley. Alfred was baptised on 23rd April 1832 at the Methodist New Connection Church at Madeley, and Henry was baptised at the same church on 13th July 1835.

He died on 16th February 1845[1], at which time he was described as a 'China Gilder', aged 49 years, and was living at Madeley Wood.

[1] Civil Register, Deaths, March Quarter 1845, Madeley, Volume 18 Page 845.

Joseph Bullock (junior)

Joseph Bullock was the son of Joseph Bullock senior, who was a gilder at the Derby Factory in the eighteenth century. He was christened at Brookside Chapel Independent, Derby, on 12th June 1795. He would have been apprenticed at Derby as a gilder in about 1807, and have finished his time by 1814.

He was married to Elizabeth Clark on 16th June 1817. The couple's first child, William, was christened at St. Alkmund's, Derby on 1st December 1817. At this time he is described as a 'China Painter', and was living at Bridge Gate. He continued to work at Derby until at least 1827 as a daughter, Ann, was christened at St. Alkmund's, Derby, on 15th April of that year.

He appears to have left the factory shortly after, as a son, James, was christened at Swinton by Sheffield on 24th May 1829, where he is described as a 'China Painter'. How long he stayed at the Rockingham factory is not known.

Alwyn and Angela Cox, in their book, *Rockingham 1745-1842*, state that a man called James Bullough worked at Swinton as a potter and that in a document dated 1829 he is described as 'a sorter of biscuit ware'. They say he was subsequently trained as a china painter, since he is so described in both the 1828 Militia List and the parish registers in 1829. I would respectfully suggest that the man who was described as a potter and sorter of biscuit ware was another workman, and that the entries in both the Derby and Swinton registers record the name Joseph Bullock and his wife Elizabeth.

However, he had returned to Derby by 1834[1] as a son, John, was born in Derby at this time. In 1841 his wife Elizabeth died, and on 20th October 1846, he was married to Maria Broughton, the widow of Thomas Broughton, a former Derby gilder who had died in 1845 whilst working at the Coalport factory[2]. On the marriage certificate he is described as a widower, aged 50, and his occupation is given as a 'China Painter'. The address for both parties is given as Bridge Street, Derby.

He is next found in the 1851 census returns for Derby, where he is described as a 'China Painter'. At this time he was probably working at the King Street factory and was living with his wife Maria, his children John, Joseph and Eliza, and the three children of his wife's former marriage, Alfred, Henry, and Ann, at 85 Nun Street.

1 John's age and place of birth taken from 1851 Derby census returns.

2 Civil Register, Marriages, December Quarter 1846, Derby, Volume 19 Page 566.

John Buxton

John Buxton was christened on 3rd January 1813 at St. Alkmund's, Derby, and would probably have been apprenticed at Derby as a gilder about 1825, finishing his time around 1832. He is also in the list of workpeople at the factory in 1832, where he is recorded as a gilder.

He was married to Ann Dallison at St. Alkmund's, Derby on 26th December 1835, and the couple's first child, a son, Charles, was baptised at St. Alkmund's King Street Wesleyan Methodist, on 9th September 1836. He is next found in the 1841 Derby census returns, where he was living with his wife Ann and their two children, Charles and Ellen, at William Street, at which time he was described as a 'China Painter'. He continued to work at Derby until at least 1842 when a son, Richard, was christened at St. Alkmund's, Derby. The family was still living at William Street and he was again described as a 'China Painter'. He probably remained until the closure of the factory, in 1848.

There is some evidence that he worked at the King Street factory at some time, as when his son Richard was married at St. Alkmund's, on 23rd December 1871, his father's occupation was recorded as a 'China Painter', and he was living in Quarn Street, Derby.

Philip Clavey

Philip Clavey was born in the parish of St Peter, Derby, in 1779[1]. Haslem says that he was contemporary with the Tatlows and that he learned flower painting at Derby. He excelled particularly in the painting of single plants and decorated numerous dessert services in this manner.

From the date of his birth, it would seem that he was probably apprenticed at Derby in about 1791, finishing his time around 1798. He was married to Mary Gaskell at Duffield, Derbyshire, on 6th February 1803 and the couple's first child, a daughter, Elizabeth, was baptised at St. Alkmund's, Derby, on 17th January 1804. Another daughter, Sarah, was baptised at St. Alkmund's in 1806.

Shortly after this, he left Derby to work at the

Coalport factory in Shropshire. Proof of this is to be found in the parish register at Madeley, where five of the couple's children were baptised on 12th April 1814. The entries state the sons and daughters to be the children of Philip and Mary Clavey, living at Ropers Hill, and the father's occupation is given as 'China Painter'. Unfortunately, the registers do not record either the dates or locations of the births. However, evidence that indicates their date of arrival at Coalport comes from the later census returns for Derby.

Haslem, in his book *The Old Derby China Factory,* states that, 'After leaving the works he (Philip Clavey) for many years kept a glass and china shop at the bottom of Sadler Gate, Derby, close to the bridge'. It is certain, considering the previous evidence that this would be after he returned from Coalport. That he did return is confirmed by the fact that three of his children, all baptised in Madeley, were married at St. Werburgh's, Derby. The first, Edward, was married there in 1833 and at the marriages of Sarah, on 1st August 1843 and Ann, on 25th December 1846, their father was described as a 'China Painter'.

Other evidence which confirms his return and which supports Haslem's statement concerning Clavey having kept a shop in Sadler Gate is found in *Pigot's Commercial Directory of Derbyshire 1835.* In a section under Glass, China & Earthenware Dealers is an entry: 'Clavey, Philip, Sadler Gate'. He also appears in both the 1841 and 1851 census returns for Derby. In the 1841 census he is described as a 'Dealer in Glass', aged 60, born in the county and living at Sadler Gate. In the 1851 census he is described as a 'Retired Glass Dealer', aged 72 years, living with his wife Mary, daughter Ann, and her husband William Upton, at 31 Sadler Gate. This area was also described as 'Clavey's Yard'.

In the 1851 census for Derby, Ann Upton, née Clavey, was recorded as aged 40 years (born in 1811, in Madeley, Shropshire). Edward Clavey, also born in Madeley, was recorded as aged 43 years (born in 1808) and subsequently, in the *Whites Directory for 1857*, was described as a 'Victualler' at the 'Half Moon', Sadler Gate. At his death in 1873, he was recorded as aged 66 years. It seems then, that Philip Clavey and family left Derby for Coalport sometime between 1807 and 1808, and stayed there until at least 1814.

---

[1] Inferred from 1851 Derby census returns.

George Potts Cocker

Haslem, in his book *The Old Derby China Factory,* states that George Cocker was apprenticed to figure making at the Derby factory early in the nineteenth century and that he left in 1817, a year or two after serving his apprenticeship.

This information seems to be in accord with the fact that he was born in 1794[*], and that he was married to Sarah Stanley at Duffield on 1st January 1816. This would probably mean that he would have been apprenticed at Derby, about 1806, at the age of 12 years, and that he would have finished his apprenticeship around 1813. It seems that many of the Derby apprentices married within a few years of the end of their time.

Haslem goes on to say that after he left Derby in 1817 he worked for Coalport and then Worcester, but only for a short time as he returned to Derby in 1821. He was then employed once again at the factory until 1825.

I cannot find any evidence that positively supports the information concerning Coalport and Worcester, but neither is there any to disprove it. There is an element of confusion in the baptismal register of St. Peter's church concerning what at first appears to be two families. One family has children registered to George Potts and his wife, Sarah, and the other to George Potts Cocker (or just George Cocker) and his wife Sarah. The confusion actually started with the marriage at Duffield, registered as between 'George Cocker Potts and Sarah Stanley'. However, I am convinced that the two families are in fact just one, that of George Potts Cocker and his wife, Sarah (née Stanley). If this is indeed the case, the couple's first child, a son, Douglas, was baptised at St. Peter's on 5th January 1817, at which time George was described as a 'Modeller', and was living at Brookside.

George Cocker was definitely back at Derby in 1821, as his daughter, Elizabeth, was christened at St. Peter's, Derby, on 16th December of that year. In the register he is described as a 'Potter', living at South Street, Derby.

According to Haslem, Cocker left the factory in 1825 to set up in partnership with John Whitaker senior, a gilder, and commenced making china figures in Friar Gate. The partnership lasted for only a year, but Cocker continued with the concern until 1840, when he moved to London.

When his daughter, Emma, was christened at St. Peter's, Derby on 16th July 1826, he was described as a "China Manufacturer" and was still living at

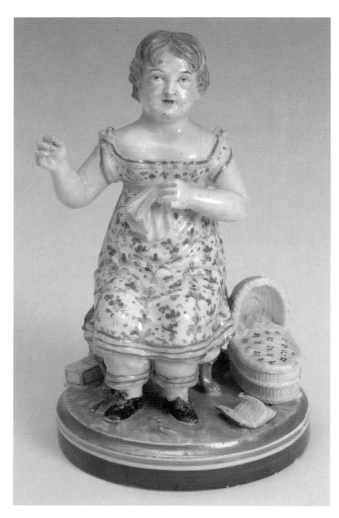

Colour Plate 33. Decorated figure from the time of Cocker's manufacturing establishment c.1825-1840. Perhaps decorated by John Whitaker. 'Cocker Derby' under base.
Derby Museums and Art Gallery.

South Street. However, at the christening of his son, George, at St. Peter's, on 20th September 1829, he is described as a "China figure maker" and was then living at Friar Gate. The couple's last child, Edwin Potts Cocker, was christened at St. Peter's, Derby, on 10th January 1834. Edwin was later also to become a figure maker and to work in the Potteries. George Cocker appears in *Glovers Directory of the County of Derby 1829*, under an entry, ' Cocker George, ornamental porcelain manufacturer, friar gate', and in *Pigot's Commercial Directory of Derbyshire 1835*, under a section entitled 'Glass, China & Earthenware Dealers', is an entry 'Cockers George (and Modeller) 4 Friar Gate'.

There is some evidence that Cocker made a number of moulds for the Rockingham factory between about 1829 and 1831, but although he is in a militia list for 1831, he does not appear to have been employed at Swinton. The entries in the baptismal registers for 1829 and 1834, and the entries in Pigot's and Glovers Directories, indicate that he

was still living in Derby. It is probable that he supplied these moulds when trading as an independent manufacturer. In the recent book, *Rockingham 1745-1842*, by Alwyn and Angela Cox, it is stated that there is a signed base of a master model incised with the date March 12th 1829, which was recovered from the Rockingham site. The inscription implies that he had by then produced a series of twenty-nine figures for the Bramelds. The are also many similarities between models made at Derby and those made at Swinton, and between those at Swinton and later models made at Fenton in the 1850s.

Haslem's assertion that George Cocker had moved to London by about 1840 is backed by an entry in the *London Post Office Directory, 1841*, which reads '8 Chenies Street, Cocker George, china manufacturer'. Other evidence to support his stay in London comes from the parish registers of St. James, Westminster, where his daughter Sarah Potts Cocker was married to John Douglas Snowball, a tailor, on 23rd June 1853. The witnesses were his son, Edwin Potts Cocker, and his daughter, Emma Potts Cocker. The address given for both the bride and the groom was 3 South Row, Westminster, and the bride's father's name and occupation was registered as 'George Cocker, Modeller'.

Further information is found later in the parish register of All Souls, St. Marylebone, where his son, Edwin Potts Cocker, was married to Anne Baxter, on 9th August 1859. Although George Cocker is said to have left London in 1853, his son seems to have stayed for at least a further six years.

After leaving London in 1853, George Cocker went to live in the Potteries, and was employed by Herbert Minton for about two years. Afterwards he worked for John Mountford and then several other manufacturers until his death, on 19th January 1869[1]. At this time he was described as a 'Figure Maker', aged 74 years, living at High Street, Fenton.

Edwin Cocker left London shortly after his marriage, and had joined his father in the Potteries by 1860. On 24th April of that year, his daughter, Annie Elizabeth, was born at 1 Queen Street, Stoke-on-Trent[2,] at which time he was described as a 'Parian Figure Maker'.

By 1866, Edwin had moved to Fenton, as a daughter, Alice Ada, was born there in that year[3]. Later, at the birth of his son, George Edwin[4], on 13th June 1872, at Trent Terrace, Fenton, he was described as a 'Figure Maker'. He is next found in the 1881 census returns[5] where he is described as a 'Potters Figure Maker', living with his wife, Anne, and three children, at 28 Richmond Street, Stoke-on-Trent.

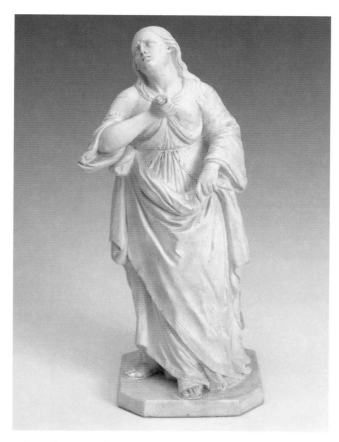

Colour Plate 34. A biscuit porcelain figure of Lucretia, stabbing herself with a dagger. The dagger has broken off and is missing. Inscribed 'Cocker Derby' under base c.1825-40. *Derby Museums and Art Gallery.*

Colour Plate 35. A biscuit porcelain figure of a cobbler whistling to his caged bird c.1825. This model bears a very close similarity to an example illustrated in Rockingham 1745-1842, by Alwyn and Angela Cox, figure 298. This example is not marked but is incised No 39.

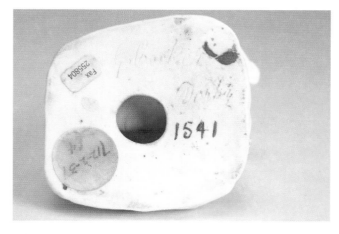

Colour Plate 36. Rockingham model of a dog watching a caged rat. The cage is detachable and has been lost. This model is strikingly similar to one illustrated in Derby Porcelain 1748-1848, An Illustrated Guide, by John Twitchett, page 63. The latter example was signed 'G. Cocker Fenton' in script and inscribed 110.

Colour Plate 35a. Base of model above showing inscription 'G. Cocker Derby' c.1825-40. Colour Plate 35 and 35a. *Derby Museums and Art Gallery.*

Colour Plate 36a. Base of Rockingham Dog model showing impressed Griffin mark and inscribed No 80. Colour Plates 36 and 36a. *Sam Collins Collection.*

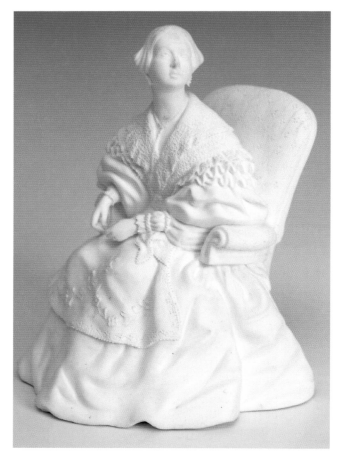

Colour Plate 37a. Reverse of chair showing inscription 'Modelled by D. Cocker 8 Chenies Street Bedford Square' c.1840-1853. This article was modelled by Douglas, the eldest son of George Cocker. The address, which is a workshop, is the one given by Haslem in his book, *The Old Derby China Factory*. Colour Plates 37 and 37a. *Derby Museums and Art Gallery.*

Colour Plate 37. Biscuit porcelain model of Queen Victoria.

Colour Plate 38a. Base of Model of girl with a lamb showing inscription 'D. Cocker Derby'. Colour Plates 38 and 38a. *Derby Museums and Art Gallery.*

Colour Plate 38. Model of a girl holding a lamb c.1825-40.

Interestingly, his wife was also described as a 'Potters Figure Maker'. At the time of the 1901 census, he is described as a 'Retired Potters Manager'.

The mystery of the inscribed signature, 'D.Cocker', found on articles manufactured at both Derby and London (*see Colour Plates 37,37a, 38 and 38a*) is solved by the discovery of a certificate recording the marriage of **Douglas Potts Cocker** and Mary Wyborn[6]. The marriage took place in the Ebenezer Chapel, Ramsgate, Isle of Thanet, Kent, on 2nd November 1842. The certificate records Douglas Potts Cocker as an 'Image Moulder', whose address is given as 233 Tottenham Court Road, London. His father's name and occupation is recorded as 'George Cocker, Modeller'.

Douglas Potts Cocker was baptised at St. Peter's, Derby, on 5th January 1817. He was registered as 'Douglas Potts' (part of the confusion mentioned earlier) and would almost certainly have been apprenticed to his father, as would his brother Edwin. At the time of writing, no further information concerning the career of Douglas Potts Cocker is available.

* Birth date inferred from death certificate.

[1] Civil Register, Deaths, March Quarter 1869, Stoke-on-Trent, Vol 6b Page 164.

[2] Civil Register, Births, June Quarter 1860, Stoke-on-Trent, Vol 6b Page 195.

[3] Information gathered from 1881 British census returns.

[4] Civil Register, Births, September Quarter 1872, Stoke on Trent, Vol 6b Page 237.

[5] 1881 British census returns, RG11 2728/130 Page 11.

[6] Civil Register, Marriages, December Quarter 1842, Isle of Thanet, Volume 5 Page 661.

Joseph Cope

Joseph Cope was christened on 7th September 1794, at St. Alkmund's, Derby. It is not known for sure but it is extremely likely that he was apprenticed at the Derby factory sometime around 1806 and would have finished his time by 1813.

He was married to Mary Rawson at Nottingham on 24th December 1818. The couple's first child, James, was baptised at St. Alkmund's, Derby on 30th January 1820, at which time he was described as a 'China Painter' and was living in Orchard Street. The couple had a further five children baptised in Derby at either St. Alkmund's or St. Alkmund's King Street Wesleyan Methodist, between the years 1820 and 1836, at which time they were living firstly at

Orchard Street and then at Brooke Street. On these occasions he was described in the register as a 'China Painter'.

He is not in the list of workpeople at the factory in 1832, which tends to suggest that either the list is incomplete or that he was working for an outside decorator. He is, however, in the 1841 Derby census and is listed as a 'China Painter', now living back at 5 Orchard Street. He probably continued until the closure of the works in 1848.

William Corden

According to William Bemrose[1], William Corden was born at Ashbourne, Derby on 28th November 1797. He would probably have been apprenticed at the Nottingham Road works in about 1809, finishing his time by 1816.

He was married to Ester Simpson on 25th September 1816 at St. Alkmund's, Derby. The couple's first child, a son, William, was baptised at St. Alkmund's, Derby on 19th August 1819, at which time he was described in the register as a 'China Painter', and was living at Chester Road. He continued there until at least 26th April 1821, when, at the baptism of a son, John, at St. Alkmund's, he is again described as a 'China Painter'.

By the time his daughter, Jane, was baptised at St. Alkmund's, Derby on 3rd March 1824, he had changed his address to Bridge Street, and was now described as a 'Portrait Painter'. His family remained in Derby at this address until at least 18th October 1829, when his son, James Robert, was christened. At this time he is described as a 'Painter'. Although his family remained in Derby, from the various addresses given at the times he exhibited at the Royal Academy, it seems he was a much-travelled man. Haslem states that Corden first tried his fortune in London in 1824, and some evidence of his presence there comes from portraits on porcelain plaques of a Joseph Moore and his son, also Joseph, which are signed and dated April 1825, and give Corden's address as 51 Oxford Street (*see Colour Plates 44,44a, 45, and 45a*). It is surmised that this address is that of a rented artist's studio.

Almost all of the information given by Haslem agrees with the facts above and is worth repeating here.

Haslem states that, 'While at the works he turned his attention to the painting of portraits and figure subjects. About 1820 he left the china works, and devoted himself to portrait painting. Shortly before he left he painted the greater part of a dessert service with subjects copied from Thurston's illustrations to Tegg's edition of Shakespeare's plays (1812), (see *Colour Plate 42*). These proved that, although somewhat deficient in the drawing of the human figure, he excelled as a colourist, and that his hatching and stippling manipulation was excellent.'

Haslem goes on to say, 'Corden also painted several plates with views of Continental cities, &c (*see Colour Plate 43*). They were copied from plates which the late Duke of Devonshire, who took a great interest in the china works, had purchased on the Continent, chiefly with the intention of lending them as an incentive to the production of works of a similar high character at Derby. Not only were the paintings on these plates excellent, but the gilding and chasing of the different borders were of the highest class; and the manner in which all this was imitated proved that talented artists were at the time employed at the works.'

After leaving the factory he painted a number of portraits in Derby and Nottingham. He exhibited at the Royal Academy for the first time, in 1826, and although his family continued to reside in Derby, the address from which the painting was exhibited was given as 33 Chapel Street, Grosvenor Place. The title of the work was 'Hebe', and was enamel on china. Haslem says that his name was in the catalogue for 1829, but for some reason there was not a picture by him in the exhibition that year. The reason for this is that he exhibited a sculpture that year entitled 'Musidora'. The address that this was exhibited from was given as Bomley House, Nottingham.

About 1829-30, he moved from Derby to Windsor, where the Marchioness of Cunningham introduced him at the Castle. King George IV promised to sit for him, but the plan was curtailed by the King's illness and subsequent death.

Haslem says that in 1831, Corden was engaged to paint some of the articles of a very large service, consisting of 144 plates and 56 large pieces, which was made for William IV by the Rockingham factory. The service cost £5,000, but the costs involved were not covered by this sum, and it is said to have helped to ruin the firm. However, there is no direct evidence that Corden did paint any of this service, as an article in the *Yorkshire Gazette* for 1832 listing the artists employed on this service did not include his name.

He once again exhibited at the Royal Academy in 1836 from 17 Brunswick Terrace, Windsor. The title of the exhibit was 'Portrait, Sir Walter Scott; enamelled on china from the original by Sir Thomas

Colour Plate 39. Derby coffee can painted with a panel inscribed 'Cupid disarmed and bound' by William Corden. Marks: Bloor circular mark in red. Height 2½ in. *Peter Jackson Antiques.*

Lawrence in the collection at Windsor Castle, by His Majesties permission'.

Corden continued to live in Windsor, where he sometimes painted in oils, and was also employed by Queen Victoria to paint some small enamel portraits. In 1844 the Prince Consort employed Corden, assisted by his son, to travel to Coburg to copy several life-size portraits of his ancestors. In Osborne House on the Isle of Wight are two paintings by William Corden. They are portraits of two of the nieces of Queen Victoria. The first is of HSH Princess Feodore of Hohenlohe Langenburc and the second of HSH Princess Ada of Hohenlohe Langenburc.

In 1854, Corden left Windsor to go to the Potteries. He later entered into a partnership with a Mr. Scaife, a miniature painter and photographer, in an effort to combine enamelling with photography. During the last few years of his life he lived in Nottingham, where he died at Arkwright Street, aged 72, on 28th June 1867[2]. The death certificate records him as a 'Portrait Painter'.

His son, **William**, who had assisted him in Coburg, also had a career as a painter and exhibited many times at the Royal Academy. William Junior was baptised at St. Alkmund's, Derby, on 19th August 1819 and was presumably apprenticed to his father as a painter.

In 1843, from 5 Queens Road, Pimlico, he exhibited a Portrait entitled 'A Family Picture', which would be extremely interesting should its whereabouts ever be ascertained. From Old Windsor, in 1845, he exhibited 'Study of a Head' and from Vine Cottage, Old Windsor, in 1846, he exhibited 'The Windmill Man'. From the same address in 1847 he exhibited a painting entitled 'Early Grief'. There was then a break of a few years until in 1854, from Trinity Place, Windsor, he exhibited a painting entitled 'Queen Mab. Soul of Ianthe, awake! etc.' He then exhibited his last two paintings in 1855 from the same address. They were entitled, 'Consulting the Oracle' and 'Indecision'.

In the 1881 census[3] he is described as an 'Artist Painter', living at High Street, Datchet, Buckinghamshire, with his wife, Elizabeth, and his son, Victor Milton, who was described as an 'Art Student'.

[1] Quoted in *Derby Porcelain 1748-1848, An Illustrated Guide*, by John Twitchett, from papers in the Royal Crown Derby Museum. However, according to his death certificate, he died aged 72 years, which would mean that he was born in 1795.

[2] Civil Register, Deaths, June Quarter 1867, Nottingham, Volume 7b Page 152.

[3] 1881 British census returns, RG11 1458/11 Page 16.

Colour Plate 40. Portrait of an unknown gentleman on a porcelain plaque painted, signed, and dated May 1824, by William Corden. Dimensions: 3¾ in X 4½ in.
Sam Collins Collection.

Colour Plate 41. Portrait of Dr. Paris on a porcelain plaque painted, signed, and dated by William Corden.
Private Collection.

Colour Plate 42. Dessert plate from the 'Shakespeare Service' painted by William Corden. Adapted from Thurston's illustrations of Tegg's edition of Shakespeare's plays (1812) c.1820. Marks: Crown, crossed batons, dots and D in red. Diameter 8³/₄ in. *Private Collection.*

Colour Plate 43. 'Berlin Plate' from 'Continental Cities' series, painted by William Corden. Marks: Crown, crossed batons, dots and D in red. Diameter 9³/₄ in. *Private Collection.*

Colour Plate 44. Porcelain plaque with a portrait of 'Joseph Moore' a shipbuilder from Plymouth. *Peter Jackson Antiques.*

Colour Plate 44a. Reverse of above plaque showing title, subject details and address at which the portrait was executed.

Colour Plate 45. Porcelain plaque with a portrait of 'Joseph Moore', son of the above, a Doctor of Medicine. *Peter Jackson Antiques.*

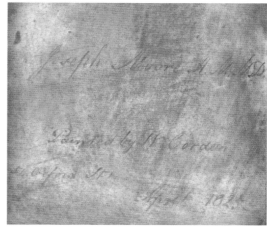

Colour Plate 45a. Reverse of above plaque showing title, subject details and address at which the portrait was executed.

51

John Cresswell

Haslem names this painter as William Cresswell. The painter's name was actually John Cresswell. The proprietor Robert Bloor discharged him in 1821, due to a recession in trade, along with Thomas Brentnall, Jesse Mountford, William Hall and James Farnsworth. He, along with the others, went to work at the Coalport Factory, where he stayed until 1826.

Support for these statements come from various Parish registers. He married Elizabeth Harris on 2nd September 1816 at Whitwick, Leicestershire and his first child, William Brentnall Cresswell, was christened at St. Alkmund's, Derby on 26th November 1820. At this time he was described as a 'China Painter', and was living at King Street.

He then, as suggested by Haslem, moved in 1821 to work at the Coalport factory, and his second child, George, was christened at Madeley on 27th November 1823. His stay at Coalport was to last only a further three years.

On 17th November 1826, he joined Messrs. Brameld & Co (Rockingham), and signed articles of agreement with them for five years, at 7s. 6d. per day for the first three years; 9s. 3d. per day for the fourth year, and 10s. 6d. per day for the fifth year. He was probably on trial at Rockingham before he signed this agreement, as evidence of his arrival at Swinton is provided by the birth of his third child, Henry, who was christened at Swinton by Sheffield on 17th June 1826. Alwyn and Angela Cox, in their book, *Rockingham 1745-1842,* state that there are further references to John Cresswell in the militia lists for 1828 and 1829 and also say that there was an invoice from the pottery dated 14th December 1829 which reads:

'To John Creswells wages/in painting Plants &c at Wentworth House ....£5 5-'

Haslem states that, after leaving Coalport, Cresswell worked at a Manufactory in France until 1848, and thereafter worked in the Potteries, until his death in 1870, at which time he was a dancing teacher. I am unable to verify any of these later facts which, considering his move to Rockingham after Coalport, do not accord with Haslem's statement and are therefore open to doubt.

Colour Plate 46. A signed example of John Creswell's flower painting, probably the plaque presented by Earl Fitzwilliam to Miss Edmonds. Inscribed on the reverse: Creswell Pinxt; No 15. Red mark c.1826-1830. *Private Collection.*

Colour Plates 47 and 47a. Both sides of a romantically named 'vomit pot'. Width at top of pot 7 in, height 8 in. This item bears the early mark of a griffin 'statant'. This mark was used for only a few months at the end of 1826. Painted by John Creswell. *Sam Collins Collection.*

53

William Dexter

William Dexter was born in Melbourne, Derbyshire, on 11th March 1817, the son of William Bull Dexter and his wife Jane (formerly Smedley). No record of his baptism has been found, but from other records such as census returns, and letters from him to his wife, his birth date has been deduced[1]. His father, William Bull Dexter, was a lace manufacturer and inventor, who, with John Dunnicliff, patented the Jaquard warp lace machine. One of William junior's brothers, Walter Dexter, was a lace designer. The family were Baptists, and were associated with Melbourne Baptist Church. After the family moved to Nottingham around 1830, all the brothers were baptised at Barker Street Chapel in Nottingham's Lace Market.

William was either apprenticed to the Derby factory at what must have been a very early age, or more likely, he was one of the 'boys' (apprentices) mentioned in the list of people working at the factory in 1832. At this time he would only have been 15 years old. If he had begun his apprenticeship at 12 years of age, then he would have finished his time by about 1836.

William appears not to have stayed too long at the factory after his apprenticeship. Haslem, in his book *The Old Derby China Factory*, states, 'After serving his apprenticeship, he did not remain altogether at the old works more than a few years and his after career was of a somewhat erratic character'.

There are not often occasions when stories of a personal nature, concerning an artist's work, come to light. One such, however, is in a manuscript, held in the Derby Public Library, called *Derbyshire Worthies*, by John Joseph Briggs[2]. I do not know of its truth or otherwise but it can do no harm to repeat it here:

'In the possession of Mr. William Bemrose junior, of Derby, is an exquisite little painting on china of a dead titmouse (blue tit), which for fidelity to nature, we think cannot be surpassed. It was executed under the following circumstances. During a stroll in the dinner hour at the back of the China Works one of the factory hands threw a stone at a tom-tit and killed it. The factory bell rang and he ran back to work with the tit in his hand, and on passing Dexter he laid the bird on his bench as depicted in the picture, with a landscape background which Dexter saw through the factory window.' This painting was apparently painted on the bottom of a broken plate.

Information received from a descendant states that he and his brother Walter spent some time in France in 1839, and Haslem adds that William worked at a manufactory in Paris for about a year at this time, painting on china. He then returned to England and moved to Nottingham, where his family had relocated in about 1830. In the 1841 census returns for Nottingham, the family was living on Babbington Street, where William was described as a 'China Painter'. It was in Nottingham, at the Parish Church of St. Nicholas, on 29th July 1841, that William Dexter and Caroline Harper were married[3]. On the marriage certificate he is described as a 'Painter' and she as a 'Watchmaker', sharing the same address. His wife, Caroline, was born in Nottingham in 1819[4], where her father had a business as a watchmaker and jeweller. Whether they had met in Nottingham earlier, where both their families lived, or in France, where Caroline had been sent to complete her education, is not known. However, it was to France, after a short stay in London, that the couple made their way in 1842. They remained in France until the mid-forties, after which they again took up residence in London. It was at this time that Haslem says that Dexter worked for a short time for George Mellor junior, decorating oriental china.

Colour Plate 48. Self-Portrait of William Dexter.
Photograph courtesy of Melbourne Library, Australia.

Colour Plate 49. Watercolour of bird's nest surrounded by flowers, painted and signed by William Dexter c.1840. 11½ in diameter.
Photograph courtesy of the Melbourne Historical Research Group.

Colour Plate 50. Watercolour of bird's nest surrounded by summer flowers, painted by William Dexter c.1840. 11½ in diameter.
Photograph courtesy of the Melbourne Historical Research Group.

Colour Plate 51. Watercolour of Bird's nest and plants by William Dexter. *Photograph courtesy of Royal Crown Derby Museum.*

Their next move, again after a short period, was back to Nottingham. Here, in July 1847, he issued a circular advertising himself as: 'Chinese Enameller to Louis Philippe, King of the French, and MMSAR the Duke de Nemours,' and says:

'In soliciting the Patronage of the Gentry of Nottingham and its neighbourhood, W.D. begs to submit for inspection specimens of Painting executed himself in all the various branches of oil and water colour, viz: Portrait Painting in every possible style; Landscapes, Flowers, Fruit, &C., accurately copied from Nature or Originals of the best Masters. Chiffoneers, Work Tables, Pre Screens, and Ornamental Work of every description completed to order. India Cabinets, and other Foreign articles, cleaned, repaired, and beautified. Oriental and other china imitated so as to match sets or services that have been broken. Enamel Painting taught and materials furnished. No 1, Milton Street.'

Lascelles & Hagars Trade Directory for 1848 lists them as living on George Street, Nottingham. She was described as a teacher of languages, and he as a portrait and animal painter. True to Haslem's statement that Dexter's career 'was of a somewhat erratic character', and probably because his advertisement had not brought in sufficient work, the couple once again moved to London, where, according to Haslem, he was 'chiefly employed in painting in water colours, varying his subjects with the seasons; thus, in spring, doing bits of banks, showing a few early spring flowers and birds' nests; flowers in summer; fruits in autumn and dead birds and game in winter. These, although slight, were executed in a clever and pleasing manner, and he found a ready sale for them at Ackerman's and other artistic establishments', (*see Colour Plates 49 to 51*).

In 1851, he exhibited a picture entitled, 'Dead Birds' at the Royal Academy. After, at a party given for the artist and academicians, where guests were asked to wear 'evening dress', Dexter appeared in Hungarian costume, adding to the illusion that he was a foreign artist by wearing a beard. Haslem described his somewhat eccentric character in the following manner. 'The Hungarian costume being in favour with Dexter, he often wore it in the streets during the time he resided in London. His appearance therefore usually attracted some attention, particularly among the rising generation. It was not unusual to see him on a Sunday morning sitting in that costume, at the door of his residence in Holloway, smoking his hooka, somewhat to the astonishment, if not to the scandal of his church-going neighbours.' In 1852 he again exhibited a picture at the Royal Academy entitled 'The lark and her young – Aesop's Fables'.

Later that same year, Dexter decided to emigrate to Australia, and Haslem comments, 'When Dexter had decided to try his fortunes at the Australian gold diggings, he considered it desirable to acquire some practical knowledge of the kind of labour which would be of use to him when there, and a railway being in he course of construction in the neighbourhood of Holloway, he occasionally borrowed the tools of one of the navvies and, much to the men's astonishment, would work earnestly with them for an hour or two. The navvies, unable to understand anybody doing that kind of work from choice, entertained some doubts touching the painter's sanity.'

Some supporting evidence of these previous statements is found in the 1851 census returns for London, where the entry reads:

14 Burnard Terrace (off Eden Grove) Holloway.

William Dexter (head) married, age 34 born Melbourne, Derbyshire, Animal artist.

Caroline Dexter (wife) married, age 33 born Nottingham, formerly watchmaker.

Mary Harper (mother) widow, age 54 born Nottingham, formerly embroideress.

Edward Punce? (entry almost indecipherable) Unmarried, age 25, born Derby, artist.

Although the last entry is not entirely legible, it is thought that this refers to the Derby painter, Edwin Prince.

As mentioned earlier, in 1852, William Dexter emigrated to Australia, arriving there, on the ship *Bank of England*, on 8th October of that year. His wife did not travel with him but eventually joined him there on the last day of 1854.

At one stage he took a job as a teacher in art and design at St. Mary's Lyndhurst School, where he was given the title of Professor of Drawing and Painting. Much more of the story of his life in Australia, and the life of his wife, Caroline, an early feminist, both in England and Australia, is compre-

Colour Plate 52. An example of the bird and fruit painting of William Dexter. 16½ in X 11 in.
Photograph courtesy of Mr. Philip Heath.

hensively covered in the book, *Folie A Deux, William and Caroline Dexter in Colonial Australia.* William Dexter died of tuberculosis, on February 4th 1860 at Redfern, Sydney, Australia[5].

[1] Age given on marriage certificate, on 1851 census and on death certificate establish year of birth while a letter written on March 6th 1859, by Dexter to his wife, in the collection at La Trobe Library, Melbourne, Australia, establishes the day and month.

[2] MSS of John Joseph Briggs, of Melbourne, Derby, 'Derbyshire Worthies', vol. vii, Page 47. In Derby Local Studies Library.

[3] Civil Register Marriages, September Quarter 1841, Nottingham, Volume 15, Page 753.

[4] Age and place of birth on 1851 census, father's occupation on marriage certificate.

[5] Death certificate of William Dexter, Sydney Register Office, Australia.

Richard Dodson

Richard Dodson was born in about 1795, probably in Derby. He was the son of William Dodson, who was Overlooker of the painting department after the departure of Thomas Soar, in 1810. According to Haslem he was apprenticed at Derby as a painter, and if so, this would have been around 1807, finishing his time by 1814.

He was married to Charlotte Welch at St. Alkmund's, Derby, on 4th November 1816. The couple's first child, John, was baptised at St. Alkmund's King Street Wesleyan Methodist, Derby, on 3rd March 1818. Four more children were baptised at this church between the years 1820 and 1825.

Haslem says that he left the works shortly after the death of his father, William, in 1820 and for a few years had a small establishment for enamelling china, on Nottingham Road, which in Haslem's time (1875) had become the 'Plough' public house. This information accords with the evidence from the church registers. However, he left Derby sometime between mid-1825 and mid-1827 as a fifth child, William, was baptised at the Wesleyan Chapel, Hanley, Staffordshire, on 5th May 1827.

Colour Plate 53. Watercolour of a wading bird signed by Richard Dodson. Dimensions: 7 in X 5 in. *Dr. John Freeman Collection.*

Colour Plate 54. A Derby bleu celeste small tureen and cover c.1815. Painted by Richard Dodson. 4 1/2 in high, 7 in over handles. Crown, crossed batons, dots, D and numeral 36 in red-brown. Late Anthony Hoyte Collection.
Photograph Courtesy Neales Auctioneers of Nottingham.

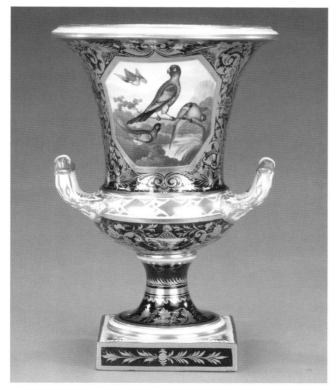

Colour Plate 55. Campana Vase c.1815. Painted by Richard Dodson with two canted rectangular panels of exotic birds in river landscapes. 13 1/4 in high, 9 in over handles. Crown, crossed batons, dots, and D in red. Numerals 10 in red and 58 in blue. The Late Anthony Hoyte Collection.
Photograph Courtesy Neales Auctioneers of Nottingham.

Colour Plate 56. Derby bleu celeste plate c.1815. Painted by Richard Dodson with exotic birds in a river landscape. 8 3/4 in diameter. Crossed batons, dots, and D in red. Gilder's Numeral 33 for Thomas Till. The Late Anthony Hoyte Collection.
Photograph Courtesy Neales Auctioneers of Nottingham.

Joseph Eccleshare

Joseph Eccleshare was born on 10th March 1793. He married Matilda Hart on 4th July 1825 at Aston Juxta, Birmingham. These records suggest that at this time he may have been employed in the jewellery trade at an enamel works in Birmingham.

The christening of their first child, Marianne, took place at St. Alkmund's, Derby on 14th May 1826, at which time he was described as a 'China Painter', and the family were living in St. Helens Street. Three further children were christened in Derby. The last, John, was christened at Brook Street Baptist, Derby, on 3rd February 1835.

He appears in the Gilding department in the list of workpeople at the factory in 1832, and continued to work at Derby until at least 1841, where he is found in the census returns, living at 40 Willow Row. He almost certainly continued working at the factory until his death on 6th June 1846. In *Pigot's Commercial Directory of Derbyshire, 1835*, is an intriguing entry under a section entitled 'Straw Hat Makers' which reads, ' Joseph Eccleshare, 40 Willow Row'. This entry is explained later, as his wife, who continued to live in Derby, is found in the 1851 Derby census returns, living with her daughter, Emma and her two sons, John and Frederick, at 47 Willow Row, in which census she and her daughter are listed as 'Bonnet Makers'.

James Fairbanks (senior)

James Fairbanks was christened at All Saints, Dilhorne, Staffordshire, in 1787. When he first worked at Derby he was employed at the 'new' works, erected for the purpose of making creamware and earthenware. He later made a statement, quoted by Haslem, to the effect that the making of both creamware and earthenware had ceased shortly before Robert Bloor took over in 1811.

He was married to Sarah Simpson at St. Peter's, Derby on 26th December 1808. At the christening of their second child, William, on 13th January 1814, at St. Alkmund's, he is described as a 'Potter' and was living at Bridge Gate, Derby. The couple had a further four children christened at Derby, between the years 1811 and 1820. James, their first child, was to follow his father's trade and to work at the Derby factory.

In 1822 James senior became foreman of the potters, taking over from William Porter who had died the previous year. He is shown as Overlooker of the potting department in the list of workpeople at the factory in 1832, and continued in this role until his own death, in 1837.

James Fairbanks (junior)

James Fairbanks' father was the foreman of the potting department at Derby between 1822 and 1837. James junior was christened at St. Alkmund's, Derby, on 7th October 1811. By the usual calculation he would have been apprenticed at the Derby factory, as a potter, about 1823 and would have finished his time by 1830. However, his christening must have been quite delayed after his birth, as he was married to Martha Hancock at Duffield, Derby, on 8th June 1828. Also, as his father was foreman of the potting department he probably started his apprenticeship at an earlier age.

The couple's first child was baptised at St. Alkmund's, Derby, on 9th August 1828, at which time he is described as a 'Potter' and was living at Erasmus Street. He continued to work at Derby and is found in the list of workpeople at the factory in 1832, in the potting department.

He continued to work at the factory until at least the end of 1839, as the couple's last child, Elizabeth, was baptised at King Street New Jerusalemites, Derby, on 13th October 1839. However, he must have left shortly after this, as he is not found in the 1841 Derby census returns.

James Farnsworth

James Farnsworth was the son of Isaac Farnsworth, who was an ornamental repairer and Overlooker of that department. He was baptised at All Saints, Derby, on 24th April 1776. An indenture exits which states, 'James Farnsworth, son of Isaac Farnsworth of Derby Repairer, put himself apprentice to learn the art of painting or embellishing porcelain or earthenware for the term of 7 years'. Unfortunately the document is not signed and is only partly filled in. There is no starting date as this only takes the form of 17xx. However, this date would probably have been around 1786/87, which means that he would have finished his time around 1793/94.

James Farnsworth worked at the factory until 1821, when Haslem says that he was discharged along with several others and that he joined the Coalport factory at this time.

Samuel Fearn

Samuel Fearn was christened at Etwall, Derbyshire on 18th September 1808. He was apprenticed at the Derby factory as a potter, and would have started his apprenticeship about 1820, finishing his time by 1827.

He was married to Elizabeth Band at All Saints, Derby, on 25th October 1829. The couple's first child, Robert, was christened at St. Werburgh's, Derby, on 7th February 1830. At this time he is described as a 'Potter', living at Bridge Street. He continued to work at Derby and is in the list of workpeople at the factory in 1832, in the potting department. A further two children were christened at Derby between the years 1832 and 1834.

He is found in the 1841 Derby census returns, where he is described as a 'Potter' and was living at Green Street. He continued working at Derby until the closure of the factory, in 1848, after which he, John Henson, Samuel Sharpe, James Hill, all former workmen at the Nottingham Road factory, together with Sampson Hancock, commenced the manufacture of china on premises at King Street. He is found in the 1851 Derby census returns, living at 22 Gisborne Street, with his wife, Elizabeth and two sons, Robert and Edwin. He is described as a 'Porcelain Manufacturer', his son Robert as a 'Painter', and his younger son, Edwin, as a 'Painter Apprentice'.

John Fearn

John Fearn, the older brother of Samuel Fearn, who was a proprietor at the King Street factory, was baptised on 10th May 1807 at Etwall, Derbyshire. He was apprenticed at Derby as a China Painter in about 1819, and would have finished his time by 1826.

He was married to Eliza Tomlinson at St. Werburgh's, Derby on 7th April 1828, at which time he was described as a 'China Painter'. The couple's first two children were christened on the same day, 21st February 1829, at St. Werburgh's, Derby, where he is again described as a 'China Painter' and was living at Hill Street.

At some time between 1829 and 1832, he left the factory to become a commercial traveller, as he is not in the list of workpeople at the factory in 1832. He is described as such at the christening of his third child, Marianne, on 30th May 1839, at St. Alkmund's, Derby. However, in the Derby census returns of 1841, he is described as a 'Dealer in colours' and was living at William Street.

James Goadsby

I cannot find any record of the baptism of a 'James Goadsby' born in the forty years between 1770 and 1810. It is possible that the surname has been misspelt and could of course be in the registers variously as Gadsby or Goodsby etc. However, a James Goadsby was married to Elizabeth Redfern at All Saints, Derby, on 27th June 1815. Elizabeth was then twenty-one years of age. Her husband was almost certainly at least twenty-one years of age at this time. Haslem states that Goadsby was apprenticed as a figure maker at Derby, and with the usual calculation that apprentices joined at twelve years of age, he would have started his apprenticeship around 1806, finishing his time by 1813.

He continued to work at the factory, and the next occurrence placing him in Derby is his attendance as a witness, along with Ester Mountford, at the wedding of John Whitaker and Ednah Mountford at All Saints, on 2nd February 1829. His wife Elizabeth must have died during the intervening years as a few weeks later, on 21st March, James Goadsby and Ester Mountford were married at St. Alkmund's, Derby.

He is in the list of workpeople at the factory in 1832, where he is listed as a Figure Maker. He died shortly after this time, as his widow, Ester, was married to John Moscrop, the Overlooker of the painters and gilders, on 6th April 1833.

William Gould

William Gould was baptised at All Saints, Derby, on 1st September 1800. He was apprenticed at Derby, as a china painter, in about 1812 and would have finished his time by 1819.

He was married to Mary Smith at St. Werburgh's, Derby, on 23rd November 1824 and at the time of the wedding he is described as a 'China Painter'.

Unfortunately it is at this point that the information concerning this workman at Derby expires. However, Lockett, in his book *Davenport Pottery and Porcelain 1794-1887*, when discussing a letter from John Davenport to his son, concerning the Royal Service made for Queen (then Princess) Victoria in 1830, states, 'Here we have documentary evidence that William Pitts was to design the shapes of the service and that the centre groups were painted by Gould. Unfortunately, nothing further is known of this artist'.

Although there is no proof that this is the same William Gould as at Derby, the flower groups that make up the decoration on this service are definitely in the Derby style.

William Hall

William Hall was born in 1797 in Staffordshire. The date that he arrived at Derby is not known. However, if Haslem is correct when he says that William Hall was apprenticed at Derby, then his starting date would be about 1809, finishing his time around 1816.

He continued to work at Derby until 1821 when, according to Haslem, he was discharged, along with four other painters, due to a recession in trade. He then went to work, along with the others, at Coalport. Haslem also says, 'The year after leaving Derby, and when at Coalport, he painted a plate with a basket of flowers in the centre, which he presented to Mr. Thomason: it is now in the possession of the writer (Haslem) and gives a favourable impression of Hall's talent.'*

On leaving Coalport, in about 1830 or 1831, he went to work in the Staffordshire Potteries, where he was employed at Messrs. Alcocks, as Foreman. In 1838, he had apparently fallen on hard times and was out of employment, as an advertisement in the *Staffordshire Advertiser* of 28th July 1838 clearly shows:

THE COURT FOR RELIEF OF INSOLVENT DEBTORS.

The Matters of the Petitions and Schedules of the Prisoners hereinafter named, (the same having been filed in the Court) are appointed to be heard as follows: -At the Court House, at STAFFORD, in the county of Stafford, on the 16th day of August 1838, at the hour of ten in the forenoon precisely.

WILLIAM HALL, formerly of Shelton, in the parish of Stoke-upon-Trent, Staffordshire, Artist, China Painter and Overlooker for Messieurs Allcock's, Burslem, Staffordshire, China Manufacturers; then of the same place, China Painter, Color maker, and Retail Brewer; and late of the same place, China Painter and Artist, but out of employ.

Haslem, in his book *The Old Derby China Factory*, says that William Hall also worked for Alderman Copeland at Stoke-on-Trent and that he died in February 1861, aged 61. The rather sad end to this biography is that William Hall, described on his death certificate as a 'Beerseller', aged 61, resident in Bethesda Street, Shelton, died of cirrhosis on 17th February 1861.

Colour Plate 57. Moulded plate c.1820 with double-barred scrolls gilt against a deep chrome green ground; central decoration of a basket of flowers on a brown wooden table by William Hall. Marked with the brown-printed Society of Arts 'Coalport Felt Spar Porcelain' backstamp.
Cheltenham Art Gallery and Museums.

* Here is Haslem's description of a plate given to Mr. Thomason and dated 1822 as item 139A in his catalogue.

'Embossed plate, probably Coalport, insects and gilding in border, basket of flowers standing in a landscape in the centre. Painted and presented to Mr. Thomason by William Hall, whose initials with the date, "1822", are at the back of the Plate.

'William Hall was apprenticed at the Derby Factory, left 1820 or 1821, was employed at Coalport and afterwards in the Staffordshire Potteries, where he died in 1861, aged 61.'

According to Michael Messenger: 'The description of the plate is not dissimilar to an unmarked Coalport plate in Cheltenham Museum and Art Gallery; this has double-barred moulded scrolls in low relief around the rim, painted insects *(sic)* and gilding within the chrome green border, and a central painting of flowers which is far from typical of the standard Coalport flower painting of the period and which may be tentatively attributed to Hall'.

John Hancock (junior)

John Hancock junior was the grandson of John Hancock, the discoverer of silver and steel lustres, and the man dubbed by many as 'The Father of the Potteries'. His father, also John, was a colour maker and groundlayer at the Derby factory.

John junior was born in 1804 in the Potteries and was almost certainly apprenticed there. It is not known when he joined the Derby factory, but if, as according to Haslem, he had accompanied his father in 1820, he would have been only sixteen years of age, and presumably still an apprentice painter. Haslem goes on to say that, 'About 1823 or '24, Hancock painted a large bowl and jug to match, each capable of holding between three and four gallons. They were both profusely covered with flowers, boldly executed, and were kept as show-pieces in the Warehouse at Derby for many years before they were disposed of.' Again, according to Haslem, John Hancock painted birds, fruit, flowers, figures and armorial bearings equally well.

He continued working at the factory, and on 5th April 1830 he was married to Mary Harrison at

Colour Plate 59. Watercolour of birds in a river landscape signed and dated March 1835, by John Hancock junior. Dimensions: 9 in X 7 in. At the time this was painted he was working at the Derby Factory. *Dr. John Freeman Collection.*

Colour Plate 60. Derby Empire style vase c.1825 painted by John Hancock junior. Height 10 in. Marks: Crown, crossed batons, dots and D in red. *Sam Collins Collection.*

Colour Plate 61. Watercolour painted, signed and dated 1837 by John Hancock junior. Dimensions: 9 in X 5 in. At the time this was painted he was working for the textile firm of Messrs Cowsels of Blackford Bridge, near Bury. *Royal Crown Derby Museum.*

Colour Plate 62. John Hancock junior. Bird Studies. *Derby Museums and Art Gallery.*

Colour Plate 63. John Hancock junior. Bird Studies. *Derby Museums and Art Gallery.*

Colour Plate 64. John Hancock junior. Bird Studies, possibly
a design for transferring onto porcelain.
Derby Museums and Art Gallery.

Colour Plate 65. John Hancock junior. Bird Studies, possibly a design
for transferring onto porcelain. *Derby Museums and Art Gallery.*

Colour Plate 66. Study of Insects. *Derby Museums and Art Gallery.*

Colour Plate 68. John Hancock junior. Flower study.

Colour Plate 67. John Hancock junior. Plant study with butterflies.

Colour Plate 69. John Hancock junior. Flower study.
All studies Derby Museums and Art Gallery.

Colour Plate 70. Porcelain plaque painted, signed and dated 1834 by John Hancock junior. Dimensions: 8½ in X 6½ in. At this time he was working at the Derby Factory. *Sam Collins Collection.*

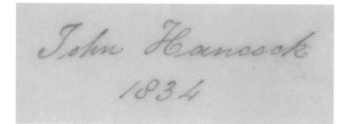

Colour Plate 70a. Reverse of porcelain plaque above.

Colour Plate 71. Signature on Exotic Magpie watercolour (Colour Plate 61).

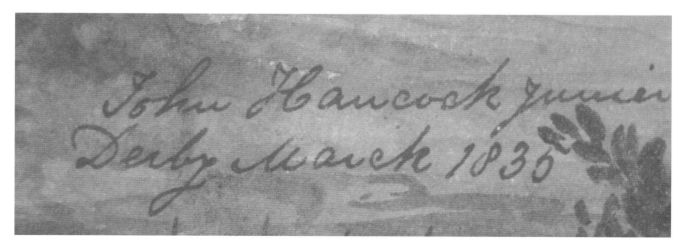

Colour Plate 72. Signature on Birds in Landscape Watercolour (Colour Plate 59). Note: Signature specifically identifies John Hancock junior and the signatures on the other items match, thus identifying those items as by John Hancock junior, not John Hancock senior as formerly attributed by previous authors.

St. Peter's, Derby. The couple's first child, a son, George, was baptised at St. Peter's, Derby, on 8th June 1831. At this time he was described in the register as a 'China Painter', and was living in Traffic Street. He was also found in the in the list of workpeople at the factory in 1832, in the painting department. The couple's last child, a daughter, Anne Elizabeth, was baptised at St. Peter's on 26th February 1834, and at this time he was again described as a 'China Painter', still living at Traffic Street.

Haslem states, 'In 1836 John Hancock left Derby, having entered into an engagement, as pattern designer, with Messrs. Cowsels, whose works were at Blackford Bridge, near Bury, in Lancashire; another proof that his talent had a wide scope. Here his designs for waistcoat pieces and patterns for ladies' dresses were very successful, as also were several toilet table cloths; one in particular, in the centre of which was a portrait of the young Queen, had an extensive sale. He died of consumption, accelerated, probably, by close application, in April 1839, aged 34 years.'

Haslem's information proved to be accurate as John Hancock's death certificate states that he died of consumption on 8th April 1839[1]. At the time of his death he was living near Blackford Bridge and was described as a 'Designer'.

[1]   Civil Register, Deaths, June 1839, Bury, Vol 21 Page 239.

Thomas Hardy

Thomas Hardy was christened at All Saints, Derby on 22nd December 1801. His apprenticeship as a gilder began at Derby in about 1813, and he would have finished his time by about 1820.

He was married to Catherine Thorpe at Duffield, Derbyshire, on 27th January 1822, and at the christening of the couple's second child, Elizabeth, at St. Alkmund's, Derby on 25th April 1824, he was described as a 'China Painter', living at Welches Yard.

He continued to work at Derby and is recorded in the gilding department in the list of workpeople at the factory in 1832. He is also found in the 1841 Derby census returns, where he is described as a 'China Painter' and was then living at Hill Street.

The couple had a further four children christened in Derby, between the years 1826 and 1844. At the last, Kate, christened at St. Peter's on 14th January 1844, he is again described as a 'China Painter', and was now living at Borrows Walk. It is highly prob-

able that he continued working at Derby until the closure of the factory in 1848, as he is also listed in the 1849 *Glovers Directory* for Derby.

James Hill

James Hill was baptised on 2nd March 1791 at All Saints Church, Derby. He was apprenticed to the Nottingham Road Factory in about 1803, and would have finished his time around 1810. He was married to Mary Swindall at All Saints, Derby, on 28th February 1814.

He appears in the list of workpeople at the factory in 1832, in the gilding section. He next appears in the 1841 census returns for Derby, where he is recorded as living with his wife Mary at Parker Street[1]. At this time he was described as a 'China Painter'. He continued to work at Derby until its closure. In the 1851 Derby census returns, he is again listed as a 'China Painter'; now living at number 43 Parker Street. After the closure of the factory, in 1848, he had joined the new firm in King Street as a partner, and he remained as such until his death in 1854.

An obituary notice appeared in the *Derby Mercury* of May 3rd 1854.

'On Tuesday week, in Parker Street, Mr. James Hill, in the 64th year of his age; an artist of considerable ability. The numerous specimens of flower painting produced by him at the china works in the town are characterised by an almost inimitable delicacy and beauty.'

Haslem's response to this obituary was as follows: 'Hill's flowers did not merit such an encomium, as they were slight, and were always done at one burning; indeed, he was wont to say he considered himself a gilder, and not a flower painter. A pattern, which was well known, and which was called "Hill's Flowers", he did in large quantities, and this, from long practice, he painted with great facility; it consisted of one group, with several sprigs scattered about. The group was formed of one large rose, and a few small sprigs of different colours. These were more conventional than natural. The lights of his roses were taken out in a series of straight cutting lines, and there was no variety in the colouring of the foliage.'

The gilder number used by James Hill was 21, which was probably allocated around 1810, and would have been used by him until 1848.

[1]   *Glovers Directory* of Derby 1842 reveals the address to be No 26 Parker Street.

Colour Plate 73. Watercolour of 'In Lovers Walk, Matlock' attributed to James Hill. Diameter 6 in. A paper on the reverse, in pencil, has the inscription 'James Hill'.
Dr. John Freeman Collection.

Colour Plate 74. Watercolour of fruit and flowers painted and signed by James Hill.
Derby Museums and Art Gallery.

Colour Plate 74a.
Signature on Watercolour.

Colour Plate 75. Derby oval dish painted in Sèvres style with scattered roses by James Hill. Marks: Printed Bloor Derby circle in red. 21 in red for gilder James Hill. Diameter 13¾ in. *Royal Crown Derby Museum.*

Thomas Hill

Thomas Hill was baptised at St. Werburgh's Derby, on 19th October 1806. He would have been apprenticed as a modeller about 1818, and finished his time around 1825.

He was married to Rebecca Maskery at All Saints, Derby, on 10th June 1827 and the couple's first child, Harriet, was baptised at All Saints, Derby, on 30th December 1827. At this time he is described as a 'China Potter', living at Willow Row. At the baptism of their next child, Joseph, on 11th March 1830 at St. Alkmund's, he is described as a 'China Worker' and was then living at Darley Lane.

He continued to work at Derby and is recorded in the list of workpeople at the factory in 1832, in the figure makers section. It is not known how long after this time that he left the factory, but he is not listed in the 1841 census for Derby.

Since there were only five modellers, including the overseer, in this section, a good proportion of the figures, from 1825 until at least 1832, must have either been modelled or 'repaired' by this workman.

William Hill

William Hill was christened at St. Peter's, Derby, on 23rd February 1807. He was apprenticed at Derby as a gilder, about 1819 and would have finished his time around 1826.

He was married to Ann Marshall at St. Alkmund's, Derby on 28th December 1829 and at the christening of the couple's first child, Sarah, he is described as a 'China Painter', living at River Street.

He continued to work at the Derby factory and is recorded in the list of workpeople at the factory in 1832, in the gilding department. He is also found in the 1841 Derby census returns, where he is described as a 'China Painter', and was then living at Bath Street.

Between the years 1830 and 1842 the couple had a further two children christened at St. Alkmund's. The last, John, was christened on 26th June 1842. It is very probable that he continued to work at the factory until it closed in 1848, as he appears in the 1849 *Glovers Directory* for Derby.

Edward Hopkinson (senior)

Edward Hopkinson was christened at Ashover, Derbyshire, on 1st July 1787. Haslem states that he was apprenticed to William Smith as a gilder.

He was married to Constance Webster at St. Alkmund's, Derby on 30th March 1807. They had a large family of eight children, between the years 1809 and 1832, two of which, Edward and Richard, also became gilders and worked at the factory. Another son, William, was apprenticed at the works as a figure maker.

At the baptism of their son, Richard, on 20th January 1814, at St. Michael's, Derby, he is described as a 'China Painter', and was living at St. Michael's Lane. At the baptism of subsequent children in Derby, he is again described as a 'China Painter', and had moved firstly to Darley Lane, then to River Street and finally to Bath Street.

Edward snr. is in the 1832 list of workpeople at the factory but probably moved to Stoke long before the closure in 1848, as he is not found in the 1841 census returns for Derby. No gilder's number is given for him in the 1820 list, but as the workmen normally retained their number until they either died or left the factory, it shouldn't be too hard to identify his work, executed using the same number, over a period of thirty plus years.

Haslem says that after the factory closed, 'Hopkinson and his sons were employed by different firms in Staffordshire and that he and his son, William, carried on a small concern there, manufacturing figures, vases, and other ornaments, some of them from two to three feet in height. Their vases ornamented with raised flowers possess considerable merit, and as they somewhat resemble those made at Derby, are sometimes sold as such.'

Another son, **Frederick Ambrose**, born in 1832, was probably apprenticed to his father at the time they were operating their own manufacture in Stoke. Later, in the 1881 census[1], he is described as an 'Earthen Manufacturer and Grocer employing 17 males and 12 females' and at this time he was living at Basford Bank, Stoke upon Trent.

[1] 1881 British census RG11 2729/75 Page 33.

Edward Hopkinson (junior)

A son of Edward Hopkinson snr., he was christened at All Saints on 19th September 1809, and was apprenticed at the Derby factory as a gilder about 1821. He would have finished his time by about 1828. He is then found in the list of workpeople at

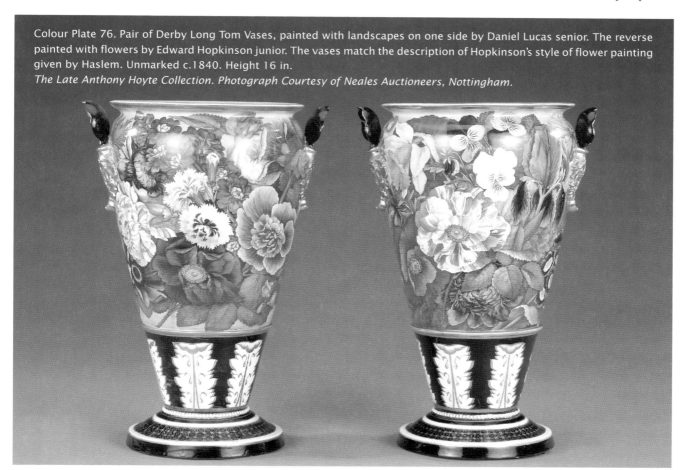

Colour Plate 76. Pair of Derby Long Tom Vases, painted with landscapes on one side by Daniel Lucas senior. The reverse painted with flowers by Edward Hopkinson junior. The vases match the description of Hopkinson's style of flower painting given by Haslem. Unmarked c.1840. Height 16 in.
The Late Anthony Hoyte Collection. Photograph Courtesy of Neales Auctioneers, Nottingham.

the factory in 1832, in the gilding section.

He was married to Ann Thompson at St. Peter's, Derby on 1st February 1834. The couple had two children, the first baptised in 1834 at St. Peter's, and the second in 1837 at St. Werburgh's, at which time they were living firstly in Bath Street and then in Green Lane, Derby. At both of these events he was described as a 'China Painter'.

Haslem tells a tale that 'an order for a large service, decorated with flowers, having to be executed in haste, all who could paint flowers were employed on it. Young Hopkinson, having shown some taste for flower painting, was, against his wishes at the time, put to work at this order, and gave so much satisfaction that he was afterwards a good deal employed as a flower painter'. He also states that 'Hopkinson's style of painting was so much like Edwin Steele's that it is sometimes difficult to tell his better things from Steele's – the chief difference is that the central flowers in his groups have usually so cutting an outline as to seem to be detached from the rest of the composition'.

He then continued until the closure of the factory, in 1848. Like his father, his gilder number is not given in the 1820 list. It may, however, be possible to identify some of his flower painting from the description given by Haslem.

After the closure of the factory he went to the Potteries where he died in 1868.

Richard Hopkinson

Richard Hopkinson was the son of Edward Hopkinson senior and was baptised on 20th January 1814. The date of his apprenticeship as a gilder is not known, but would probably be about 1825, finishing his time around 1832. He was married to Maria Bacon at Duffield, Derbyshire, on 16th June 1832. Two children were baptised at St. Alkmund's, Derby. Edward was baptised on 30th April 1833, and Emily on 14th December 1834. At this time he is described as a 'China Painter', living at Bath Street.

He is in the list of workpeople at the Derby factory in 1832, where he is listed as a gilder. Haslem says that he left to work in the Potteries after the closure of the factory in 1848. This is not entirely correct as he is found in the 1851 census returns for Worcester. At this time he was living as a lodger in London Road, St. Peters, which was near to the Worcester porcelain factory. He was described as a 'China Painter' born in Derby in 1814. It seems that at this time he had left his family in Derby while establish-

ing himself at the Worcester factory. His family joined him at some time, as five years later a son, Frank, was born on 11th May 1856 at Park Terrace, St Martins, Worcester[1]. The birth certificate confirms that this is indeed the correct family as it records that the father, Richard Hopkinson, was a china painter and that his mother's name was formally Maria Bacon. Richard was probably at this time still working at the Worcester china factory, but it is not known how long he remained there.

However, he was certainly working in the Potteries in 1881, as he is in the 1881 census for Shelton[2], where he is described a 'Gilder (Potter)', aged 68, living with his wife, Maria, and his son, Frank, at 22 Queen Ann Street, Shelton. Frank, whose age was 24, was shown as born in Worcester.

The rather sad end to the story is that Richard Hopkinson died on 12th April 1884, in the workhouse in Stoke-on-Trent[3]. The death certificate records that he was aged 70 years and was described as a 'Potter's Ground Layer of Shelton'.

[1] Civil Registration, Births, June Quarter 1856, Worcester, Volume 6c Page 311.
[2] 1881 British census returns RG11 2727/94 Page 2.
[3] Civil Register Deaths, June Quarter 1884, Stoke-on-Trent, Volume 6b Page 127.

William Hopkinson

William Hopkinson was the eldest son of Edward Hopkinson and was born in Derby in 1808. He was apprenticed at Derby, as a figure maker, in about 1820, and would have finished his time around 1827.

He was married to Louisa Baddeley at St. Alkmund's, Derby, on 28th June 1831, and three children were born to the couple, at Derby, between the years 1831 and 1839. He is in the list of workpeople at the factory in 1832, and continued to work at Derby until about 1840. Although Haslem says that he left Derby at the closure of the works, along with his father and brothers, this is not borne out by the evidence, as according to the 1851 census for Stoke a son, Edward, was born well before the closure, in Hanley, in 1842. This information also negates the assertion by other authors that he joined the King Street works on their foundation in 1849. However, he did return to Derby to work at King Street at a later date. His wife Louisa (née Baddeley) is also found in the 1832 list as a burnisher, which fact, together with certain others, leads me to suspect that this list was drawn up somewhat earlier than

1832, as she is found under her maiden name.

He remained in the Potteries and is found in the aforementioned Stoke-on-Trent census for 1851, where he was described as a 'Potter Presser', living at Hope Street, Stoke, with his wife, Louisa, who is again described as a 'Burnisher', and his four children. His sons, Samuel, aged 19 and William, aged 12 are described as figure makers. Later, in the 1881 census, Samuel is described as an 'Artist', living in Lambeth, Surrey[1]. William, in the same census, is described as a 'China Potter Figure Maker', living in Fulham, London, with his wife, Mary, who is described as a 'China Printer'[2].

In the recent book *Old Crown Derby Works, The King Street Factory 1849-1935* by Cherryl Head and Robin Blackwood, it is stated that amongst the King Street Archives are three invoices from an outside modeller called William Hopkinson. These were sent from 3 Burlington Gardens, Burlington Road, Fulham, London, and cover the period 1871 to 1872. In view of the previous information, I suggest that the person concerned was the son of William Hopkinson senior, who, as we shall see, was currently working at King Street, and who might well have recommended his son's talents to Sampson Hancock. In 1875 William junior was living at 53 High Street, Fulham.

Haslem says that William senior returned to Derby to work for Sampson Hancock at the King Street works, and writing in 1876 says that he had worked there until recently. He had certainly returned to Derby by 1867, as on 3rd December of that year his wife had died at 2 Noel Street, Derby. On the death certificate she is described as 'Wife of William Hopkinson China Potter'[3].

Two years later, on 2nd October 1869, he was married at St John's Church, Derby[4], to Annie Maria Louisa Breen; a widow aged 40 years. On the marriage certificate he is described as aged 62, a widower whose occupation is given as 'Potter'. The residence shown for both parties was Ashbourne Road, Derby. His father is described on the certificate as 'Edward Hopkinson, Painter'.

By the time of the 1871 census for Derby they had moved address, and William was described as a 'China Potter', living with his second wife, Ann, at 26 Green Street, Derby.

There is an interesting story about William Hopkinson in the recent book by John Twitchett, *Derby Porcelain 1748-1848,* which appears to have come from the Bemrose Papers. It tells of an encounter between William and the man who was to become the Prime Minister, William Gladstone, and took place at an exhibition of workmen's craft in London, after a dinner with Gladstone and twenty of the workmen.

'After the repast Mr. Gladstone took his visitors round his gallery of pictures and showed them various cabinets of china – for the ex-Chancellor of the Exchequer has a great love for old china. On coming to the splendid case of Dresden china, Mr. Gladstone remarked that he had been told that two vases, which he pointed out, ought properly to be placed in the next cabinet of Darby china. Hopkinson, who was a tall man, stood rather behind the rest and replied, "Yes, sir, they are Darby". Mr. Gladstone turned sharply round and said, "Who said that? Let him come here." So Hopkinson stepped forward, when the following conversation took place. Mr. Gladstone: "How do you know they are Darby?" Hopkinson: "Why sir! They were made in the same room where I worked as an apprentice at the Darby Works, and a man called Gadsby made them, and they were painted by Lucas." Mr. Gladstone: "Now how old were you then?" Hopkinson: "I was about 18 years of age." Mr. Gladstone: "Very good"; and turning to Mrs. Gladstone, he said that the two vases were to be removed into the "Darby cabinet, as Darby should not be robbed of any of its well earned honours."'

The making of the vase would have occurred in 1826 since that is the year that William Hopkinson would have been 18 years of age. I believe that the man referred to as Gadsby was in fact James Goadsby, who was a figure maker at Derby at this time. The 'Lucas' referred to was, of course, Daniel Lucas senior. As to why William was in London at the time of the exhibition, there is some small evidence that he may have worked there, as in the 1881 census both of his sons, as mentioned earlier, were living and working in London.

[1] 1881 British census RG11 0596/127 Page 26.

[2] 1881 British census RG11 0074/15 Page 30.

[3] Civil Register Deaths, December Quarter 1867, Derby, Volume 7b Page 261.

[4] Civil Register Marriages, December Quarter 1869, Derby, Volume 7b Page 745.

Samuel Keys

Samuel Keys was christened at All Saints, Derby, on 24th December 1770. He was apprenticed to the Derby porcelain factory, as a gilder, in 1785 and

Colour Plate 77. Derby porcelain model of Palemon and Lavinia c.1820. Gilded by Samuel Keys senior. Marks: Crown, crossed batons, dots and D in red. Large number 1 on base. *Royal Crown Derby Museum.*

would have finished his time by 1792. He was married to Hannah Ault on 28th November 1792 at St. Peter in Sheffield.

The couple's children were christened at All Saints and St. Alkmund's, Derby, between 1793 and 1816. At the christening of a daughter, Sarah, at St. Alkmund's, Derby on 12th April 1816 he is described in the register as a 'China Painter' and was living at Bridge Street.

Samuel's wife, Hannah, must have died within the next few years, as on 11th June 1821, at St. Mary, Nottingham, he was married to Elizabeth Ferneyhough. The couple had two children, christened at St. Alkmund's, Derby, Henry in 1822 and Elizabeth in 1823. At this time he is described as a 'China Painter' and was still living in Bridge Street. Two further children, Frances and Anne, were christened at St. Alkmund's King Street Wesleyan Methodist, in 1826 and 1827 respectively.

He worked for a considerable time at Derby and probably took over the gilder's number 1 soon after Thomas Soar became Overlooker of the painting department, in 1796. Haslem states that: 'Keys was one of the best gilders of his day, excelling in gold arabesque ornamentation, in which he sometimes introduced coloured scrolls. He more particularly excelled in the elaborate decoration of china figures in the Dresden style at which kind of work he could not be surpassed'. Haslem goes on to say that Samuel Keys left Derby, 'some years before the close of the factory, and during the latter part of his life he was employed by the late Herbert Minton at Stoke-upon-Trent by whom his work was greatly appreciated. To the last the wonderful delicacy of his execution did not forsake him.'

Godden, in his book *Minton Pottery and Porcelain of the first Period*, states that he found Samuel Keys' name in the wages book under 'Painters and Gilders' from October 1831 to November 1836. He also draws our attention to a miniature of Samuel Keys painted by John Simpson at Minton in 1838. Godden also quotes John Keys from his *Sketches of Old Derby and Neighbourhood* (1895) who records that Thomas Steel and Samuel Keys were very close friends who 'worked at one table together for nineteen years under Messrs Minton & Co'.

Documentary evidence seems to contradict the foregoing statements, and it is improbable that Samuel Keys worked for Minton for nineteen years, if at all. The information concerning Keys having worked for the Minton factory does not seem to be valid, for the following reasons. The entry in the Minton wages book must concern another person of the same name, as the name of Samuel Keys is also in the list of workpeople at the Derby factory in 1832, and he therefore could not have been at the Minton factory at this time. Secondly, he is listed in both the Rates Book for the parish of St. Alkmund's dated 14th February 1840, at 8 Bridge Street[1], and the 1841 Derby census returns, where he was living with his second wife, Elizabeth, and his two daughters, Elizabeth and Ann, at the same address. He is also listed in *Glovers Directory* for 1842. Bridge Street is the address at which he resided earlier, when the children of his first wife, Hannah, and the first two children of his second wife, Elizabeth, were christened. The rest of his children with his second wife may also have also been born in Bridge Street, but the Methodist registers do not give addresses. Also, his daughter, Anne, then aged 22 years, who would surely be living in her father's house, was married to a William Gawthorne at St. Alkmund's, Derby, on 28th August 1849, at which time her father is described as a 'China Painter'. Lastly, Samuel Keys died at Derby in 1850, also in Bridge Street, as is shown by his obituary in the *Staffordshire Advertiser*, in its edition of 18th October 1850.

'On Tuesday, the 8th instant, after a lingering illness, Mr Samuel Keys, Bridge Street, Derby, in his 80th year. Deceased had followed his business as ornamental gilder in the china-painting department for upwards of 60 years, and was much respected by his fellow workmen. His death is deeply lamented by his family and a large circle of friends and acquaintances.'

As to why he would be in Derby, when Haslem says that he was working at Mintons at this time, is puzzling. However, that the Samuel Keys who lived in Derby with his second wife, Elizabeth, did die in 1850 is confirmed by the fact that Elizabeth Keys is found in the 1851 Derby census returns. Here she is listed as a widow, living with her daughters, Elizabeth and Frances, at the same address the family had lived at as shown in both the 1840 Rates, and the 1841 census, namely number 8 Bridge Street, Derby.

It is possible that if the 1832 list was drawn up at a slightly earlier date, then Samuel Keys could have been at Mintons between 1831 and 1839, as there is no direct evidence, other than the list, of his presence at Nottingham Road between these dates. Perhaps this is the reason for Haslem's statement, although he doesn't say that Keys returned to the Derby factory, which this evidence suggests that he did. On the balance of evidence, however, it is more likely that Samuel Keys was employed at the Nottingham Road factory for all of his working life.

The portrait plaque, in the British Museum, by John Simpson, must therefore either be a likeness of another Samuel Keys, or painted from memory by him from an earlier time. I have always considered him rather young looking to be the 68-year-old gilder from Derby.

¹ Rates for the parish of St. Alkmund, Derby. Derby Local Studies, Irongate, Derby.

Edward Keys

Edward Keys was baptised at All Saints, Derby, on 23rd August 1795 and was the eldest son of Samuel Keys, the well-known Derby gilder. He was apprenticed at Derby as a modeller around 1807, would have finished his time by about 1814 and continued to work at the factory until 1826.

Haslem states that 'Edward Keys left Derby about 1826, and went into the Staffordshire Potteries, where he worked first for Messrs. Daniell and afterwards for Messrs. Minton and other firms. He was the modeller of a number of figures which were issued at Derby; among them were twelve or thirteen different statuettes of Dr. Syntax which, as they were brought out shortly after the publication of Combe's graphic adventures of the Doctor, had a large sale. He also modelled portrait statuettes of George IV and Napoleon, ten or twelve inches in height, together with several smaller figures and animals, a set of grotesque monkey musicians, some of the characters in Pierce Egan's then popular work, *Life in London, &c.*'

Godden, in his book *Minton Pottery and Porcelain of the First Period*, says, 'he was at first employed at Henry & Richard Daniels' works at Stoke, but by at least 1831 he had moved to Mintons where he remained until 1842. Several early Minton figures were undoubtedly modelled by this former Derby hand, whose name heads the section "Modeller, Figures & Flowers" in the porcelain sections of the

Colour Plate 78. Derby figure of 'Dr Syntax at the Booksellers'. Modelled by Edward Keys c.1820. Marks: Bloor Derby below a crown in red. Height 5½ in. *Dr John Freeman Collection.*

Colour Plate 79. Derby figure of Billy Waters the Black musician. Modelled by Edward Keys. Marks: On base, crown and D in puce. Height 4½ in. *Derby Museums and Art Gallery.*

Colour Plate 80. Derby figure of Dr. Syntax mounted on Horseback (front legs damaged). Modelled by Edward Keys. *Derby Museums and Art Gallery.*

Colour Plate 81. A rare figure of an Elephant and Driver modelled by Edward Keys c.1825. Marks: Crown over DERBY in red and numeral 34. Length 6¼ in, height 5¾ in. *Harry and Valerie Cordwent Collection.*

Colour Plate 82. Pedestal figures of Admiral Lord Nelson (unmarked) and George IV (marked with crown, crossed batons, dots and D in red) c.1820. Height 4½ in. Modelled by Edward Keys. *Harry and Valerie Cordwent Collection.*

Colour Plate 83. Bloor Derby Model of Napoleon by Edward Keys c.1825. Height 7 3/4 in. *Private Collection*. Compared with a rare miniature model of Napoleon again by Edward Keys c.1825. Height 3 1/8 in., 53 in red.
Harry and Valerie Cordwent Collection.

Minton wages book from October 1831 (the first available record) to December 1835 when the modellers are given a separate entry. He was the head of a team listed as "Edward Keys & Co" having two men and five boys under him in 1831. There are several entries of extra payments to Edward Keys, which refer to new figures *modelled* by him, as one entry of July 1833 has the "figures" added. In 1842 he started on his own, but this venture failed and from 1845 to 1853 he was employed by Wedgwoods.'

There is some evidence that helps to unravel the sequence of events. Firstly, Edward Keys was married to Mary Fish at Uttoxeter, Staffordshire, on 1st August 1835. I cannot find any proof that directly after he left Derby he went to work for Messrs. Daniell, but by 1831 he had gone into business for himself. Sadly, ultimately, he did not succeed.

Initially, it appears that he contracted out himself, his brother Samuel, and five boys, to Mintons, in about 1831. It seems that, in modern parlance, they were 'subcontracted' to make figures and flowers for Minton. It is not clear whether he was making the finished articles at his own manufactory, which from a notice in the *Staffordshire Advertiser* had been established for some time, or merely the moulds. Either way this would explain the extra payments to Edward Keys described by Mr. Godden. There is also an entry in *White's History, Gazetteer and Directory of Staffordshire, 1834,* which reads 'Keys Edward Modlr. George St.' As to his having started his manufacturing venture in 1842, I think it is clear from the following notice that he had commenced sometime before, and that the year 1842 was the eventual failure of the enterprise. There is also the fact that earlier, in the 1841 census returns for Stoke-on-Trent, he is described as a 'Manufacturer', living in Brown Street, with his wife, Mary, and son, John. In the *Staffordshire Advertiser* of 14th May 1842 a bankruptcy notice was issued against him:

WHEREAS a Fiat in Bankruptcy is awarded and issued forth against EDWARD KEYS, of Hanley, in the County of Stafford, China Manufacturer, and he being declared a bankrupt is hereby required to surrender to the major part of the Commissioners named in and authorized by the said Fiat, on Wednesday, the 18th day of May instant, at the Wheat Sheaf Inn, Stoke-upon-Trent, at eleven of the clock in the forenoon, and on Tuesday, the 21st day of June next, at the Wheat Sheaf Inn, Stoke-upon-Trent and make full discovery and disclosure of his estate and effects, when and where the creditors are to come prepared to prove their debts, and at the first sitting to choose Assignees, and at the last sitting the said bankrupt is required to finish his examination, and the Creditors present are to assert to or dissent from the allowance of his certificate; and all persons indebted to the said bankrupt, or that have any of his effects, are not to pay or deliver the same but to whom the Commissioners shall appoint, but they are to give notice thereof to Mr. JOHN ADAMS STEVENSON, Solicitor, Stoke-upon-Trent, or his Agent, Mr. CORNWELL BARON WILSON, 13, Furnival's Inn, London.
H.A. WEDGWOOD,
T.C. SNEYD KYNNERSLEY,
R. STEVENSON, Jun.

This was followed in the next edition of 21ˢᵗ May by an advertisement as follows:

'TO SELL BY PUBLIC AUCTION,
Mr, DAVIES
Has received instructions, from the Assignees of
EDWARD KEYS,
TO SELL BY PUBLIC AUCTION,
On Monday, the 23ʳᵈ day of May next, at one
o'clock precisely, at the
House in BROWN STREET, HANLEY;'

There then followed a list of household furniture and effects.

Of more interest was the second part of the advertisement:

'Also,
TO BE SOLD BY PRIVATE CONTRACT,
The UTENSILS and STOCK-IN-TRADE of the said Bankrupt, at the Manufactory in High Street.
The Manufactory may be taken at a moderate rent.'

He is next found in the 1851 Stoke-on-Trent census returns, where he is described as a 'Potter Modeller', and was living with his wife, Mary, at Etruria. This information accords with the statement made by Geoffrey Godden in his book, *Minton Pottery and Porcelain of the First Period*, that he worked for Wedgwoods between 1845 and 1853.

John Keys

John Keys was the son of Samuel Keys senior, a very well-known gilder, who worked at the Derby factory for many years. John was christened at St. Alkmund's, Derby, on 8ᵗʰ September 1797. He served his apprenticeship at the Derby factory as a flower painter, and would have started in about 1809, finishing his time by 1816.

According to Haslem, 'he attained considerable proficiency as a flower painter, his manner being between that of Billingsley and the more florid style which the flower painters afterwards practised'.

He left the factory shortly after his apprenticeship to practise as a teacher of flower painting in the town. In addition to his work on Derby china he also painted watercolours. He died in 1825 at the age of twenty-seven and his obituary appeared in the edition of the *Derby Mercury* on 27ᵗʰ April 1825:

'On Thursday (Ap.21. 1825) aged 27, after a long and protracted illness Mr. John Keys of this place, flower painter. As an artist, though almost self-taught, he ranked high, and has left behind specimens of his superior abilities; his style which was entirely his own, is allowed to be chaste and masterly, all his studies and best pictures are from nature which he closely copied.'

Colour Plate 84. Derby Porcelain card rack painted by John Keys. Marks: Crown, crossed batons, dots and D in red c.1820. Height 1¾ in, diameter 8¾ in. *Derby Museums and Art Gallery.*

Colour Plate 85. Derby shell-shaped dish decorated with alternating floral and landscape panels, and a central floral group. The landscapes painted by William Corden and the floral decoration by John Keys c.1820. Marks: Crown, crossed batons, dots and D in red. *Royal Crown Derby Museum.*

Samuel Keys (junior)

Samuel Keys was the son of Samuel Keys senior, who was a well-known gilder at the Derby factory. He was christened at St. Alkmund's on 29th November 1804 and was apprenticed at Derby as a modeller. By the usual calculation, this would have been in about 1816, finishing his time around 1823 Four years later in 1827, he became Overlooker of the Ornamental Potting Department.

He was married to Mary Hazeldine at St. Werburgh's on 29th March 1828. Haslem says that two years later, in 1830, he left Derby to work in the Potteries. He was employed at several firms and for a time he was in partnership with John Mountford making Parian figures.

Haslem also says that between 1820 and 1830 he modelled many theatrical statuettes, amongst whom were, "Liston in the role of Paul Pry", two figures of Madame Vestris in "Buy a Broom", Miss Foote, afterwards Countess of Harrington, in the Little Jockey and several others. Shortly before he left Derby, he made a pair of large figures: one of Innocence, and one of Hebe, twenty eight inches in height, which were richly decorated in colours and

gold by his father; some flowers on one of the pedestals, against which the figure leans, being done by Leonard Lead.'

After leaving Derby he was working at Mintons, initially contracted to them by his brother Edward's firm, but by June 1833 was entered in Mintons' wages book as an employee. He continued at Mintons until 1849, when he went into partnership with John Mountford, another former Derby workman, manufacturing 'Statuettes, animals, ornaments, and all kinds of Fancy Articles, in Porcelain and Statuary, at Stoke-on-Trent, under the firm of "S. KEYS and MOUNTFORD". This firm continued until 15th October 1853, when a notice to dissolve the partnership appeared in the *Staffordshire Advertiser* of 22nd October 1853. This notice also stated that they were manufacturers of Parian, under the style of Keys and Mountford. He also seems to have had other irons in the fire as an entry in *History, Gazetteer, and Directory of Staffordshire, 1851*, under a section entitled 'Beer Houses' states, 'Keys Samuel (& Manufacturer) John St.'

Some time after the dissolution of the partnership he appears to have gone into business selling china. A hint of this can be gleaned from an advertisement in the *Staffordshire Advertiser* of 21st February 1857:

TO CHINA MANUFACTURERS AND OTHERS
TO BE SOLD BY PRIVATE CONTRACT,
A number of DEAL COUNTERS, fitted with cupboards and Drawers with shelving above, supported on turned pillars, deal Partitioning, the whole of which are in excellent condition, having been recently made expressly for the exhibition of the products of the Potteries, and will be sold in one or more lots to suit purchasers – Apply to Mr.S.Keys, John-street, Stoke-upon-Trent.

After this enterprise he went back into manufacturing. Two more advertisements in the *Staffordshire Advertiser* on 27th June 1863 and 19th December 1863 give us an insight into the business. The first advertised the sale of the working plant, goodwill, and fixtures of a small manufactory. The second shows the nature of the business and was as follows:

TO BE LET, a Small MANUFACTORY, in Copeland-street, Stoke-upon-Trent, comprising one Six-mouth oven with a majolica and enamelling kiln, with work benches, throwers, wheel and engine lathe, boards, sagars, and every convenience for carrying on a good business in the lamp stand or door furniture – Apply to S.KEYS, Stoke-upon-Trent.

Haslem, writing in 1875, states, 'Of late years he has been engaged in designing and modelling both useful and ornamental articles for Majolica and Terra Cotta manufacturers in which his brother John's drawings and studies of flowers and foliage are of great assistance'.

Colour Plate 86. Derby Figure group of 'Tyrolean Minstrels' modelled by Samuel Keys junior c.1827. Central figure height 6¼ in. *Derby Museums and Art Gallery.*

* These models of the Ranier family, a troupe of musicians and dancers, who visited Great Britain in 1827, were based on a print published in 1828. Although the entry in the list of figures is not entirely clear, they have formerly been attributed to Edward Keys. However, if Haslem is correct in stating that Edward Keys left Derby in 1826, then this cannot be the case. Samuel Keys was certainly in Derby in 1828, and it was probably he who modelled these figures.

Edward Kirkland

Edward Kirkland was baptised on 16th December 1804 at Spondon. He would probably have been apprenticed around 1816 and finished his time by 1823.

He was married to Mary Ann Crooks at Wirksworth, Derbyshire, on 11th October 1829. The couple's first child, John Edward Crooks, was baptised on 23rd October 1831, at St. Alkmund's, Derby. At this time he was described as a 'China Painter', living at King Street. He is recorded in the list of workpeople at the factory in 1832, in the gilding department. At the baptism of his second child, Sarah Ann, on 7th July 1834, at St. Alkmund's, he is once again described as a 'China Painter' and was still living in King Street. However, at the baptism of another daughter, Elizabeth, at St. Alkmund's, on 7th August 1836, he is described as a 'Publican' and had moved to Nottingham Road. He may have originally taken this on as a second source of income, which in those days was not unusual.

Joseph Kirkland

Joseph Kirkland was christened at Edlaston, Derby on 23rd September 1787, and according to Haslem was apprenticed to William Smith. This would have been about 1799, finishing his time around 1806.

He was married to Elizabeth Moore at St. Alkmund's on 12th November 1811. At the baptism of the couple's second child, Anne, at St. Alkmund's, Derby, on 25th December 1814, he is described as a 'China Painter', and was living at King Street. The last documentary evidence of his stay at the Derby factory is the baptism of a son, James, on 18th February 1816 at St. Alkmund's, where he is once again described as a 'China Painter'.

Thomas Kirkland

Thomas Kirkland was born in about 1801. He would probably have been apprenticed in 1813 and finished his time by 1820.

He was married to Anne Shipley at St. Werburgh's on 3rd July 1821. The couple's first child, William, was christened at Brook Street Baptist, Derby, on 21st February 1823. Three other children, Emily, Mary Anne, and Alfred Thomas, were christened at Brook Street Baptist between the years 1826 and 1832. At the christening of Eliza at St. Alkmund's,

Derby, on 25th June 1837, he was described as a 'China Painter' and was living at Mansfield Road.

Strangely, he is not included in the list of people working at the factory in 1832. He is, however, found in *Pigot's Commercial Directory of Derbyshire 1835*, under a section entitled 'Grocers and Tea Dealers' where the entry states, 'Thomas Kirkland, Mansfield Road'. He also appears in the 1841 Derby census returns where he is described as a 'Grocer'. His daughter Emily, however, was working at the china factory at this time.

William Kirkland

William Kirkland was born in about 1807 but it is not known where he came from or where he was apprenticed. However, he was married to Sarah Emberton on 14th August 1827 at St. Alkmund's, Derby.

The couple's first child, Edwin, was christened at St. Alkmund's, Derby, on 4th November 1827, at which time he is described as a 'China Modeller', and was living at Bridge Gate. Two more children were baptised at St. Alkmund's, Derby between the years 1829 and 1831 and at this time he is described as a 'Potter'. He is subsequently found in the list of workpeople at the factory in 1832, in the potting department.

Edwin Kirkland

Edwin Kirkland was baptised at St. Alkmund's, Derby, on 4th November 1827 and was the son of William Kirkland, a potter at the Derby factory. It is surmised, because of subsequent events, that he was apprenticed as a china gilder at the Derby factory. If this were so, he would probably have started his time around 1839 and would have finished by 1846.

On the occasion of his marriage to Susannah Slater, on 18th December 1849, at St. Oswald's, Ashbourne, he is described as a ' Reporter', and his father's occupation was given as a 'China Potter'. As this was after the closure of the factory, it is possible, as was the case with several others, that he was finding work at whatever trade he could at this time.

He is next found in Leith, Midlothian, Scotland, in 1855 where a daughter was baptised on 18th September of that year. Five further children were baptised in Leith and he remained in Scotland until at least 1862, when the last baptism, that of his daughter, Isabella Margaret, was recorded on 18th November of that year.

His next move was to Hanley, Stoke-on-Trent, where a son, Albert, was born on 26th June 1867[1]. At this time he was living at Cooks Buildings, Shelton, and was described as a 'China Gilder'. On the certificate his wife's name is confirmed as Susanna, 'formerly Slater'. Whilst in Hanley his daughter, Mary, was married to Thomas Allen, a kiln man, in 1873.

His next move was his return to Derby. He is found in the 1881 census returns, where he is described as a 'China Decorator', and was a widower, living with his children, William and Albert, and his son-in-law, Thomas Allen, a kiln man, at 57 Bainbrigge Street, St. Werburgh's, Derby[2]. It is possible that both he and his son-in-law were working for the King Street factory at this time.

[1] Civil Register Births, Stoke-on-Trent, September quarter 1867.

[2] 1881 British Census RG11 3400/92 Page35.

Leonard Lead

Leonard Lead was a flower painter, who was born in Staffordshire, in 1787, and was the son of Leonard Lead senior, a woodcutter and charcoal burner. He worked with his father and brother at Pinxton from December 1798 until April 1799. Since the Pinxton factory book does not record his job or status, it is possible that he was an apprentice and that he carried on into the Coke period. Alternatively he may have been assisting his father at Pinxton, and been apprenticed at Derby about 1800. In his 19th year, in 1805, he joined the 'Fox and Owl' Benefit Society.

His first marriage was to Mary Morlidge on 27th August 1810 at Duffield in Derbyshire. At the baptism of the couple's second child, Sarah, at St. Werburgh's, Derby, on 27th July 1814, he is described in the register as a 'China Painter', living at Searl Street. A further child, William, was baptised at St. Werburgh's on 7th May 1817, at which time he is again described as a 'China Painter' and was still living at Searl Street. Unfortunately, his wife, Mary died at the early age of 29 years, and was buried at St. Alkmund's, Derby, on 25th March 1821.

His next marriage was to Ann Vernon at All Saints, Derby on 23rd June 1822 and at the christening of their second child, John, who was later to be apprenticed at the factory, they were residing at Lodge Lane where he was again described as a 'China Painter'. Their last child, Oswald Vernon, was christened at King Street Wesleyan Methodist Church on 11th August 1833, and by this time the family had moved to Chester Place.

He appears in the list of workpeople at the factory in 1832, as a painter. He seems to have been away visiting on the evening of the Derby census of 1841, as he is not recorded with his wife and the rest of his family at Chester Place at this time. However, in the 1851 Derby census returns, he is described as a 'China Painter', living at 5 Arthur Street, Derby. According to Haslem, 'After the close of the old works, and until near the close of his life, he was employed in painting Derbyshire spar ornaments in varnish colours, a style of work which will not prove so durable as that which he has left on Derby china'. He also says that Leonard Lead worked at Derby for more than forty years, which this evidence entirely supports.

He died at the age of eighty-two, at the house of William, one of his sons, at 10 Samuel Street, Leicester, on 15th December 1869[1]. The death certificate records that he was 'Formerly a Designer on Earthenware'.

His obituary was in the *Derby Reporter*, in 1869:

'He was one of the last staff of artists at the old Derby china manufactory; by his energy and industry, he brought up a large family in a creditable manner, and after a life of honesty and with a stainless character, he died at the age of 82 years.'

Two of his sons were apprenticed at the Derby factory. His second son, **William**, who was born to his first wife, Mary, was baptised at St. Werburgh's on 7th July 1817, although he was probably born two years previously. He appears to have been apprenticed to Derby at an early age, as he is recorded in the list of workpeople at the factory as a gilder in 1832. At some time previous to 1841, he left the factory to take up residence in Leicester, where he changed his trade and became a printer.

John Lead was the first son of his second wife, Ann, and was baptised at St. Alkmund's on 4th January 1825. He was apprenticed at the factory, again at an early age, and was described in the 1841 census returns for Derby as a 'China Painter', living at Mansfield Road. He probably continued at Derby until the closure of the factory.

On February 8th 1852, he was married to Mary Chamberlain at St Margaret's Church, Leicester[2]. The marriage certificate records him as a 27-year-old bachelor and gives his occupation as an 'Artist', living at Richard Street, Leicester. His father was

Colour Plate 87. Derby pierced plate painted by Leonard Lead. Marks: Bloor circular. Diameter 10 in. *Royal Crown Derby Museum.*

Colour Plate 88. Derby Chocolate cup and saucer painted by Leonard Lead. Mark: Printed Bloor roundel in red on base of both pieces. Dimensions: Cup height 3¹/₄ in, Dia 3³/₄ in, saucer dia 6¹/₄ in. *Derby Museums and Art Gallery.*

recorded as Leonard Lead whose occupation was also given as an 'Artist'.

At some stage after his marriage he moved to the Potteries and changed his profession, as on 2nd June 1870 a son, Richard was born at Globe Street, Burslem[3]. On Richard's birth certificate his mother was recorded as Mary Lead formerly Chamberlain and his father's occupation was described as 'Potter'. Later, in the 1881 census returns for Stoke-on-Trent[4], he is again described as a 'Potter', living with his wife Mary, and their two children, Leonard and Richard, at 24 Reid Street, Burslem.

[1] Civil Register, Deaths, December Quarter, 1869, Leicester, Volume 7a Page 128.

[2] Civil Register, Marriages, March Quarter 1852, Leicester, Volume 7a Page 252.

[3] Civil Register, Births, September Quarter, Wolstanton, Volume 6b Page129.

[4] 1881 British census returns RG11 2714/15 Page 23.

workpeople at the factory in 1832, where he is recorded as a gilder. He is also found in the 1841 census returns for Derby, where he was described as a 'China Painter', and was living at 16 Exeter Place. He is finally found in the 1851 Derby census returns, where he is described as a 'Retired China Painter', aged 74, and was living with his son-in-law, George, and daughter Jemima, at 14 Midge Street.

As he started work at the factory towards the end of the 18th century, he must surely have been issued a fairly low gilder numeral. The fact that he left the factory meant that he lost that number but, as he had returned by 1813, his number must still have been a fairly low one. The length of time that he continued at the factory (1813 to 1848), the consequent amount and type of work that he must have accomplished, means that with research his number could possibly still be discovered.

[1] Birth date taken from 1851 Derby census returns.

William Longdon (junior)

William Longdon was born in 1777[1] and baptised at St. Michael's, Derby, on 28th January 1780. He was apprenticed at the Derby factory on 5th July 1790, when he was 13 years of age. He would therefore have finished his time by about 1797.

On 25th March 1800, he was married to Catherine Smedley at St. Alkmund's, Derby. His first three children were christened in Stoke-on-Trent, the first in 1803 and the third in 1806. His fourth child, Mary, however, was christened on 29th May 1813, at St. Alkmund's, Derby, and on the occasion of the baptism of his daughter, Anne, at St. Alkmund's on 26th October 1815, he was described as a 'China Painter', living at Darley Lane. Obviously, shortly after his marriage, the couple had left for the Potteries, where he worked for at least three years. By 1813 he was back in Derby, and remained to work at the factory until its closure in 1848.

Haslem states that 'he was much employed at the Chantilly Pattern, and in the course of time got to think so much of it, and of what he considered his masterly execution of it, that had he been employed on the most artistic work in the factory he could not have thought more highly of himself or of his great importance in the establishment'. I personally think that this is a trifle harsh, as it is not wrong to be proud of the work that one does, even if it is of a comparatively minor nature.

He continued to work at Derby and is in the list of

John Lovegrove

John Lovegrove was born in Chaddeston[1], Derby in about 1794. It is possible that he was the John Lovegrove baptised at Duffield on 23rd March 1794 to Henry Lovegrove and his wife, Ann. He was apprenticed as a gilder to William Smith, a former Derby hand, who, when leaving the works, had commenced enamelling china in a court in St. Alkmund's churchyard. Smith was also a maker of enamel colours and the well known dark blue used on Derby china was made by him.

On 11th July 1814, John Lovegrove was married to Elizabeth Rutland at All Saints, Derby, and a year later, in 1815, left Smith's employment and joined the Derby factory. The couple had two sons, James, born 1816, and William, born 1821, both of whom followed their father to become china painters. His wife, Elizabeth, also worked at the factory and is in the list of burnishers in 1832.

He is in the list of the people working at the factory in 1832, where he is recorded as a gilder. He is also in the 1841 Derby census, listed as a 'China Painter', living at 43 Erasmus Street with his wife Elizabeth and his son William. It is not clear whether he was working at the factory at this time, or had already started in business for himself, as in the 1849 *Glover Directory for Derby* is an entry which states, ' John Lovegrove & Son China Manufacturers 32 Traffic Street'. There is also an entry in the 1851 Derby census returns where he is listed as living with his wife Elizabeth, his son William and his daughter Emma. Unfortunately the entry is badly faded but the column for 'Occupation', in both his and William's case, reads as follows, '*Inde-cipherable* of China'.

Haslem states that, 'After the close of the factory, Lovegrove worked in London, and afterwards in Yorkshire. When in London he was chiefly employed in gilding china with leaf gold for a shop in Tottenham Court Road, which advertised to supply the article cheap "to persons about to marry!"' There are some discrepancies in Haslem's statement, as it makes no mention of Lovegrove being in business for himself after the closure of the factory.

At some time later he returned to Derby and died, after several years of infirmity, on 24th February 1873. His age was recorded as 76 years (the age given on the certificate is in error) in the Union Workhouse at Litchurch[2]. On his certificate he was described as 'Formerly a China Painter'. There is a certain poignancy about his death in this particular place, as only three years later the workhouse was purchased by a newly formed company and became part of the site of The Derby Crown Porcelain Company.

[1] Information taken from 1851 census returns, Derby.
[2] Civil Register, Deaths, Derby 1873 March Quarter, Volume 7b, Page 290.

James Lovegrove

James Lovegrove was born in Derby in 1816 and was the son of John Lovegrove, a gilder at the Derby factory. He was apprenticed at Derby in about 1828 and would have finished his time around 1835. He was married to Mary Smith at St. Alkmund's, Derby, on 24th December 1838 and at the time of his wedding was described as a 'China Painter', living at Erasmus Street.

He continued to work at the factory and is found in the 1841 Derby census returns, where he is again listed as a 'China Painter' and was living with his wife, Mary, at 14 Derwent Row.

Whether he remained at the Derby factory until its closure in 1848 is not certain, but he is found in the 1851 census returns for Stoke-on-Trent. His wife, Mary, having died sometime between 1841 and 1851, he is now listed as living with his new wife, Harriet, and his one-year-old daughter, Elizabeth, at Sutherland Road. At this time he is described as a 'Painter and gilder', born in Derby.

William Lovegrove

William Lovegrove was born in Derby in 1821, and was the son of John Lovegrove, a well-known gilder at the Derby factory. He was apprenticed as a painter around 1833, and would have finished his time by 1840. Haslem states that he painted flowers and birds.

He is found in the 1841 census returns for Derby, in which he is described as a 'China Painter', living with his father at 43 Erasmus Street, and at which time he was probably still working at the factory. However, some time between then and the time of the publication of *Glovers Directory* in 1849 (probably at the closure of the factory, in 1848), he left the factory to join his father's business in Traffic Street.

On 29th November 1849 at St. Peter's Church, Derby, he was married to Emma Thorpe[1]. The marriage certificate records him as a 'China Painter', living at Siddals Lane. Emma was described as a 'Lacemaker', and was living at Devonshire Street. On the certificate his father's name was given as John Lovegrove, whose occupation was 'China Painter'. He is next found in the 1851 census returns for Derby, living with his parents and wife, Emma, at Siddals Lane.

By the year 1860, he had moved to Staffordshire, where his son, Samuel William, was born on 17th October of that year[2]. On the birth certificate, William Lovegrove is described as a 'Potter, Painter', and was living with his wife, Emma, at Dresden, in the district of Trentham.

However, by 1868 he had returned to Derby, and was possibly working at the King Street factory, although in light of subsequent documents, it is more likely that he was in business for himself (see following paragraph). His first wife, Emma, had died sometime between 1860 and 1868, as on 12th August 1868 he was married to Sarah Taylor at St. Peter's, Derby[3]. On the marriage certificate he was described as a widower, and his occupation was recorded as 'China Painter'. The address given for both bride and groom was Osmaston Street. On this document his father's name was recorded as John Lovegrove, whose occupation was given as 'China Painter'.

He is next found in the 1871 census returns for Derby, where he is described as a 'China Painter and Designer', aged 50 years, living with his wife, Sarah, and his son, Samuel, at 47 Osmaston Road (*sic*). An entry in C.N. *Wright's Directory of South Derbyshire, 1874* states, 'Lovegrove Wm. Glss. & China dlr. 47 Osmaston St.'

In the 1881 Derby census he was described as an 'Earthenware Dealer', and was still living at 47 Osmaston Street[4]. He was still described as a dealer, although this time as a 'China Dealer', in the 1891 census returns for Derby, where he was still at the same address.

He died on 16th January 1897 at his home in Osmaston Street, at which time he was described as a 'China Flower Painter'[5].

[1] Civil Register, Marriages, December Quarter, Derby, Volume 19.

[2] Civil Register, Births, December Quarter 1860, Stone, Volume 6b Page 39.

[3] Civil Register, Marriages, September Quarter 1868, Derby, Volume 7b Page 588.

[4] British Census 1881 RG11 3395/66 Page 14.

[5] Civil Register, Deaths, March Quarter 1897, Derby, Volume 7b Page 344.

Goodwin Lowe

Goodwin Lowe seems to be a Derby workman that time forgot. He was christened at St. Alkmund's, Derby in 1775. By the usual timing he would have been an apprentice sometime between 1785 and 1789, finishing between 1792 and 1796. Since his profile would surely have been higher, had he been a painter, it is surmised that he was apprenticed as a gilder.

He married Sarah Rogers at St. Alkmund's, Derby on 14th April 1800. Seven children were baptised at St. Alkmund's between the years 1802 and 1816. At the christening of their last child, a daughter, Harriott, on 7th August 1816, he was described as a 'China Painter', and was living at Bridge Gate, Derby.

George Lowe (senior)

George Lowe was born in Derby in 1805 and was apprenticed at the Derby factory as a gilder in about 1817, finishing his time around 1824. He was married to Elizabeth Marshall at St. Alkmund's, Derby on 4th April 1825. The couple's first child, George, was baptised at Brook Street Baptist, Derby, on 20th March 1826, at which time he was described as a 'Gilder'.

He continued to work at the factory and is re-corded in the list of workpeople at the factory in 1832, in the gilding section. His last child, Josiah, was baptised at Brook Street Baptist, Derby, on 18th April 1837. He seems to have left the factory shortly after this time as only his son George (an apprentice china painter at the factory) is found in the 1841 census returns for Derby, living with the family of Joseph Bentley and his wife.

In the 1881 census he is found living in Cumberland with his second wife, Margaret, at which time he is described as a 'Retired China Painter'.

[1] British Census 1881 RG11 5144/42 Page 5.

George Lowe (junior)

George Lowe was the son of George Lowe senior, a gilder at the Derby factory. He was baptised at Brook Street Baptist, Derby, on 20th March 1826. He would have been apprenticed as a gilder about 1838, finishing his time by 1845.

He is found in the 1841 Derby census returns living with Joseph Bentley, a china painter, and his wife Elizabeth, at 23 Bridge Gate, where he is recorded as a 'China Painter' aged 15. This fact, and that of his still being an apprentice at this time, suggests that his parents had moved away from Derby by this date. He most probably stayed until the closure of the factory in 1848.

However, he seems to have moved to the Potteries shortly after the closure, as he was married to Mary Ann Hulson at St James' Church, Longton on 9th December 1849[1]. The certificate records him as a 'Gilder', living in Fenton. It also records the name of his father as George Lowe, whose occupation was also a 'Gilder'.

His son, Thomas, was born in Stoke-on-Trent in 1860, and on 22nd October 1861 a daughter, Sarah Jane Bishop, was born at South Street, Fenton[2]. On the birth certificate George Lowe is recorded as a 'Potters Gilder'. He remained in the Potteries and is next found in the 1881 census returns for the area, living at 136 Hope Street, Stoke-on-Trent, with his wife, Mary, and his three children, Thomas, Joseph, and Sarah[3].

[1] Civil Register, Marriages, December Quarter 1849, Stoke-on-Trent.

[2] Civil Register, Births, December Quarter 1861, Stoke-on-Trent, Volume 6b Page 167.

[3] British Census 1881 RG11 725/47 Page 45.

Daniel Lucas (senior)

Daniel Lucas was born in 1785, in Ashbourne, Derbyshire[1], the son of John Lucas, a farmer[2]. He was a landscape painter, and in early life he is reputed to have worked for Messrs. Davenport. In 1804 he married Rebecca Edden at Old Church, St Pancras, London, and on 25th December 1809, two children, John and Mary, were christened at Burslem, Staffordshire.

Haslem states that, 'for a quarter of a century prior to the closing of the Derby factory, he was the principal landscape painter employed at Derby; his work, therefore, is probably oftener met with than that of any other of the Derby landscape painters. His colouring lacked variety, and his style was heavier than that of the painters before his time'.

Haslem's statement puts Daniel Lucas's arrival at Derby loosely around 1823. Twitchett suggests 1820, and Godden, in the book *Davenport China, Earthenware & Glass 1794-1887* puts it at 1818. However, the christening of a daughter, Anne, on 13th July 1814, at St. Alkmund's, Derby, is proof of an earlier date. As his son William was born in Burslem in 1812[3], it follows that he arrived at Derby sometime between these two dates. Three further children were christened between the years 1816 and 1823, all at St. Alkmund's, Derby. During this period he lived firstly at Nottingham Road and then at Navigation Row and was, at this time, described as a 'China Painter'.

He continued to work at Derby and appears in the list of workpeople, as a painter, at the factory in 1832. Haslem says that he occasionally painted in oils, and that some of the best public house signs in Derby were done by him: among them being the 'Old Boat' in the Morledge, the 'Jolly Toper' near St. Mary's Bridge, the 'Plough' and the 'Peacock', both on the Nottingham Road, the 'Hare and Hounds' in Erasmus Street (where incidentally, many of the workmen lived), and others.

Haslem also says that he was an expert fisherman and liked to spend time on the banks of the Trent, in the neighbourhood of Twyford.

Rebecca, his first wife, appears to have died sometime after 1823, as on 31st December 1840 he was married to his second wife, Frances Barker, a widow, at St. Peter's, Derby[4]. At this time he was living at Traffic Street and was described as a 'Painter'.

He continued working at the factory and is found in the 1841 Derby census returns living with his second wife, Frances, and two young children, Thomas, aged 2 years and Henry, aged 3 years. On the closure of the factory he left Derby and went to work in Birmingham, where he is found in the *History, Gazetteer and Directory of Warwickshire, 1850*, described as an 'Artist' living at 37 Cross Street, Birmingham. He is later found in the 1851 census returns, again described as an 'Artist', living with his wife, Fanny (Frances?), his married daughter Mary, and grandson, William, at 14 Severn Street. He continued to live in Birmingham until his death, in 1867.

[1] Age and birthplace taken from 1851 census for Birmingham.
[2] Information taken from second marriage certificate.
[3] Birth date taken from 1851 census for Stoke.
[4] Civil Register, Marriages, December Quarter 1840, Derby, Volume 19 Page 478.

Colour Plate 89. Oval Derby Dish with a central landscape painted by Daniel Lucas senior. Marks: Bloor circular and named description in red. Length 11 in.
Royal Crown Derby Museum.

Colour Plate 90. Garniture of three Derby vases painted by Daniel Lucas senior. Views of 'Kedleston Hall', 'Repton near Derby' and 'View of Derby'. Marks: Printed crown and Gothic D in red c.1835. Height 11½ in and 9 in. *Late Anthony Hoyte Collection. Photograph Courtesy Neales Auctioneers of Nottingham.*

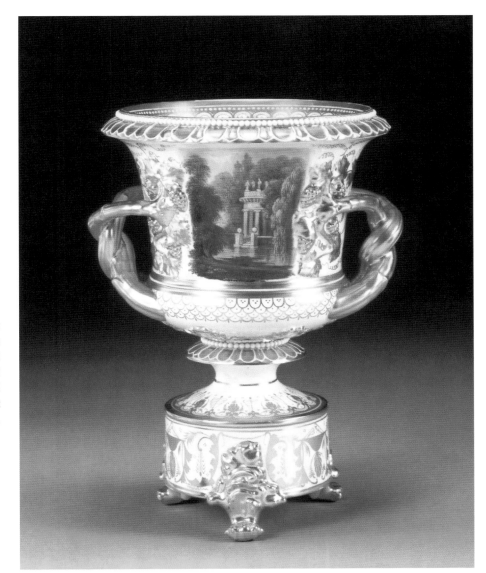

Colour Plate 91. A Derby porcelain Warwick vase. The two centre panels painted with 'View of Italy' and 'Willersley Castle Derby[sh]' by Daniel Lucas senior. Marks: Hand painted Bloor circle mark. Titles in red script c.1820. Size 11 in tall, 7½ in wide. *Peter Jackson Antiques.*

Colour Plate 92. A pair of Derby bough pots painted by Daniel Lucas senior. Description on base of left hand item 'View of Darley near Derby'. Description on base of right hand item 'Matlock Church Derbyshire'. Marks on both: Crown, crossed batons, dots and Derby in red. *William Allen Collection.*

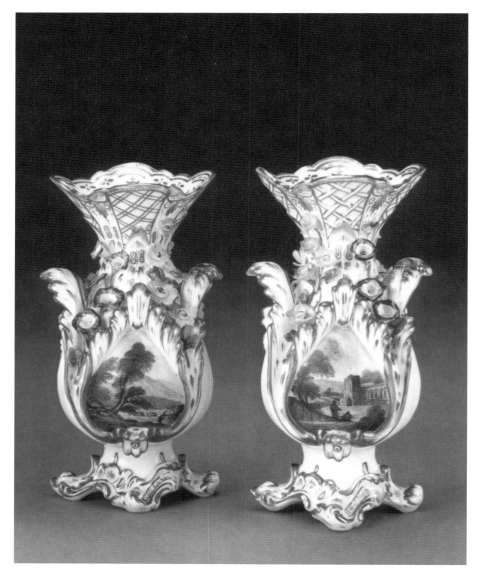

Colour Plate 93. A pair of Derby porcelain Rococo Revival vases. Although the four landscapes are not named, one can be identified as the classic view of the Derby Silk Mill, All Saints Church, the Shot Tower, 18th century town houses, River Derwent and bridge. The other three scenes are of typical Derbyshire views with rivers, stone bridges, and mountains of the Dovedale and Matlock Vale areas. Measurements: 6½ in tall, 3½ in wide. Marks: Printed crown over Derby enclosed in a banner ribbon in red c.1835/1840.
Peter Jackson Antiques.

John Lucas

John Lucas was christened on 25th December 1809 at Burslem, Staffordshire, and was the eldest son of Daniel Lucas, the well-known Derby landscape painter. He was also apprenticed at Derby, and according to Haslem, learned landscape painting under his father. He left Derby shortly after his apprenticeship to go to the Rockingham works at Swinton, Yorkshire. Haslem also says that he painted in the manner of his father but that his execution was more refined.

If he had started his apprenticeship at the usual age of 12 years, he would have begun about 1821, finishing his time around 1828. However, it can be seen from the illustration that his talent was well advanced at the age of thirteen, and he most probably started his apprenticeship earlier. He was still working at the factory in 1832, when the list of contributors to the King's Gift was drawn up.

He then moved to the Rockingham works but as he died and was buried on 7th May 1833 at Swinton, he can only have worked at Rockingham for a very short time. There are, however, known to be two Rockingham plaques painted by him.

Colour Plate 94. Porcelain plaque of 'Rivalx Abbey' painted by the 13-year-old John Lucas. His palette seems much influenced by that of his father, Daniel Lucas senior. *Derby Museums and Art Gallery.*

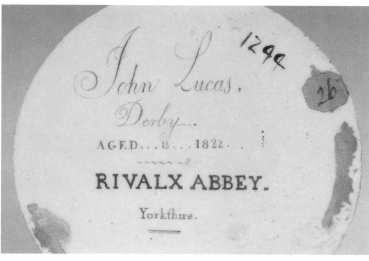

Colour Plate 94a. Reverse of Plaque showing inscription. *Derby Museums and Art Gallery.*

Daniel Lucas (junior)

Daniel Lucas junior was the son of Daniel Lucas, the well-known Derby landscape painter. He was christened at St. Alkmund's, Derby, on 5th September 1816, was apprenticed at Derby around 1828 as a landscape painter, and would have finished his time by about 1835. Haslem says that 'on leaving Derby he worked at the Coalport factory for many years and afterwards at Copeland's'. Godden, in his book *Coalport and Coalbrookdale Porcelains,* has Lucas's dates at Coalport between 1845 and 1861.

Unfortunately, this does not seem to be supported by the evidence.

Although his wife, Mary Bill, was born in Market Drayton in Shropshire, the couple were married in Burslem Parish Church, on 2nd May 1840[1]. Their first child, Frances, was born in Burslem in 1842, and subsequently, three more children were baptised in the Stoke area in 1846, 1848 and 1850. He appears in the 1851 census for Stoke-on-Trent, and was living with his wife, Mary, and their children, Frances, Mary, Rebecca and George, at 51 Swinford Road. At this time he is described as a 'Landscape

Colour Plate 95. Copeland Jug from the 'Rivers of France' breakfast service c.1862. Painted by Daniel Lucas junior. Probably issued from his decorating establishment in Longton. *Vega Wilkinson Antiques.*

Colour Plate 96. Close up of landscape painting on one side of the jug from the 'Rivers of France' breakfast service. *Vega Wilkinson Antiques.*

Colour Plate 96a. Close up of Landscape painting on reverse side of jug from the 'Rivers of France' breakfast service. *Vega Wilkinson Antiques.*

Colour Plate 97. Porcelain plaque of fishing boat sailing up the Inner Sound past Banburgh Castle painted and monogrammed by Daniel Lucas junior. Dimensions: 5 X 4 in. *Private Collection.*

Painter on China'. Two years later, on 9th March 1853, his son, John Bill, was born at Oakhill, Stoke-on-Trent, at which time he was described as an 'Artist'.

According to the later 1881 census returns for Stoke-on-Trent, the couple had a further child born in the Stoke-on-Trent area, as a daughter, Rebecca (the second child in the family by that name) was born there in 1855.

In his book, Geoffrey Godden states that Daniel Lucas' name is found in the Coalport wages book for 1859, but that his name is not in the Coalport census returns for 1861. He goes on to say that he painted Copeland vases for the 1862 Exhibition. Another statement, supporting Daniel Lucas having worked for Coalport around 1860, comes from William Scarratt in his book, *Old Times in the Potteries.* In it, whilst describing a number of artists who had previously worked for John Ridgway at Cauldon Place, he includes 'Mr. Daniel Lucas, from Derby, now at Coalport, 1860'. Not only does this support the Coalport theory but it also gives us an insight into where he may have been working previously.

Other documentary evidence of his stay at the Coalport factory comes in the form of two entries in the records of the Madeley Wood Wesleyan Methodist Church, in the baptismal register. Francis Morris Lucas was born on 16th January 1858, and Annie Millicent was born on 28th October 1859. Both children were baptised on 22nd January 1860. From this it appears that the 1881 census returns are not entirely accurate, as Annie Millicent (called just Millicent in these returns) was born in 1859, not 1861 as her age of 20 years would suggest. The civil register reveals that another daughter, Caroline Eliza[2] (almost certainly the "Lizzie" in the 1881 census returns) was born on 18th May 1861 at Coalport, at which time he was described as a 'China Painter'. However, as Daniel Lucas does not appear in the 1861 census returns for the area, it can be surmised that, although his family are still in the area at this time, he may already have left Coalport to work in the Potteries, his family following shortly.

It can be seen from the foregoing that Daniel Lucas could therefore only have been at Coalport

Colour Plate 98. Spode porcelain tray painted by Daniel Lucas junior c.1860. *The Potteries Museum and Art Gallery.*

from about 1856 until early 1861, before the date of the census. It seems that Haslem had the sequence of events incorrect and that Lucas did not work for Coalport directly after leaving Derby.

Haslem also says that on leaving Copeland's he started a decorating establishment in Longton, where he and his sons decorated china for different manufacturers. The 1881 census returns for Stoke-on-Trent show that Daniel Lucas was described as an 'Artist', and was living with his wife, Mary, and four of their children at 37 Sutherland Street[3]. One of his children, John Bell (sic), was also described as an 'Artist'. Another son, Francis Morris, was described in these returns as a 'Landscape Painter (Potter)' and was living at Victoria Street, Stone, Staffs.

According to the available evidence, the correct sequence of events would seem to be that Daniel Lucas junior left Derby between 1835 and 1840 to work at Ridgways at Cauldon Place. From there he moved to Coalport, where he worked for a period between 1856 and early 1861. His next move was to Copelands where, according to Haslem, he had left

by 1876, and was at that time residing in Longton where, with his sons, he had started his own decorating establishment.

Daniel Lucas died on 31st October 1898[4], aged 80 years, at which time he was described as an 'Artist (Painter) Retired', and was living at 69 Peel Street, Longton.

1 Civil Register, Marriage, June Quarter 1840, Wolstanton, Vol 17 Page 231.
2 Civil Register, Births, June Quarter 1861, Madeley, Vol 6b Page 617.
3 British Census 1881 RG11 2734/138 Page 4.
4 Civil Register, Deaths, December Quarter1898, Stoke-on-Trent, Vol 6b Page 180.

William Lucas

William Lucas was the second son of Daniel Lucas, the well-known Derby painter, and was born in Shelton, Staffordshire in 1812. He came to Derby with his family in about 1814, and would have been apprenticed as a gilder about 1824, finishing his time around 1831. He married Sarah Ride at St. Peter's, Derby, on 29th September 1835, and their children were christened at St. Alkmund's, Derby between 1836 and 1846. At this time he is described as a 'China Painter', and the family were living firstly at Green Lane, then St Helen's Street and finally Goodwin Street.

He is recorded in the 1832 list of workpeople at the factory, in the gilding department. He continued to work at the factory, and is found in the 1841 Derby census returns, where he is listed as a 'China Painter', living with his family and his brother George, aged 15, who is also listed as a 'China Painter.'

Haslem states that he was trained at the Derby porcelain factory as a gilder, and says that he 'probably excelled more in that branch of the art than his father did as landscape painter'. He further states that on leaving Derby, William was employed at Messrs. Mintons and died at Stoke-upon-Trent in early life.

It can be seen, from the above, that William Lucas did not join Mintons until at least 1846 and probably didn't leave Derby until the closure of the factory, in 1848. He is found in the Staffordshire census returns of 1851 which list him as a 'China Gilder', aged 39, living at High Street with his wife, Sarah and their children, Rebecca aged 14, John aged 11, William aged 9 (who later became a Methodist Minister), all born in Derby, and a daughter, aged 1, born in Staffordshire. Their sons, John and William, were both described in the census as 'Potters'.

George Mellor (senior)

A gilder and Japan painter, he was born at Derby, in St. Peter's parish, in 1780[1], and would have been an apprentice gilder, at Derby, in about 1791-2. He was at Pinxton from 1796 until 1799, which raises the intriguing probability that he finished his apprenticeship under William Billingsley. He was in Staffordshire in 1801, where it is alleged he met Billingsley, who was there to purchase china, in the white, for decorating at his Mansfield establishment.

He was married to Sarah Eccles at Madeley on 10th September 1800 and other information, which states that he was working at Coalport until 1811, is substantiated, as three children; Mary, christened 20th June 1802; George, christened 1st February 1807; and John William, born 29th May 1809, were all born in Madeley, Shropshire. It is interesting that although John William was born in Madeley and baptised, he was not registered at that time. It therefore appears to researchers when viewing the registers that he was christened at St. Alkmund's, Derby in 1819. However a note in the St. Alkmund's register explains that two of the children, John William and Malcolm, had been baptised before but not registered. John William, who was born in Shropshire, was duly registered and Malcolm, who was born on 10th July 1815 in Derby, was registered by another curate on 25th May 1821. These notes were all entered at the christening of Eliza Mellor on 26th May 1821 at St. Alkmund's, Derby. Why the children were not registered at Madeley is not clear.

Two further children were christened at St. Alkmund's; Caroline in 1823 and Harriet in 1825. The statement, therefore, that after returning to Derby he remained at the factory until 1830, is at least partly supported. His daughter Sarah Ann (who is not found in the parish register at Madeley, but according to the later 1851 census returns was born there) appears in *Pigot & Co's National and Commercial Directory, 1828-29* under a section entitled 'Glass, China & Earthenware Dealers' at 8 Victoria Street. It then appears that shortly after leaving the factory he joined with her in the business. He is found in the 1841 Derby census returns, where he is listed as a 'China Dealer', and was living in Victoria Street. The enterprise must have thrived, for in the 1851 census, his two daughters, Sarah Ann, who had been a paintress at the factory, and Caroline Ann were running the business. Caroline was by this time married to a William Price.

George Mellor is listed as an 'Enameller' and was possibly painting pieces for the shop. The two ladies were living at the premises in Victoria Street, along with their father, their mother, Sarah, her grandsons, George and Malcolm, who were the children of George Mellor junior, and were born in London, and their granddaughters, Sara Ann Eliza and Sarah Ann Price. The business is listed in *Freebody's Directory of Derby, Chesterfield etc, 1852*, under 'China and Glass Dealers' at 24 Victoria Road *(sic)*. The business was still running in 1857 as an entry in *Whites Directory for Derby* in that year confirms – 'Mellor Sarah Ann, Glass, China and Earthenware Dealer, 22 Victoria Street'.

George Mellor died on 9th September 1862 aged 82 years, at Colyear Street, Derby[2].

[1] Birth date taken from 1851 Derby census returns.
[2] Civil Register, Deaths, September Quarter 1862, Derby, Volume 7b Page 270.

George Mellor (junior)

George Mellor was the son of George Mellor senior, a gilder at the Derby factory. George jnr. was christened on 1st February 1807, at Madeley, Shropshire, where his father was then working at the Coalport manufactory.

He was apprenticed as a Japan painter and gilder at the Derby factory in about 1819 and would have finished his apprenticeship by about 1826. He was married to Ann Brown on 6th May 1832 at St. Alkmund's King Street Methodist. At this time he is described as a 'China Painter' and his address is given as Broadway, London.

Haslem, in his book *The Old Derby China Factory,* states that George left the Derby factory in 1828 and, writing in the present tense, in 1875, says that he 'has since that time resided chiefly in London, where he has been in the habit of buying oriental china, quantities of which are at times brought from India, in an unfinished state, by trading vessels; this he has been in the habit of decorating in the oriental style.'

We can infer from this information that George left the Derby factory only a couple of years after the end of his apprenticeship and that he came back to Derby to marry a local girl.

John William Mellor

John William Mellor was the son of George Mellor, a gilder at the Derby factory. Haslem says that George Mellor had two sons brought up to the business, and who were apprenticed at the Derby factory. George, he says, was a gilder but nothing was known of the other son's career.

John was born on 29th May 1809, at Madeley, Shropshire, where his father was working at the Coalport manufactory. He was apprenticed as a potter at the Derby factory around 1821, and would have finished his apprenticeship about 1828.

He was married to Emma Wright at Duffield, Derbyshire on 8th June 1829 and at the christening of their first child, Harriott Ann, at St. Alkmund's,

Derby, on 20th December 1829 he is described as a 'China worker', living at Exeter Street. At the christening of subsequent children (the couple had seven children between the years 1829 and 1840), he is described as a 'Potter' and had changed his address to Parker Street. During this time he was working at the factory, and is recorded as a potter at the factory in the 1832 list of contributors to the King's Gift, although under the name William Mellor. He appears to have dropped his first name and was using his middle name instead. In spite of that fact, all the evidence points to this being the same person as in the parish registers. Finally, he and his family are found in the 1841 Derby census returns, where he is listed under his official name, John Mellor, living at Devonshire Street, Derby and is described as a 'China Potter'.

Nothing is known of the individual items made by this potter, but he would have had a hand in many of the 'useful wares' manufactured by Derby during the 1830s and 1840s.

The rather strange ending to this story suggests that he worked at the Derby factory until it closed, in 1848, and then changed his career completely! He is next found in the 1851 Derby census returns, living with his wife, Emma and his family of seven children, at New Market, Derby, where he is described as a 'Police Officer'. At this date he must have been one of the first provincial policemen.

One wonders about the 'cultural shock' he received on joining the newly formed police force. The Municipal Corporations Act of 1835 had meant that boroughs and cities outside of London (the new Metropolitan Police Force, which had been formed by Peel, only covered London) had to form their own forces. These new 'Corporations', as they were called, were allowed to set up their new police forces as they thought fit. However, it was not until 1862 that all of the counties had formed their own forces.

The conditions endured by these early policemen were quite harsh. The required dress standards were very particular and woe betide any officer whose turnout fell short of these required standards. An officer was issued with one uniform each year and was given the opportunity to purchase his last year's uniform to use as second best. The pay for an officer was three shillings a day, and had earlier been set at this low level by Peel as a way of controlling the type of man he wanted to join his new force. He wanted working class men and not those who would be disruptive by giving themselves a 'superior' status.

Discipline was very strict and policemen were

dismissed for a variety of reasons, including if a member of the public complained about them, or if they committed any offence, kept bad company or broke police regulations such as being late on duty, being improperly dressed or leaving a beat. Apparently, the usual cause for dismissal was being drunk (not necessarily on duty).

Physically the job was very demanding. A constable on night duty walked on average twenty miles a night, in all weather conditions, seven days a week. Until the end of Queen Victoria's reign, a police officer was not entitled to any refreshment break, and no hot meals. If he was wet at the start of his shift, he remained that way until his duty ended. Constant patrolling in unsuitable boots also injured the police officer's feet and legs.

As for time off, the following story illustrates the attitude by superior officers to constables requesting leisure time. A constable in a rural location requested to have a Sunday off. He gave his reason as being for the purposes of 'sport and recreation'. Upon receiving his request his Superintendent waited for the Sunday in question and sent an urgent message to the constable's sergeant, requesting that he send the constable to his superintendent's office to collect an important note. The constable duly arrived on the day that he had requested as a rest day, and marched the 15 miles to the superintendent's station to collect the 'urgent' letter only to find it was addressed to his sergeant. He delivered the letter and his sergeant opened it. The letter read: 'Now ask this silly blighter if he has had enough sport and recreation'! Apparently, such instances were not rare. All in all, I wonder whether John Mellor rued the day the Derby factory closed!

Post Script!

Whatever the privations, John William Mellor seems to have been successful in his career, as in the *Whites Directory for Derby* in 1857, he is recorded as having reached the rank of 'Police Serjent' *(sic)*, and was living with his family at Corn Market.

Francis Sprig Moor

Francis Sprig Moor was christened at St. Alkmund's, Derby on 16th October 1779. He was probably apprenticed at Derby as a china painter, sometime around 1791.

He was married to Hephzibah Griffiths on 25th October 1801 at Duffield, Derbyshire. The couple's first child, Charlotte Griffiths, was christened at

Tabernacle Independent, Hanley, on 20th September 1802, suggesting that he had left Derby shortly after his marriage to work in the Potteries.

However, sometime between 1802 and 1814 he had returned to Derby, as on 12th May 1814, a son, George Griffiths, was christened at St. Alkmund's, Derby. At this time he is described as a 'China man', and was living at Darley Lane. Another child, Marianne, was christened at St. Alkmund's on 26th May 1816, at which time he is described as a 'China Painter' and is at the same address. It is not known how much longer he stayed at Derby, but he is not included in the 1832 list of workpeople at the factory.

Matthew Morledge

Matthew Morledge was christened at All Saints, Derby in 1791. He was apprenticed at the Derby works as a gilder, about 1803, and would have finished his apprenticeship by about 1810.

He was married to Ann Cotton at St. Alkmund's, Derby on 26th December 1816. The couple's first child, Elizabeth, was christened at St. Alkmund's, Derby on 1st April 1819. At this time he is described as a 'China Painter' and was living at Goodwin Street. The couple had three more children christened at St. Alkmund's, between the years 1821 and 1827, by which time the family had moved to Darley Lane. He is in the list of workpeople at the Derby factory in 1832, and is found in the gilding department.

One of his sons, **Frederick**, was to follow in his father's footsteps both in becoming a china painter and in working at the Derby factory. He is found in the 1841 Derby census returns, where he is described as a 'China Painter', and was living at Rivett Street.

John Moscrop

John Moscrop was born in Rowsley, Derbyshire in 1786. He was apprenticed to Derby around 1798, as a gilder, and would therefore be working, as an adult, in about 1805.

It is known that he had been married, and that his wife had died some time between 1805 and 1833, as on 6th April 1833 he was married at St. Alkmund's, and on that occasion he was described as a widower. He was married to Ester Goadsby, the widow of James Goadsby, who was a modeller at the factory. She was also the daughter of Thomas Mountford (her maiden name was Esther Mountford), the enamel kilnman at the factory.

Colour Plate 99. Tureen and Cover painted with a spray of flowers. Marks: Crown, crossed batons, dots and D in red. 18 in red for the gilder John Moscrop. Dimensions: Tureen length 5 in, width 7 in. *Derby Museums and Art Gallery.*

Colour Plate 100. A Derby dessert plate painted by Richard Dodson. Gilded by John Moscrop c.1815. Marks: Crown, crossed batons, dots and D in red, gilder's numeral 18 in red. Diameter 8³/₄ in. *The Late Anthony Hoyte Collection. Photograph Courtesy of Neales Auctioneers of Nottingham.*

He was allocated number 18 as his gilder number, which is shown in the 1820 list. It is probable that he would have been allocated this relatively low number quite a few years earlier, since he had been working at the factory from about 1805. Munday Simpson was allocated 19, and he had been at the factory since about 1809. Haslem says the general rule was that the workmen kept their numbers until they left the factory, at which time another workman took it over. Moscrop continued to work at the factory and in 1832 is shown as the Overlooker of the gilders, in the list of workpeople at the factory. He is next found in the 1841 census returns for Derby, living at 25 Erasmus Street, where he is described as a 'China Painter', aged 50. He then continued working at Derby until the close of the factory in 1848. He is further found in the Derby census returns for 1851, and is again described as a 'China Painter', aged 65, still living in Erasmus Street, this time at number 16. This evidence raises the possibility that he was working for the 'King Street' factory.

It is amazing that John Moscrop, who worked both at Nottingham Road and possibly the King Street factory, man and boy, for 50 years, has previously hardly been mentioned in the literature concerning these factories.

Thomas Mountford

Thomas Mountford was born in Staffordshire, and was almost certainly trained in the Potteries. Haslem says that he had acquired some proficiency in the making of colours.

He was married to Mary Barnett at St. John's, Burslem, on 6th June 1795. The couple had nine children christened at Hanley or Burslem, Staffordshire, between the years 1796 and 1813.

Their last child, John, was christened at Burslem, Staffordshire, on 26th January 1817, which means that their arrival at Derby was after this time. Haslem says that he was 'enamel kiln fireman' at the Derby factory for many years.

He is found in the list of workpeople at the factory in 1832 and is described as enamel kilnman. How much longer he continued to work at the factory is not known, but he is not found in the 1841 Derby census returns.

Jesse Mountford

Jesse Mountford was christened on 9th September 1798 at Hanley in Staffordshire. Haslem states that his father, Thomas, was enamel kiln fireman at the Derby works, and also states that Jesse served his

Colour Plate 101. Watercolour with a house and bridge. Inscribed by Bemrose lower left 'Mountford'. 6½ in X 10½ in. *Royal Crown Derby Museum.*

Colour Plate 102.
Porcelain plaque painted
by Jesse Mountford.
Diameter 3 in.
*Dr. John Freeman
Collection.*

Colour Plate 103. Derby
saucer painted with views
in Leicestershire by Jesse
Mountford.
*Derby Museums and
Art Gallery*

Colour Plate 104. Coalport Hanging Note Rack c.1825, with landscape painting by Jesse Mountford. Bearing the Society of Arts 'Coalport Improved Feltspar Porcelain' on the reverse. *Cheltenham Art Gallery and Museums.*

apprenticeship at Derby.

The claim that he served his apprenticeship at Derby is probably incorrect. It does not tally with the information in the registers, as John Mountford, the brother of Jesse, and the youngest son of Thomas Mountford, was christened in Burslem, Staffordshire, on 26th January 1817. This suggests that the family did not arrive in Derby until after this time, and it would not seem logical that the young Jesse would leave the family to be an apprentice in Derby, especially since his father was gainfully employed in a pottery in Stoke. These facts indicate that Jesse was not Derby trained, and that he served his apprenticeship in the Potteries.

On 25th August 1819, he married Mary Mayblin at Spondon in Derbyshire and his first child, John, was christened at St. Alkmund's, Derby, on 20th June 1820. At this time he was described as a 'China Painter', and was living at Nottingham Road. He continued to work at Derby, until he was discharged, along with four other painters, in 1821.

Haslem says that Jesse Mountford worked at Coalport for fifteen years after he left Derby. This is supported in large measure by the christening of four children in Madeley, starting with Eliza, on 18th April 1824 and ending with Maria on 3rd August 1831. Also, a daughter, Jane, was buried at Madeley Wood, on 2nd June 1833.

On leaving Coalport, Haslem says that he went to the Davenport factory at Burslem, and was employed there as a landscape painter for twenty-five years. Also, Godden says that Mountford had left Coalport by 1835, as a child, Jesse, was born in Staffordshire at this time.

Information in the 1851 census returns for Stoke support this assertion as he is described as a 'Painter of China', living in Chapel Lane with his wife, Mary, and two children, Jesse, aged 16 and Eliza, aged 15, both born in Shelton, Staffs. His son is described as a 'Painter of China' and his daughter as a 'Burnisher of Gold'.

He continued to work at Davenport until he died on 28th March 1861, at which time he was described as a 'Potter', and was still living at 5 Chapel Lane, Burslem. He was said to have been an expert angler and was preparing, in the evening, for the next day's fishing, when, as Haslem says, 'the summons came which for ever put an end to both his artistic and piscatorial pursuits'.

His son **Jesse** carried on the family's tradition, and in the 1881 census returns for Stoke was described as a 'Potters Decorator', living with his wife and children at 11 Waterloo Road, Burslem.

John Mountford

John Mountford was the son of the Derby enamel kilnman, Thomas Mountford, and was christened on 26th January 1817 at Burslem, Staffordshire. He was apprenticed at Derby, as a potter, around 1828, and would have finished his time about 1835.

On the 25th December 1835 he was married to Anne Peach, at St. Peter's, Derby, and the couple's first child, Isabella, was born in Derby in 1836. A further child, Thomas, was born in Derby in 1838.

He seems to have left Derby shortly afterwards, as his next child, Mary, was born in Stoke-on-Trent, Staffordshire, in 1840. He then worked for Alderman Copeland until 1849, and whilst there he discovered the Parian china body. He was held in very high regard at Copelands, as an article in the *Staffordshire Advertiser* of 17th November 1849, on the occasion of a dinner given to celebrate the start of a partnership between Mountford and Samuel Keys Jnr, indicates:

THE FIGURE TRADE

A party of about forty, chiefly workmen in the employ of Alderman Copeland, M.P., with other friends, met to partake of supper at host Key's, of Stoke, on Friday evening, the 9th inst. The chief object was to present Mr. John Mountford with a tribute of respect, consisting of a silver-gilt snuffbox, the gift of the figure makers. It bore the following inscription: 'This box is presented to John Mountford, by his fellow-workmen in the employ of W. T. Copeland, Esq., M.P., believing that the services he has rendered to the trade, have assisted to promote its growth and importance.' Mr. Mountford returned thanks in a neat speech, and concluded by proposing the health of the worthy Alderman, his late employer, which was drank with acclamation, and was followed by the song, 'There's room enough for all.' Amongst the other toasts were – Mr Copeland, jun., Mr. Battam, and Mr. Horton Yates; and the company did not separate, without wishing success to Mr. Mountford, in his business connection with Mr. Keys.

In the same edition was the formal announcement of the partnership between the two men.

In 1850, yet another article appeared describing an 'Exhibition of Art and Manufactures', at the Stoke-upon-Trent Athenaeum. Several of the major manufactories had exhibits, including Copelands, Mintons and Wedgwood. The exhibits from the firm of Keys and Mountford were described as follows:

'The firm of Keys and Mountford, of Stoke, also made a good show of statuettes. We may mention a copy of Canova's "Theses (sic) vanquishing the Centaur", "Venus extracting the thorn", "Andromeda exposed to the Sea Monster", "Group of boys supporting a Dessert-basket", "Boys representing the Seasons", by Flamingo; "Italian Shepherd", from Landseer's picture; a Greyhound Bitch, with Whelps, by Thompson, after Gott, the original in the possession of the Duke of Devonshire at Chatsworth, &c, &c.'

He is next found in the 1851 Stoke-on-Trent census, where he is described as a 'Porcelaine Manufacturer' *(sic)*, living at Cliff Bank, with his wife Anne, and their children, Isabella, Thomas, Mary and John. His son Thomas is described as an Apprentice 'Pottery Painter'. Later, a son, Charles Barnett, was born on 10th October 1855 at Liverpool Road, Stoke upon Trent, at which time the certificate records his father as a 'Parian Manufacturer'.

The partnership between Samuel Keys and John Mountford continued until 15th October 1853, when a notice dissolving the partnership appeared in the *Staffordshire Advertiser* of 22nd October 1853. However, John Mountford carried on alone, and managed to continue with the business until February 1860, when he appears to have encountered some difficulties. An advertisement in the *Stafford-* *shire Advertiser* on 25th February 1860 was placed for the sale of the stock, fixtures, utensils, ovens, moulds and materials of a Parian manufacturer. Buyers were asked to apply to Mr. J. Mountford, Liverpool Road, Stoke-upon-Trent.

Yet another advertisement appeared in the *Staffordshire Advertiser* on 7th April 1860 as follows:

To be SOLD by AUCTION, by Mr. CHEADLE, at the WHEAT SHEAF HOTEL, STOKE-UPON-TRENT, on Wednesday, the 18th day of April, 1860, at seven o'clock in the evening, by direction of the Mortgagees, and subject to conditions to be then declared, all those valuable POTWORKS, BUILDINGS, and PREMISES, very eligibly situated in John Street, Liverpool Road, in the centre of the town of Stoke-upon-Trent, now and for many years past in the occupation of Mr. John Mountford, Parian Manufacturer.

The buildings, which are of recent erection, have a considerable frontage to John-Street, and comprise two ovens and suitable workshops and warehouse room, and are well adapted for the manufacture of parian or china.

The property, with the exception of a small part, which is leasehold, is copyhold of the Manor of Newcastle-under-Lyme, and will be sold subject to all fines and Manorial rights.

Colour Plate 105. Parian figure group of 'Theseus vanquishing the Centaur', shown at the Stoke Athenaeum exhibition in 1850. Inscription on reverse "Keys and Mountford" c.1850.
Clive and Lynne Jackson.

Unfortunately the sale did not save him from further problems, and a string of advertisements from March until June 1860 show his creditors investigating his affairs, and forcing his bankruptcy. He was finally issued his certificate on 30th June 1860, after some of his creditors had objected. The reason for the objection was that one of the creditors had alleged that Mountford had taken some of the furniture from his house and sold it without permission. Mountford explained to the judge that he had in fact sold furniture to the value of £20 because he did not have any money to live on.

Some time later he returned to Derby, where he is reputed to have worked for Sampson Hancock at the King Street works. He was certainly back in Derby by 1871, as he is listed in the 1871 census returns for Derby, where he is described as a 'Potter', living with his wife Anne, two children, and two grandchildren at number 12 Burton Road. He may have returned to Derby several years earlier as Herbert Jewitt, the son of the ceramic historian Llewellyn Jewitt, is reported as having trained under him at King Street in 1866. There is an entry in C.N. *Wright's Directory of South Derbyshire, 1874,* which reads, 'Mountford John, Earthenware Dealer & Miss Annie, Milliner & dressmaker, 12 Burton Road'.

He is next found in the 1881 Derby census, and at this time he is described as a 'Dealer in Glass and China', and was still living at 12 Burton Road. It seems his entrepreneurial spirit was still with him! However, by the time of the 1891 census he is described as a 'China Worker', living with his wife and three grandchildren at the same address. At this time he was almost certainly working at the King Street factory, although an entry in *Kelly's Directory of Derbyshire, 1891,* reads, 'Mountford John, Glass & China Dealer, 12 Burton Road'.

An interview with Sampson Hancock was published in the *Yorkshire Weekly Post* on 12th May 1894 in which he recalled John Mountford.

'If you had paid me a visit a few days ago, you might have seen John Mountford, whom I employed. He was apprenticed at the Old Works, in Derby, but he left early in life, and came to Messrs. Copeland and Garret's at Stoke-on-Trent, to start the figure trade there. While in their employ he brought out the composition known to the trade as Parian, or imitation marble, which has done more to increase that branch of the potter's art than anything invented in the present century. The name of this man will be recorded in time to come among those of famous potters, and he is the oldest potter from the original works. I regret to say that he is now suffering from a paralytic seizure.'

Just one day later John Mountford succumbed to this affliction and died at 12 Burton Road on 13th May 1894 aged 77 years, at which time he was described as a 'China Potter'.

William Musgrove

There is some confusion over the parentage of William Musgrove. A William Musgrove was christened at Mansfield in 1781 but no parents' names are given. He was, however, at Pinxton at the same time as the Musgrove family, which consisted of John and Ann Musgrove and their children Sarah and Elizabeth. According to the factory book, William worked at the Pinxton factory from 12th November 1796 until 19th January 1799 at a rate of 4d. per day. It is not clear in what capacity he was engaged, but from his wage rate it was as a junior and was most probably as an apprentice gilder.

Haslem says that George Mellor, who left Derby to work with Billingsley at Pinxton, made a statement to the effect that there were between ten and twelve painters and gilders employed at Pinxton during his time (1796 to 1799) and among the names he mentions is that of William Musgrove.

The Musgroves then went with Billingsley to Mansfield and Brampton, before returning to Pinxton in about 1803. In light of subsequent events it seems that either he stopped at Pinxton as an apprentice, or, more likely, he went to Mansfield with Billingsley, and continued his apprenticeship there.

In 1806 William Musgrove married Ann Berry at Mansfield, Notts. Their first child, Marianne, was christened at St. Alkmund's, Derby on 5th September 1808. In 1818, at the christening of his third child, Ann, the family was living at Nottingham Road and he is described as a 'China Painter'. Their last child, Samuel, was christened at St. Alkmund's on 2nd July 1826 and the family was then living in Navigation Row, where he was again described as a 'China Painter'.

This evidence points to a long career as a Derby painter or gilder, and it is surprising that his name does not feature in any Derby literature.

Henry Pedley

Henry Pedley was christened at St. Werburgh's, Derby, on 21st April 1806, and was apprenticed at Derby, as a gilder, around 1818. He would have completed his time by 1825. He continued to work at Derby, and is found in the list of workpeople at the factory in 1832, in the gilder's section.

Shortly afterwards he left Derby to take up employment in the Potteries, and was married to Mary Ann Frazer, on 22nd December 1833, at Stoke-on-Trent, Staffordshire. The couple's first child, Hannah, was christened in Stoke-on-Trent, on 29th March 1835. A further three children were born in

Colour Plate 106a. Signature of Henry Pedley on this porcelain plaque.

Colour Plate 106. Porcelain plaque of 'The Pleading of the Birds' painted by Henry Pedley. Sight measure 14 in X 12 in. This is the only known work by this artist, and, given its quality, it is mystifying that the name of this Derby trained artist has been forgotten. Herbert Allen Collection in the Victoria and Albert Museum.
Photograph shown by courtesy of the Victoria and Albert Museum.

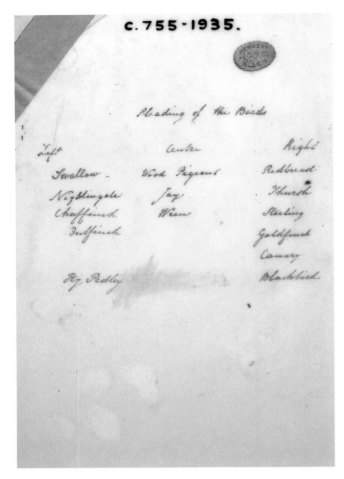

C.755-1935.

Pleading of the Birds

Left	Centre	Right
Swallow	Wood Pigeons	Redbreast
Nightingale	Jay	Thrush
Chaffinch	Wren	Starling
Bulfinch		Goldfinch
		Canary
Hy. Pedley		Blackbird

Colour Plate 107. Reverse of porcelain plaque in Colour Plate 106.

Stoke-on-Trent, the last of whom, Henry George, was born on 17th January 1838. At this time the family were living at Broad Street, Shelton, where he was described as a 'China Painter', and his wife as a 'Paintress'.

It is possible that he was working at the Copeland and Garrett works at this time, as in her book *Spode–Copeland–Spode*, Vega Wilkinson, in the section (Appendix 3) concerning 'Details taken from the Special Order Reference Books 1833-1900s – Spode Archives', has pattern number 5800 allocated to 'Pedley H'. The description of the decoration was 'Birds on each side', and the pattern number, again according to Wilkinson, was got up around 1837 (Appendix 9 of her book). Further evidence of a stay at Copeland's comes from the Allen Collection in the Victoria and Albert Museum. This collection contains a plaque signed 'Hy. Pedley', painted with various types of birds, named on the reverse. The collection catalogue reference states that 'Henry Pedley worked at Copeland's factory, Stoke-upon-Trent, and at the Old Hall Factory, Hanley'.

He left Stoke sometime shortly after and worked in a manufactory in France. His son, Thomas, was born there, in Lyons, in 1841. He was, however, back in Stoke-on-Trent, by 1851, and is found in the Stoke-on-Trent census returns at that time. He is described as a 'China Painter', and was living with his wife, Mary Ann, and his four children, at Vale Street. His daughter, Harriet, is described as an 'Apprentice burnisher', and his son, Harry, as an 'Apprentice modeller'.

There is some evidence that his next move was to the Coalport factory. Godden, in his book *Coalport and Coalbrookdale Porcelains,* says that Henry Pedley's name is in the 1859 wages list and that his remuneration was a high figure, being £2.10s.0d. per week. This was the same amount as drawn by John Randall and Daniel Lucas junior. There are also two designs allocated to him in the factory pattern books, 6/418, 'Plants by Pedley', and 6/419, 'Two birds by Pedley'. According to Godden, these pattern numbers lie between the dates 1850-1855. All the above evidence raises the possibility of a stay between c.1852-c.1860.

He died at the age of 74 years on 10th March 1880[1]. The death certificate records him as a 'Crest Painter' who was living at West Street, Stoke-on-Trent.

[1] Civil Register, Deaths, March Quarter 1880, Stoke-on-Trent, Volume 6b Page 143.

Thomas Pegg

Thomas Pegg was the elder brother of William Pegg (known as Quaker Pegg), the famous botanical flower painter at the Derby factory. He was christened at Whitmore, Staffordshire, on 27th January 1771.

He was married to Anne Hodgkinson at St. Werburgh's, Derby, on 24th July 1790. From this evidence it would seem that he was the first of the brothers to arrive at the Derby factory.

Haslem has an amusing anecdote about Thomas, which is worth repeating here. He says, 'Thomas, a brother of William Pegg, was a gilder at the Derby works, and, although he had no scruples of conscience (unlike his brother William), which caused him to prefer the making of stockings to the decoration of china, yet he had, like his brother, some eccentricity of character. One of his notions was that he was destined to gather the Jews together and take them to Jerusalem, where they were, under his auspices, once more to form a united nation; and it was said he one day started on his eastward journey with that intent, but got no farther than Borrowash, some four or five miles from Derby, where, on cool reflection over a quiet pipe and a glass of home-brewed he decided to retrace his steps. It is scarcely necessary to say that when Tom took a longer journey he left the Jews still a scattered people. Like his brother William, Tom had lost the sight of one eye. The appellation of Joshua, the Prophet, which his shopmates gave him, was by no means distasteful to Thomas Pegg.'

He was still working at the factory in 1832, when he is listed in the gilding department.

William Pegg (the Younger)

Colour Plate 108. Carte de Visite of William Pegg (the Younger) c.1860. *Royal Crown Derby Museum.*

William Pegg was born in Derby and christened at St. John's, Westminster, in about 1795. He was apprenticed at the Derby factory, as a flower painter, in about 1807, and would have finished his time around 1814. He was married to Sarah Simmonds at All Saints, Derby, on 2nd October 1817.

According to Haslem, he left the factory in 1819.

However, this does not seem to be the case, as a daughter, Mary Anne, was christened at All Saints, Derby, on 22nd May 1821. The entry in the register describes him as a 'China Painter', living at Tenant Street. Perhaps he was also a victim of the 'turnout' of painters, in 1821.

After leaving Derby, he went to work in the Potteries. John Twitchett, in *Painters and the Derby China Works*, states that, 'During the 1820s Pegg was employed by Henry and Richard Daniel at Stoke-on-Trent, and he is mentioned appreciatively in Richard Daniel's letter to his father Henry, written between 1823 and 1825, in which he says, "Do get some good flower painters if possible. I have now sold more than Pegg and Brammer and Ellis will do for six months…Take no more common painters or gilders, we must have the very best only… Now is the time or never. Everybody says they never saw such goods before. Poor Ridgway says we cut up his trade and John Rose sends out goods so bad everybody complains."'

Other evidence, which supports Twitchett's statement and places him in the Potteries at this time, comes from the parish register at Hanley, where a son, William, was christened at the Chapelry of Hanley on April 13th 1823. A further two children were baptised at the Chapelry of Hanley, Elizabeth in 1824 and Harriet in 1827.

Current information gathered from Bemrose[1] suggests that William Pegg was a friend of William Billingsley and that he worked at Nantgarw after he left the Derby works. As can be seen from the foregoing information, this is very doubtful indeed. Firstly, William Pegg was born in the very year that Billingsley left Derby, in 1795, to start his manufactory at Pinxton. Billingsley then went to Brampton in Torksey in 1803, followed by Worcester in 1808 and then to Nantgarw in 1813. Pegg meanwhile started his apprenticeship at Derby around 1807, finishing about 1814. It is very difficult to see how a friendship could have developed between them when they were hundreds of miles apart.

Secondly, Bemrose relates that Pegg and his wife 'Margaret' used to make the difficult pedestrian journey to Nantgarw. However, as previously stated, William Pegg was married to Sarah Simmonds. This again does not engender confidence in his information. Finally, Bemrose states that it was in 1819, after Pegg had left Derby, that he went to Nantgarw, when in fact Pegg did not leave Derby until after May 1821. There is also the fact that Billingsley was, at this time, supplying Mortlocks with the majority of his porcelain 'in the white', and his financial situation at the time would probably not have allowed him to employ painting staff. It seems that there is confusion between William Pegg (the Quaker) and William Pegg (the Younger) when relating stories of travels to Wales. Quaker Pegg did indeed travel to Swansea to visit the factory there. This took place in the year 1817, when his travels were meant to alleviate the trouble he was having with his failing eyesight by resting them from painting. In a letter to his wife, from Swansea on 1st August 1817, Pegg explains that his eyesight had recovered somewhat since being in Swansea, but that it had worsened again whilst writing the letter. Being a very moral man, he also explained that he had an objection to working whilst in Swansea, as it might offend his employer, Robert Bloor. He did not stay much longer in Swansea, as soon after other letters were received from different parts of the country, as he continued his tour. Sadly then, it seems that neither of the William Peggs painted on Welsh porcelain.

According to Haslem, William Pegg (the Younger) later left the Potteries, and took up residence in Manchester where 'he was for many years one of the pattern designers at Hoyle's celebrated print works in Lancashire. About 1840 he, with two other of Hoyle's hands, established a successful business in the same line at Heaton Norris, near Manchester, in the names of Taylor, Hampton, and Pegg. This William Pegg died, aged 72 years, in January 1867. Some years before his death he retired from active life; he painted flowers with great neatness and taste, and to the last amused his leisure by working in watercolours, his execution being as neat and careful as in his best days.'

It is probable that William Pegg did not leave the Potteries until after 1831, as a daughter, Eliza, aged 10 years, was listed in the 1841 census returns for Hulme, Lancashire, as having been born out of the county. In fact, the first mention of William Pegg that is found after his leaving the Potteries occurs in the *1836 Pigots Directory of Manchester*. The entry in this reads, 'William Pegg, Pattern Designer, Chapel Street, Ardwick'. Also in the same directory are three other entries of interest: 'John Hampson Calico Printer; James Hampson Calico Printer; Thomas Hoyle and Sons Calico Printers, 5 Friday Street and Mayfield Buxton Street'. This last entry may very well be where William Pegg was in employment at this time. In the *1841 Slaters Directory of Manchester and Salford*, an entry again confirms that William Pegg was a 'Pattern Designer', but was now living at 75 River Street, Hulme. This is veri-

Colour Plate 109. Watercolour of Cottage Garden Flowers. Said by Bemrose to be by William Pegg. 9³/₄ in X 7¹/₂ in. *Royal Crown Derby Museum.*

fied by the 1841 census returns for Hulme, where he is found living in River Street with his wife, Sarah, and his daughters, Mary, aged 20, Elizabeth, aged 16, Harriet, aged 13, and Eliza, aged 10 years. All of the family is stated in the returns to have been born outside the county, which as stated earlier, indicates that they were still in the Potteries in 1831.

The next phase of his life; that of being a partner in a print design company; is first encountered in 1852, when in the *1852 Slaters Directory of Manchester and Salford* there is an entry which reads, 'William Pegge (*sic*), Calico Printer (Taylor Hampson and Pegge)* Clayton Bridge, Newton Heath'. Information from *Slaters Directory* continues to show the company operating at the same address, although in 1861 the partners are given as Taylor and Pegg, and in 1863, William Pegg alone.

An indication of the family's address, in the early 1850's, comes from the marriage certificate of his daughter Mary Anne[2]. At her marriage to Edward Brooke, an artist, at the Independent Chapel, Rusholme Road, Chorlton upon Medlock, on 16th March 1854, her address is given as 32 Butler Street, Chorlton upon Medlock. Her father is recorded on the certificate as 'William Pegg, Calico Printer'.

William Pegg died in 1867 and his death certificate[3] relates that he died suddenly, at Barlow Moor on 12th January 1867. Consequently an inquest was held on 14th January, which confirmed his death was from 'Natural Causes' and also states that the inquest was held at the Bleachers Arms, Heaton Norris.

[1] Information in *Painters and the Derby China Works*, John Murdock & John Twitchett, Trefoil 1987.

[2] Civil Register, Marriages, Chorlton, March Quarter 1854, Volume 8c Page 572.

[3] Civil Register, Deaths, Chorlton, March Quarter 1867, Volume 8c Page 427.

* Please note name of partnership member is Hampson and not Hampton as stated by Haslem.

John Perkins

John Perkins was baptised at St. Peter's, Derby on 24th June 1797. He was apprenticed at the Derby factory either as a potter or figure maker in about 1809, and would have finished his time by about 1816.

He was married to Hannah Smith at St. Werburgh's, Derby, on 9th May 1825, and at the time of his marriage was described as a 'China Manufacturer'. The couple's first child was christened at St. Werburgh's, Derby on 21st October 1825, at which time he was described as a 'Potter', and was living at Agard Street. A further three children were born to the couple, in Derby, between the years 1827 and 1830, and each time he is described as a 'Potter', living firstly in River Street and then Erasmus Street. He continued to work at Derby, and is found in the list of workpeople at the factory in 1832, in the figure makers department. Haslem describes him as amongst the 'clever modellers and ornamental potters who learnt the art at Derby'.

He left Derby shortly afterwards and went to work in the Potteries. A child, Hannah, was baptised at The Methodist New Connection Church in Longton, Staffordshire, on 26th January 1834 and another, Samuel, in October 1835.

Patrick Potts

Patrick Potts was born in about 1778 in Smalley, Derbyshire, and would have been apprenticed at the factory as china painter in about 1789, finishing his time around 1796. He was married to Rachel Carrington on 1st January 1807, at Duffield, Derbyshire.

The couple's first child, Joshua, was baptised in Madeley, Shropshire on 21st July 1807, which indicates that he had left Derby shortly after the wedding, to work at Coalport. By 1810, however, they were back in Derby, where on 15th September of that year their son, John, was baptised at Smalley. When their daughter, Mary was baptised on 25th February 1814, at St. Alkmund's, he was described in the register as a 'China Painter', living at Ford Lane.

He is finally found, described once again as a 'China Painter', in the register of All Saints on the occasion of the baptism of his son, Joshua, on 10th January 1817, and was now living at Walker Lane. It is not known whether he was a painter or a gilder (he was probably a gilder as his name would surely have been known if he were a painter), nor how much longer he stayed at Derby.

Henry Lark Pratt

Henry Lark Pratt was christened at Derby St. Peter's on 16th February 1805. He was apprenticed at the Derby factory as a china painter, around 1817, and would have finished his time by about 1824.

According to Haslem, he 'only remained at the works a few years after the term of his apprenticeship had expired'. Unfortunately, I have been unable to trace any event that would definitely pinpoint the year in which he left Derby, but a statement in his obituary, in 1873, puts it at about 1830.

It is known, however, that he was working for Messrs. Minton by 1831. According to Godden in his book *Minton Pottery and Porcelain of the First Period*, he is listed in the only surviving Minton wages book under 'Painters and Gilders' from October 1831 to November 1836.

He was married to Margaret Windsor at Stoke-on-Trent on 21st May 1836 and the couple's first child, Mary, was christened at Stoke-on-Trent on 18th February 1837. A further five children were born in the Staffordshire area, and the last, William, was born in Shelton in 1843.

He apparently continued to work in the area, though not necessarily remaining at Mintons, as he is described as an 'Artist' in the 1841 Stoke-on-Trent census returns.

In his obituary in the *Staffordshire Sentinel* of 8th March 1873 it states:

'THE LATE MR. PRATT. – Our Obituary contains the name of Mr. H.L. Pratt, whose long connection with art in the district deserves more than a mere mention. Mr. Pratt was born in Derby, and served his time as a landscape painter, at the Old Derby China Works. In 1830 he came to the Potteries, and was employed at the works of Messrs. Minton. In 1844-5 he was employed by Messrs. Chapman and Hall of London in taking sketches of the baronial halls of Staffordshire, Cheshire and Derbyshire, and devoted himself, during his leisure hours, in acquiring the art of painting in oil. Of this branch of art he became passionately fond, and in Derby, Birmingham, and Coalport, left evidence of his skill. Many of the galleries of the noblemen and gentlemen of the Midland counties contain paintings by him, Mr. Pratt having been employed by, amongst others, the present Sir Robert Peel, the late and present Dukes of Devonshire, and the late Dowager Countess of Harrington. He had, also, some years ago, the honour of Her Majesty's patronage, who was pleased to purchase a tête déjeuner service, on which were views of Windsor Castle, Balmoral, &c. There was scarcely a picturesque nook in Staffordshire, Derbyshire, Shropshire, and part of Cheshire, that he had not seen and sketched, and of Dovedale he was especially fond. The love of art permeated his nature, and in the true sense of the word he was an artist.'

Possibly, as part of his employment for Chapman and Hall, he then moved to Warwickshire. His daughter, Fanny Maria, was born on 12th December 1845 at Melbourne Street, Wolverhampton, and another, Sarah, was born there in 1846, at which time he is described as an 'Artist'. By 1851 he had returned to Derby and is found in the 1851 Derby census returns again described as an 'Artist', living with his wife, Margaret, and their nine children. There is also an entry in *Freebody's Directory of the Towns of Derby, Chesterfield, Alfreton, Buxton, Bakewell, Matlock, 1852,* which reads 'Pratt Henry L., artist, 8 Larges St, Friar gate'. He had obviously had a brief sojourn in Shropshire, sometime between 1846 and 1850, as a daughter, Anne Elizabeth, was born in Stourbridge in 1850. How long he spent at Derby during this period is not precisely known, but he was certainly back in Staffordshire by 1861. He died on 3rd March 1873 at the age of 68

years, in Grant Street, Stoke-on-Trent, at which time his occupation is given as 'Artist'.

A son, also named **Henry Lark**, was born to the couple in 1839, at Stoke-on-Trent. He was to follow in his father's footsteps and become an artist. He changed his forename to 'Hilton', to avoid confusion with his father. Unfortunately, the initials remain the same, so that there is still some confusion when a painting is signed 'H.L.Pratt'. Hilton liked to paint outdoors as much as possible and almost every summer would travel to areas such as the Lake District where he would stay for a couple of months. On one occasion, whilst staying at Dalgelly in 1874, he posted an envelope on 19th August to his wife at Prospect Cottage, Penkhull, Stoke-on-Trent. The content of the envelope was a sprig of heather.

In 1867 he exhibited a painting at the Royal Academy entitled 'Cloud End, near Congleton, Cheshire. From Bosley reservoir'. Later, in 1873, he exhibited a painting entitled 'Derwentwater from Barrow' at the Society of British Artists, Suffolk Street, London. His address was given as Richmond Villas, Penkhull, Stoke upon Trent.

He died at the early age of 36 years in 1875 and the *Staffordshire Sentinel* had an obituary as follows:

'On July 31st, 1875, Mr. Henry Lark Pratt. Junr., artist, Stoke, aged 36 years.

The LATE Mr. H. L. Pratt – We regret to hear of the death of Mr. H. L. Pratt, artist, of Stoke upon Trent, after a severe illness, and at the premature age of thirty-six years. Mr. Pratt, who was the son of an artist of some repute, had by the patient and diligent cultivation of good natural abilities attained a respectable status as a landscape painter and his future career was full of promise. Most of his earlier pictures are now in the possession of local patrons, but during the last two or three years Mr. Pratt had considerably enlarged the circle of his friends. He was a conscientious student of nature, and was accustomed to spend several months of every year in out-door work, chiefly in North Wales, the Lake District, Sherwood Forest, and the more picturesque portions of North Staffordshire. "A View of Bosley Reservoir from Cloud End" was exhibited at the Royal Academy some years since and was greatly admired as a poetical rendering of the softer aspect of the scene. The time is afternoon or evening and a crescent moon is reflected, if we mistake not, in the perfectly placid waters. But it was in some of his Lake pictures that Mr. Pratt achieved his greatest successes.'

Colour Plate 110. Junction of River Derwent and Derby Canal. An oil painting c.1854 painted by Henry Lark Pratt senior. Unframed size 17 in X 24 in. *Derby Museums and Art Gallery.*

Colour Plate 111. Derby Market Place. An oil painting c.1850 by Henry Lark Pratt senior. Framed size 33 in X 44¹/₂ in. *Derby Museums and Art Gallery.*

Colour Plate 112. Derby from the East, 1857. An oil painting by Henry Lark Pratt senior. Framed size 29 ½ in X 40 ½ in. *Derby Museums and Art Gallery.*

Colour Plate 113. St. Peters Church by Moonlight c.1860. An oil painting by Henry Lark Pratt. A view of the church that Henry Lark Pratt was baptised at forty-five years earlier. Framed size 11½ in X 14½ in. *Derby Museums and Art Gallery.*

Colour Plate 114. Part of a Minton dessert service pattern number 3351 painted by Henry Lark Pratt. The original cost-estimate book c.1836 shows a Minton dessert service pattern number 3351 as 'Landscape and Marine views' painted by H.L. Pratt. For marine views on this service see *Minton Pottery and Porcelain of the First Period* colour plate V. Named views on service: Top left; Brougham Castle, Northumberland, Centre; Tivoli, Top Right; Brougham Castle, Bottom Left; Eglinton Castle; Bottom Right; Blacklong, Norfolk. *Olver Collection.*

Colour Plate 115. Minton plate from the above service with a view of Brougham Castle, Northumberland. *Olver Collection.*

Colour Plate 115a. Reverse of plate in Colour plate 89 showing title and pattern number 3351. *Olver Collection.*

Colour Plate 116. Pair of Minton 'Scroll footed jars' c.1835. 10 in to top of handles. Design number 20 in the Ornamental Design Book. Painted with shipping scenes. The painting of these vases matches the painting on an example of dessert service pattern number 3351. *Sam Collins Collection.*

Colour Plate 116a. Reverse side of the Minton Scroll footed jars showing landscape painting by Henry Lark Pratt. *Sam Collins Collection.*

Edwin Prince

Edwin Prince was baptised at St. Alkmund's, Derby, on 6th November 1825. He would have been apprenticed as a painter at Derby in about 1837, and would have finished his time by around 1844. He is listed in the 1841 Derby census returns as a 'China Painter', aged 15, and was living at Chester Place. Often classed together in ceramic literature with Richard Ablott as 'amongst the last batch of apprentices at Nottingham Road', it can now be seen that, although this may be true for Edwin Prince, Richard Ablott was born some ten years earlier in 1815, and they would certainly not have been apprentices at the same time.

Haslem, in his book *The Old Derby China Factory,* says, 'On the closing of the old Derby works Prince, for a short time, worked in London, and for more than the last twenty years has been engaged at glass painting at Messrs. Wales's *(sic)* establishment in Newcastle-upon-Tyne. Others of the old Derby apprentices found employment at the same establishment. Prince's landscapes, on Derby china, may be known by the prevalence of warm brown tints, which are used in finishing.'

Some evidence of a stay in London comes from the 1851 census for the district of Holloway in London, where a not completely decipherable entry suggests that he may have been lodging with William Dexter, another former Derby painter, and his wife Caroline, at 14 Burnard Terrace. The entry has the person as born in Derby, a 'Painter', and of approximately the correct age, namely 25 years.

He is next found in Newcastle upon Tyne, where at the parish church of St. John the Baptist, on 1st January 1857, he was married to Elizabeth Barnett (née Holland), a widow[1]. She was ten years his senior and was a British subject, born in Lisbon, Portugal[2]. The marriage certificate records him as a 'Glass Painter', living in the parish of St. John. His father, Paul Prince, was recorded as a 'Model Maker'. Edwin Prince worked for the next twenty years plus as a painter of stained glass windows for William Wailes of Bath Lane, Newcastle upon Tyne.

In the 1871 census returns for Newcastle upon Tyne he is recorded as a 'Glass Painter', aged 45 years, living with his wife, Elizabeth, aged 55 years, at 13 Blenheim Street, Westgate. Three years later, on 13th January 1874, his wife Elizabeth died[3]. The death certificate records that she was 59 years of age, the wife of Edwin Prince, 'Glass painter', and that the couple were still living at Blenheim Street.

He continued to live at this address until 1878[4], when he left to go into retirement.

William Wailes (1808-1881) was a grocer and tea dealer who in 1838 added a stained glass studio in a back room of his premises, which soon became the largest provincial studio in England. His output was vast, and the 1851 census records that he was already employing seventy-six workers. Unfortunately, no archives have survived and the identities of his workforce remain obscure. Wailes' son-in-law, Thomas Rankine Strang (1835-1899) became a partner in the business in 1861 and as Wailes and Strang the firm continued to make stained glass until c.1914. Many of the windows in St. John the Baptist, the church in which Edwin Prince was married, were manufactured by William Wailes.

The 1881 census returns confirm that Edwin Prince had retired and moved to Londs, Overstrand, Norfolk, where he is listed as a widower and 'Glass Painter Retired', aged 55, living with his sister, Sarah Payne[5]. It was during his retirement that he painted on china for Sampson Hancock, the proprietor of the King Street China Factory in Derby. The items painted by him, if the normal practice of at least two firings was required, must have been shuttled between Norfolk and Derby, and one wonders at the economics of this situation. However, they must have been satisfactory as the practice was carried on for a number of years.

Edwin Prince died in Overstrand in January 1896. An obituary was published at the time and was as follows:

DEATH OF A DERBY ARTIST – THE DEATH IS ANNOUNCED OF Mr. Edwin Prince,

Of Overstrand, Cromer, which took place on Thursday evening. The deceased was the last of the old school of china painters, employed at the old Crown Porcelain Works, Nottingham Road, and excelled particularly in landscape work. At the break up of the old factory in 1848, he went to Newcastle-on-Tyne, where he was employed for many years as a painter on glass for ecclesiastical windows. His work had a national reputation, and he executed many commissions for the Pugins. In his retirement at Overstrand he occupied his leisure in landscape painting on china for his old friend Mr. Sampson Hancock of King Street, Derby and it is a somewhat remarkable coincidence that these two links with the past should be broken within a few weeks of each other. No one who has seen specimens of Mr. Prince's work could fail to admire the extreme delicacy of its shading, and the faultless character of his perspective, in which he stood almost without a rival. Mr. Prince was a member of the old Derby family, and one of his brothers occupies a responsible position at Messrs. Haslam Union Iron Factory. At the time of his death, which was caused by bronchitis, he was in his 70th year.

1 Civil Register, Marriages, March Quarter 1857, Newcastle upon Tyne, Volume 10b Page 53.

2 Information taken from the 1871 census returns for Newcastle upon Tyne.

3 Civil Register, Deaths, March Quarter 1874, Newcastle upon Tyne, Volume 10b Page 7.

4 He is found in Ward's *Directory of Newcastle upon Tyne, Shields, Jarrow and the adjacent villages* in the 1871-1782, 1873-1874, 1875-1876 and 1877-1878 editions. In the 1879 edition, another person is living at this address. He is also in J Christie's *Annual Directory for Newcastle, Gateshead, Jarrow and all the adjoining towns and villages* in the 1870-1871, 1873-1874, and 1874-1875 editions.

5 1881 British census RG11 1925/15 Page 24.

Colour Plate 117. Italianate landscape painted by Edwin Prince. Painting is dated 'Feb 1849' and possibly signed 'Prince' (although this could conceivably have been annotated by Bemrose). Dimensions: 4 in X 5 in. *Royal Crown Derby Museum.*

Colour Plate 118. Transparent watercolour of Newton Solney near Burton upon Trent painted by Edwin Prince. Inscribed by Bemrose 'Newton Solney Prince Burton on Trent'. Dimensions: 3 in X 4½ in. *Royal Crown Derby Museum.*

Colour Plate 119. A plaque painted early in his career, with a rural scene by Edwin Prince c.1845. Plaque in view 4 in X 3³/₈ in. *Harry and Valerie Cordwent Collection.*

Colour Plate 120. Porcelain plaque 'Derby from the Meadows' painted and signed by Edwin Prince. *Private Collection.*

Colour Plate 121. King Street porcelain dessert plate c.1878-1896. Signed 'E Prince' in the painting, and inscribed 'Rotherwas'. Marks: Crown, crossed swords two sets of dots and D, with initials S & H in red. Diameter 8 in. *Derby Museums and Art Gallery.*

Colour Plate 122. King Street plate painted with a shipping scene entitled 'Bridlington Quay' and signed by Edwin Prince. Marks: Signed and titled in the painting. On reverse: Crown, crossed swords, S H and D in red c.1878/1896. *Peter Jackson Antiques.*

Colour Plate 123. King Street plate painted with a shipping scene entitled 'Mouth of the Humber' by Edwin Prince. Marks: Signed and titled in the painting. On reverse: Crown, crossed swords, S H and D in red c.1878/1896. *Peter Jackson Antiques.*

James Ratcliffe

James Ratcliffe was christened at St. Michael's, Derby on 21st August 1803. He was apprenticed as a potter about 1815, and would have finished his time by 1822.

He was married to Elizabeth Pearson at St. Michael's, Derby on 10th September 1828. The couple's first child, William, was christened at All Saints, Derby on 12th December 1830. At this time he was described as a 'Potter', and was living at 3 Morledge. He is found in the list of workpeople at the factory, in 1832, under 'Kilnmen', where he was responsible for the glaze kiln. He continued to work at the Derby factory, and a further five children were christened in Derby, between the years 1832 and 1841.

He is then found in the 1841 Derby census returns, where he continued to live at 3 Morledge. A further two children were baptised at All Saints, Derby, in 1843 and 1846 and it is probable that he continued working at the factory until its closure, in 1848.

The 1851 census shows that after the closure of the factory he became a labourer at the Derby iron foundry.

Henry Roe

Henry Roe was christened at St. Peter's, Derby, about 1798. He was apprenticed at Derby, as a potter, around 1810 and would have finished his time about 1817.

He was married to Catherine Simpson at St. Peter's, Derby, on 25th December 1823 and the couple's first child, Philip, was christened at St. Peter's on 22nd May 1825. At this time he was described as a 'China Manufacturer', living at Albion Street. Four more children were christened at St. Peter's, St. Alkmund's and Brook Street Methodist, between the years 1829 and 1837, where he was variously described as a 'Potter' and 'China factor', then living at Erasmus Street.

He is also in the list of workpeople at the factory, in 1832, under 'Potters'.

John Rogers

John Rogers was born in about 1800. It is not known where he was apprenticed. He was married to Mary Wright at Duffield on 3rd April 1822. The couple's first child, Ann Augusta, was christened at St. Alkmund's, Derby, on 6th November 1834. At this time he was described as a 'China Painter', living at Nottingham Road. He is also in the list of workpeople at the factory, in 1832, in the gilding department.

The couple's next child, Ann, was christened at St. Alkmund's, Derby on 3rd April 1836, where he was again described as a 'China Painter', and was then living at William Street. He continued to work at Derby and is found in *Glovers 1843 Directory*, described as a 'China Painter', living at Bloom Street.

Edward Rouse

Edward Rouse was born in Derbyshire c.1806 and was apprenticed at Derby as a potter, sometime about 1818, and would have finished his time by 1825.

He was married to Maria Horlow at St. Alkmund's, Derby, on 28th August 1827. The couple's first child, Henry, was christened at St. Alkmund's on 24th August 1828, at which time he is described as a 'Potter', living at Erasmus Street.

He continued to work at Derby, and is in the 1832 list of workpeople at the factory under 'Potters'. A further five children were christened at Derby between the years 1830 and 1839, and the family continued to live in Erasmus Street.

He is found in the 1841 Derby census returns where he is described as a 'China Potter', and his address is given as 12 Erasmus Street.

James Rouse (senior)

James Rouse was christened at St. Alkmund's, Derby on 27th February 1803. He was trained at the Derby factory as a flower painter, and by the usual calculation would have started his apprenticeship around 1815, and finished by 1822. On 23rd September 1823, he was married to Sarah Allsopp at St. Werburgh's, Derby. At this time he was described as a, 'China Painter', residing at London Road, Derby.

Colour Plate 124. Self-portrait of James Rouse. *Derby Museums and Art Gallery.*

Haslem, in his book *The Old Derby China Factory,* states that 'when he served his apprenticeship at the Old factory he worked in the same room with Pegg the Quaker, Cotton, Corden, and others, and that when the days work at the factory was over, Rouse and others of the boys were in the habit of attending at Pegg's house, where he seemed to take great pleasure in giving them lessons'. The period of James Rouse's apprenticeship coincides with

'Quaker' Pegg's second period of work at the Derby factory and would therefore give credence to Haslem's story.

Michael Messenger, in his book *Coalport 1795-1926,* states that he left Derby in 1826 or the following year, and says that he is reputed to have worked for a few years in Staffordshire after leaving Derby, and before moving to Coalport. This, however, is not borne out by the available evidence, as a son, Charles, was christened at St. Peter's, Derby on 18th January 1830. The family, at that time, was residing at Bradshaw Street, Derby.

Rather, he seems to have gone straight to Coalport from Derby. Haslem states that 'within a few years of Billingsley's death, Rouse was employed there', i.e. Coalport. As Billingsley died in 1828, this accords more with the documentary evidence, and would help to place his arrival at Coalport to shortly after 1830. According to Godden, James Rouse was in Coalport by 1833, as he says a son, James, was born in Madeley at this time. Documentary evidence of his presence in Coalport comes from the fact that his name is included in the list of signatories to the 1833-34 'Loyal Address', against the strike that took place at Coalport at that time. Godden goes on to say that, 'For thirty years James Rouse painted a variety of Coalport porcelain with figure and Cupid subjects as well as with fruit and flower studies. On his own admission he painted Coalport porcelain in the Nantgarw manner. A number of these pieces, apparently made at Coalport but marked either "Swansea" or "Nantgarw", do survive; some of these used the Adelaide shape which was introduced about 1831.'

Other evidence, which supports Godden's statement that Rouse was in Coalport around 1833-34, comes from the Madeley census returns. In the 1841 returns he is described as a 'China Painter', living with his wife, Sarah, and four children, in Madeley Wood. The children included William, aged 15, described as a 'China Painter', born outside the county, and James, aged 8, born in the county.

His wife, Sarah, died in Madeley in June of 1842. Four years later, he married his second wife, Jane Nickless, in the Parish Church at Dawley in Shropshire[1]. This event took place on 31st August 1846. The marriage certificate records his occupation as 'Painter', and that of his father, William, as a 'Weaver'. He continued to work at the factory, and is next found in the 1851 Madeley census returns, living at the same address. He is again described as a 'China Painter', and at this time was living with his second wife, Jane, his 17-year-old son, James, who was also described as a 'China Painter', born in Madeley, and five other children. Evidence of his presence at the Coalport factory in 1859 can be ascertained from the 1859 wages list[2], when he drew the wage of £2 14s.6d. In addition, some of his work was exhibited at the 1851 and 1862 International Exhibitions. He is next found in the 1861 census returns for Wellington (inc. Madeley) at Foxholes, where he is described as a widower aged 55, and his occupation is given as 'China Painter'. At this time he was living with his unmarried daughter, Mary, and his sons Edward, aged 15, who was described as a 'China Painter', and Charles, aged 12 years.

He left Coalport sometime in the 1860s and went to work in Birmingham, enamelling for jewellers and goldsmiths. In *White's Directory for Birmingham, Wolverhampton and Walsall of 1869* he is listed in both the alphabetical and street sections as, 'James Rouse enamel artist, 294 Coventry Road'. However, Sampson Hancock said that by 1875 he was back at Derby and working for him at the King Street works. His marriage to his third wife, Elizabeth Burton (a widow) is something of a puzzle, inasmuch as it took place in Birmingham three years later, at St. Bartholomew's Church, on 25th April 1878[3]. At this time his address was given as Duddeston Row, Birmingham, which is in the vicinity of Great Charles Street, an area well known for jewellers and goldsmiths. His age is given as 62 years, when in fact he was aged 75 years at that time (perhaps this was because his wife was only aged 54). His occupation was given as 'Artist' and his father's occupation had now changed from the earlier description of 'Weaver' to that of 'Gardner' *(sic)*. Further evidence of his association with the jewellery trade comes from the fact that one of the witnesses to his marriage, William Clifford, was described in the 1881 census as a 'Jewellery Packer'.

He is next found in the 1881 census returns for Derby, where he is described as a 'China Painter', living with his third wife, Elizabeth, and a daughter, Emily, at 44 Fleet Street, Litchurch, Derby. His wife was born in Shirley Heath, Warwickshire, and his daughter, Emily, 21, was born in Birmingham. However, I believe these returns to be in error concerning the daughter, Emily. She was almost certainly the daughter of her mother's previous marriage, and her surname should have been entered as Burton. At this time he was working at the King Street factory where, as stated previously, he had been working since 1875, and where he remained until 1882, after which time he left to join the new Crown Derby factory.

James Rouse was still painting until near the time of his death, which occurred on 25th February 1888 at the house of his son-in-law, John Hand, in Osmaston by Ashbourne[4]. At this time he was described as aged 85 years (his correct age), and his occupation was recorded as an 'Artist Painter'.

As can be seen from the foregoing, several of his sons followed their father's profession and became china painters. **William Edwin**, his eldest son, was apprenticed at the Coalport factory as a flower painter. He was born in Derby in 1824, and Godden says, 'William Rouse's name is included in both the 1841 and 1851 Coalport census returns and in the 1859 wages list, but not in the 1861 census returns'. This latter fact indicates that he had left Coalport before his father. He was married to Drusilla Parsons on 18th June 1849, at Preen Parish Church, in the district of Atcham, Shropshire[5]. Both he and his wife were described on the marriage certificate as 'Painter'. The couple's first child, John, was born on 28th February 1852, at which time they were living at Woodlands, Broseley, and he was described on the birth certificate as a 'China Painter'. At some time after his departure from Coalport, he gave up his career as a china painter, and in the 1861 census returns for Newport East, St. Paul, he is found living at 49 Cross Street in Newport, Wales, with his wife Drusilla and his son John. In these returns he is described as a 'Potato Dealer'. Later, in the 1881 census returns he is found living in Monmouth, Wales, still with his wife, Drusilla, where he is now described as a 'Milk Dealer'.

There is, I believe, a certain amount of confusion concerning the careers of James Rouse senior and his second son (i.e. the second to survive), **James**, who was born in Madeley in 1834. James junior was apprenticed at Coalport as a figure painter around 1846. In 1851 he is found in the census returns for Madeley, described as a 'China Painter', living with his parents at Madeley Wood. He continued to work at the factory, and is next found in the 1861 census returns for the area, where he was now described as a 'Porcelain Painter', living with his wife, Elizabeth, at Madeley Road. He had married Elizabeth Aston at Holy Trinity Church, Coalbrookdale, on September 3rd 1856[6], and on the marriage certificate was described as aged 23 and a 'China Painter'. Elizabeth was described as 21 years of age and also a 'China Painter'. Her father's profession was recorded as 'China Thrower'. He then remained at the factory until at least 1867, when his daughter, Mary, was born on 2nd June of that year[7]. Soon after he moved to Longton in Staffordshire. Previous authors have stated that James senior left Coalport in 1871 and worked in the Potteries for Ridgways at Cauldon Place. However, it can be seen from the above information, that James senior left Coalport in the 1860s to work in Birmingham, and that it was his son who worked in the Potteries.

James junior's wife, Elizabeth, died at Longton in 1872, and two years later he returned to Madeley to marry his second wife, Myra Jones, at Little Dawley Parish Church[8]. This event took place on 9th November 1874, and at this time he was described as a 40-year-old widower living in Longton. His occupation, and that of his father, was recorded on the marriage certificate as 'China Painter'. After his marriage he returned, once again, with his family, to work in Longton. At sometime during this period, he appears to have set himself up as an independent decorator considering the number of Minton and other factory items, including plaques, that are to be found signed by him. These items do not have the factory backstamps or pattern numbers that would normally be associated with a factory decorated article, and indicate that they were purchased in the white.

At the birth of his daughter, Henrietta, on 28th May 1876[9], he was living with his second wife Myra at George Street, Longton, where he was described as a 'China Painter'. He was still residing at this address in 1881, where he is found in the census returns for Stoke, living with his wife, Myra, and their four children at 161 George Street, Prospect House, Stoke-on-Trent. One of his children, **William Aston Rouse** was, in turn, also to become a china painter.

John Twitchett and Betty Bailey, in their book *Royal Crown Derby* state, 'James Rouse Jun. worked at Osmaston Road, it is said, in a room by himself, but little authenticated work has been seen'. The reservations indicated in the latter part of this statement prove to have substance, as James junior died at 161 George Street, Longton on 10th June 1891[10], at the same address he was resident from the early 1870s. This fact makes it improbable that James Rouse junior worked at Osmaston Road. At the time of his death, which was caused by influenza, turning into pneumonia, he was described as a 'China Artist', aged 56 years.

Another son of James Rouse senior, **Charles** (the second child in the family of this name) was born in Ironbridge, Shropshire, in 1848. He may have started his training at Coalport, but as his father left the factory in the 1860s to go to Birmingham, the indications are that Charles, aged 12, accompanied him. Charles subsequently married Mary Moore on 18th April 1870 at Edgbaston Parish Church[11]. The marriage certificate records his occupation as that of a 'Painter'. A son, William, was born in Birmingham in 1872. After a spell in Scotland, where his daughter Jessie was born in 1879, he then moved to Derby where he worked at the Crown Derby factory in Osmaston Road.

He is found in the 1881 census returns for Derby, living next door to his father at 42 Fleet Street, Litchurch[12]. The arrival of his son in Derby, to work at the Crown Derby works, may very well be the reason that James Rouse decided to leave King Street, and move to Osmaston Road in 1882. Charles continued to work at Osmaston Road, and is found in the 1891 census returns for Derby, living at number 54 Molineux Street, where he is described as a 'China Decorator'. He was living at this address with his wife Mary, his daughter Jessie, and his son **William**, who was also described as a 'China Decorator'. He and his son both worked for the factory for at least 20 years, as in the 1901 Derby census returns, Charles is described as a 'Foreman China Gilder', living at 57 Rutland Street, with his second wife Annie (née Heath), whom he had married in 1893, at Stratford, and his daughter Jessie[13]. William, who was again described as a 'China Decorator', was now living at 33 Sutherland Road, with his wife Rose and his daughter Ethel[14]. Charles may still have been working at Osmaston Road in 1915 as a 'C. Rouse' is recorded in the *Derby & District Directory for 1915/16*, as a 'China Gilder', living at 49 Olivier Street. It seems then, that not only was James senior the only workman to have been employed at all three Derby factories, but that his family was the only one to have had three generations to work at the Crown Derby factory.

Father or Son?

As well as the confusion concerning their careers, there is also uncertainty over the attribution of painting on various items to father or son, both of whom were named James. In order to identify their work (both men were active between about 1850 and 1888, when James senior died), signatures have been gathered from a number of the items in question.

Signatures on some of the early work carried out by James senior before the birth of his son are illustrated in Colour Plates 125a and 126a. A signature on a signed plate some 50 years later is illustrated in Colour Plate 132a. All work that I have seen with a signature that is accompanied with the word for senior, i.e. 'Sen' or 'Senr' is carried out in this manner, by which I mean in a cursive hand. I would therefore suggest that a signature in a cursive hand, without the accompanying word, is also by James senior.

On the other hand, the only signature that I have seen accompanied by the word 'Jun', i.e. junior, is on a portrait of his father by James junior (see

Colour Plates 134 and 134a). This signature is in a non-cursive hand. Signatures consistent with this example are to be found on a number of items (mostly plates) from several factories, e.g. Minton, Wedgwood and Aynsley (see Colour Plates 135 to 139). As mentioned earlier, these items do not appear to have been painted at the various factories, as they do not bear the relevant back stamps. They are therefore consistent with the work of an outside decorator, which I suspect was one of James junior's projects whilst in Longton.

Signatures of this type also appear on two plaques, which seem to have been painted during his stay at the Coalport factory (see Colour Plates 140 and 141). These are dated 1861 and 1862 respectively, and are important inasmuch as they help identify certain work carried out at Coalport but not previously attributed. In Michael Messenger's comprehensive work *Coalport 1795-1926*, there is not one mention of James Rouse junior, even though he was active there for nearly twenty years. However, upon viewing Colour Plate 139 one wonders whether some work previously attributed to William Cook should now be attributed to James Rouse junior!

Colour Plates 143 and 144 show an interesting comparison between the animal painting of father and son. There are examples of cattle painting attributed tentatively to other artists at Coalport, but here we have examples from both father and son, who worked there for many years, which show their talent in this genre to good effect.

[1] Civil Register, Marriages, September Quarter 1846, Madeley, Volume 18 Page 111.
[2] Coalport and Coalbrookdale Porcelains, G. Godden, 1970.
[3] Civil Register, Marriages, June Quarter 1878, Birmingham, Volume 6d Page 32.
[4] Civil Register, Deaths, March Quarter 1888, Derby.
[5] Civil Register, Marriages, June Quarter 1849, Atcham.
[6] Civil Register, Marriages, September Quarter 1856, Coalport.
[7] Civil Register, Births, June Quarter 1867, Madeley.
[8] Civil Register, Marriages, December Quarter 1874, Madeley, Volume 6a Page 1257.
[9] Civil Register, Births, June Quarter 1876, Stoke-on-Trent, Volume 6b Page 262.
[10] Civil Register, Deaths, June Quarter 1891, Stoke-on-Trent, Volume 6b Page 220.
[11] Civil Register, Marriage, June Quarter 1870, Edgbaston.
[12] 1881 British census RG11 3404/21 page 35
[13] 1901 British census RG13 3218/152 page 19.
[14] 1901 British census RG13 3206/88 page13.

Colour Plate 125. Porcelain plaque with figure painting signed and dated 1830 by James Rouse senior. Dimensions: 7½ in X 9¾ in. This would have been painted just before the end of his employment at Nottingham Road.
Sam Collins Collection.

Colour Plate 125a. Reverse of the above plaque showing the signature of James Rouse senior. *Sam Collins Collection.*

Colour Plate 126. Porcelain plaque with figure painting by James Rouse senior. Signed and dated 1830 on reverse. Dimensions: 5 in X 6 in. *Private Collection.*

Colour Plate 126a. Reverse of plaque above showing signature of James Rouse senior.

Colour Plate 127. Porcelain plaque painted by James Rouse senior, with flowers in a vase placed on a table.
Derby Museums and Art Gallery.

Colour Plate 128a. Reverse of the Coalport clock showing flower painting by James Rouse senior. The clock was designed to be viewed on a mantel with a mirror behind it. *Shrewsbury Museums Service.*

Colour Plate 128. Clock and stand manufactured at Coalport about 1837 with a profusion of modelled flowers; the small reserve of a cherub holding an hourglass painted by James Rouse senior. The clock is unmarked but the stand is marked with a printed 'Coalport Porcelain/Sparkes of Worcester' mark. The clock is 480mm high and the stand 320mm. *Shrewsbury Museums Service.*

Colour Plate 129. Small pottery bottle vase of unknown manufacture and date. Beautifully painted with an arrangement of flowers by James Rouse senior. Signed on base. *Nicholas Gent Antiques.*

Colour Plate 130. King Street plate painted with a man and his dogs in a highland setting by James Rouse Senior. Signed on reverse 'James Rouse sen.'. Marks: Crown, crossed swords, dots and initials S and H. *Nicholas Gent Antiques.*

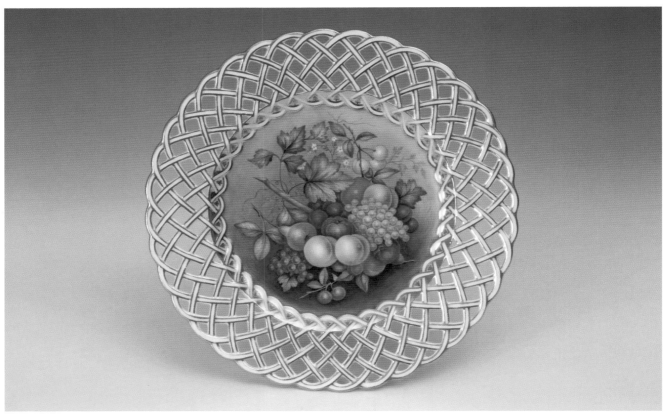

Colour Plate 131. King Street pierced plate painted with fruit by James Rouse senior. Signed on reverse 'J. Rouse. Sen.' Marks: Red crown over crossed swords and D with two sets of three dots and initials S and H. Diameter 9". *Private Collection.*

Colour Plate 132. Crown Derby plate painted by James Rouse senior. Signed on reverse 'James Rouse Senr'. Cypher mark for 1885. Impressed trefoil-potting mark for 1884. Diameter 9 in.

Colour Plate 133. Crown Derby Bute shaped coffee cup and saucer, eggshell china, with miniatures of children painted by James Rouse senior. Pattern 1599. Cup height 2¼ in, saucer diameter 4¼ in. Crown and D in red. Cypher for 1884. Assigned to J. Rouse in pattern book. *Royal Crown Derby Museum.*

Colour Plate 134a. Close up of portrait of James Rouse senior showing signature of *James Rouse junior.*

Colour Plate 134. Portrait of James Rouse senior painted by his son James junior. *Royal Crown Derby Museum.*

Colour Plate 135. Minton Plate c.1875. Painted by James Rouse junior. *Clive and Lynne Jackson.*

Colour Plate 136. Minton Plate c.1875. Painted by James Rouse junior. Part of a series entitled 'Kind Sisters'. *Clive and Lynne Jackson.*

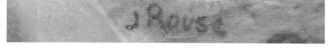

Colour Plate 137. Signature on Minton plate in Colour Plate 135.

Colour Plate 138. Wedgwood porcelain plate painted and signed by James Rouse junior. Marks: Black Wedgwood Portland Vase with printed Wedgwood beneath. Impressed Wedgwood and capital D. c.1878-1891. *Private Collection.*

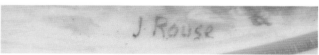

Colour Plate 138a. Signature on Wedgwood plate.

Colour Plate 139. Aynsley Plate decorated in Sèvres style by James Rouse junior. Marks: Impressed Aynsley. Diameter 8½ in. *Private Collection.*

Colour Plate 140. Porcelain plaque painted in Sèvres style. Signed and dated by James Rouse junior on scroll middle left. *Derby Museums and Art Gallery.*

Colour Plate 141. Porcelain plaque painted by James Rouse junior. Signed and dated on scroll held by right hand cherub. *Derby Museums and Art Gallery.*

Colour Plate 142. Coalport plate, part of a service supplied for the visit of the King and Queen of Sardinia in 1855. Please note similarity in painting to that of porcelain plaque in Colour plate 141. *Photograph courtesy of Ironbridge Gorge Museums Trust.*

Colour Plate 143. Porcelain plaque 1871. Painted with a pastoral scene by James Rouse junior. Signed and dated lower middle. *Seage Collection.*

Colour Plate 144. Porcelain plaque painted with cattle and signed by James Rouse senior. *William Allen Collection.*

Colour Plate 145. Crown Derby plate painted by Charles Rouse. Signed in capital letters C.ROUSE 1886. Impressed 'Derb'. *Private Collection.*

Colour Plate 145a. Reverse of plate showing signature and date.

Colour Plate 146. This was described at a sale in 1985 as 'Rare Derby plaque by William Rouse'. Dimensions: 9" X 12". The William Rouse referred to is most probably the son of Charles Rouse (see Colour Plate 145) who worked at the Crown Derby Works at Osmaston Road, starting in the 1880s. As William was born in 1872 and started at Osmaston Road in the 1880s, this plaque is most likely to be a Crown Derby plaque of this era. *Photograph Courtesy of Peter Jackson Antiques.*

had "derived inestimable benefit"; while there he had won the first prize for two years running at the Hanley Exhibition for students. Before joining Pinder, Bourne & Co, he had served an apprenticeship under the distinguished French Art Director Leon Arnoux.'

He was married to Clara Elizabeth Webb on 18th July 1867 at St. Paul's, Burslem, at which time he was described as an 'Artist'[8]. In about 1874, he succeeded his brother, Albert, at Pinder, Bourne & Co. Evidence supporting these statements comes from the 1881 census returns for Burslem, where he is described as a 'Potters Designer', aged 36, born in Derby and living with his wife Clara and three children, James, Isobel, and Joseph, at 208 Waterloo Road, Burslem[9].

Henry Doulton acquired the earthenware factory of Pinder, Bourne and Company in 1877, and in 1882 the name was changed to Doulton and Company, Burslem. In 1885, a new wing was added, and the manufacture of bone china was commenced. John Slater, who was the Artistic Director at Burslem between 1887 and 1914, invented a process by which lace was pressed into the stoneware body while still soft. It was then glazed, decorated and gilded with applied motifs. This is known as 'Chiné ware' or 'Doulton and Slater's Patent'.

[1] Civil Register, Marriages, June Quarter 1867, Derby, Volume 7b Page 698.

[2] 1881 British census RG11 2722/96 Page 10.

[3] Civil Register, Births, June Quarter 1872, Stoke-on-Trent, Volume 6b Page 231.

[4] 1881 British census RG11 2732/65 Page 9.

[5] 1881 British census RG11 2723/103 Page 42.

[6] 1901 British census RG13 2607/80 page 19.

[7] 1901 British census RG13 2607/76 page 12.

[8] Civil Register, Marriages, September Quarter 1867, Wolstanton, Volume 6b Page 108.

[9] 1881 British census RG11 2715/68 Page 34.

Colour Plate 150. Derby plate with central plant attributed to Edward Hopkinson junior and gilding attributed to Joseph Slater, by John Haslem. Marks: Printed Bloor ribbon in puce. Diameter 10½ in. *Derby Museums and Art Gallery.*

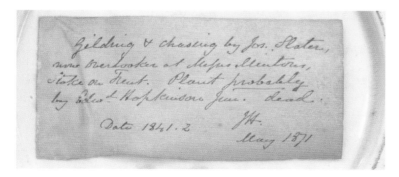

Colour Plate 150a. Reverse of above plate showing label with attributions by John Haslem, which reads: 'Gilding and chasing by Jos. Slater, now overlooker at Messrs Mintons, Stoke on Trent. Plant probably by Edw[d] Hopkinson Jun. dead.

Date 1841.2   JH

May 1871'

William Henry Slater

William Henry Slater was the son of Joseph Slater and the grandson of William Slater senior, both well-known gilders at the Derby manufactory.

He was baptised at Brookside Chapel Independent, Derby, on 2nd November 1834 and was reputed to be the last apprentice at the Nottingham Road factory, which would have been around 1845-46. Obviously, as the works closed in 1848, he would not have finished his apprenticeship there. Haslem, in his book *The Old Derby China Factory*, says, 'William, the eldest, when a boy, began his career at the Derby factory, and on its close painted for a short time at Messrs. Holmes', coach makers, of Derby. On leaving he also went into the Potteries, and, after a time, was employed at painting heraldry, &C., for Messrs. Minton and others'. If Haslem is correct then it was at Messrs. Holmes' that William finished his apprenticeship.

Scarratt, in his book *Old Times in the Potteries*, says of William Slater, 'He came to the Potteries and was a successful painter on porcelain in the style of the enamels of Limoges, for the firms of Samuel Alcock & Sons, of Burslem, also for Sir James Duke & Nephews at the same works, and he was very well represented at the exhibition of 1862 by a vase "Peace and War" designed by the late Mr. George Eyre, also a plaque, " Triumph of Venus", and other specimens of merit, along with work in arabesque and heraldic styles. He also painted the level with inserted plaques representing potting, used by Mr. Gladstone when laying the foundation stone of the Wedgwood Institute at Burslem, October 26th 1863, the whole, made and decorated by the firm of Sir James Duke & Nephews'. He goes on to say that Slater went to Mintons in 1864, where he painted for Mr. Arnoux in the style of Limoges enamel for the French Exhibition of 1867. After leaving Mintons he was manager of the decorative department for Harvey Adams & Co (this was also supported by Haslem, writing in 1875). He afterwards joined Taylor, Tunnicliff & Co., Eastwood, Hanley, and superintended the decorative department, where some very high-class lamps were made and painted. After this he went for a short time to Longton.

His second marriage took place on 23rd December 1878 when he was married to Mary Jane Forrester Billington at the parish church at Hartshill, Staffordshire[1]. At this time, he was described as a widower, living in Shelton, and his occupation was recorded as 'Designer'.

In the 1881 census returns for Shelton, he is described as a 'Designer and Earthenware Manufacturer', aged 46, born in Derby, and living with his wife, Mary Jane, and son, Albert William, at 48 Queen Ann Road, Shelton[2].

[1] Civil Register, Marriages, December Quarter 1878, Stoke-on-Trent, Volume 6b Page 273.

[2] 1881 British census RG11 2722/34 Page 9.

John Stanesby

John Stanesby was born on 3rd March 1786 and was baptised at All Saints, Derby on 11th March of that year. According to Haslem, in his book *The Old Derby China Factory*, 'at a very early age he was put to work at the old Derby china factory, where he served his apprenticeship to flower painting, attaining considerable proficiency in that branch of art. He more particularly excelled in the painting of roses, and was able to produce, with a few deft touches of his pencil, a seemingly elaborate representation of that lovely flower, with rapidity almost magical.'

If we extrapolate 'at a very early age', into say 10 years of age, we can assume that he started his apprenticeship in about 1796 and would have finished by 1803. Given what Haslem has to say about the interest taken in the apprentices by William (Quaker) Pegg in the second period of his work for Derby, I think that as a flower painter Stanesby would almost certainly have received instruction from him during Quaker Pegg's first period at the factory.

That John Stanesby was interested to further his career by private study is shown by an agreement with two of his colleagues, Joseph Bancroft and John Brewer, to purchase *The Cabinet of Arts* as a source book for their work[1].

Haslem goes on to say that, 'Feeling the daily routine of his labours at the china works irksome, and wishing for a wider field for the exercise of his talent, he, shortly after attaining his majority, removed to London, where he cultivated, as far as his opportunities would allow, his inclination for the higher branches of art'. Since he would have reached his majority, i.e. 21 years of age, in 1807, we can assume that he left sometime during 1807 or 1808.

Again we have to rely on Haslem for information concerning John Stanesby's early activities in London. I have no positive proof of what he says, although some secondary evidence of his stay in London is available. Subsequent evidence from parish records concerning his movements to and fro from London to Derby also give confidence in Haslem's information.

Referring to Stanesby's time in London, Haslem states, 'At this time he executed many beautiful specimens of china painting, and also practised extensively painting on glass. In glass painting he was for some time in partnership with an enterprising man named Backler, and the firm executed some ambitious works in the form of windows for public buildings, and also established public exhibitions of glass painting in London which were visited by many distinguished personages, including the allied sovereigns, in 1814 and also Prince Leopold (afterwards King of the Belgians).' Haslem then goes on to say that Stanesby subsequently took to the practise of portraiture, and was an occasional exhibitor at the Royal Academy prior to 1825 when he returned to Derby, where, for some years, he practised as a portrait painter.

I can find no references to his exhibiting at the Royal Academy. However, he may have exhibited at one of the other societies. That he was in London until at least 1821 is proved both by the birth of a daughter, Mary Anne, who was baptised at Fetter Lane Independent, London, on 22nd June 1817 and the birth of a son, John, who was born in 1819, but was christened on 29th March 1821 at Tottenham Court Road Independent, St. Pancras, London. In each case the parents were given as John Stanesby and Mary Eleanor.

That he had returned to Derby by 1825 is also proved by the birth of a daughter, Hannah Spencer, at Brookside Chapel Independent, Derby, on 13th October 1825. Again the parents were given as John Stanesby and Mary Eleanor. Several other children were born in Derby. A son, Joshuah, was baptised at Brookside Chapel Independent, on 4th May 1828. A further two sons, Samuel and Alexander, were born in 1830 and 1832 respectively. Unfortunately I have been unable to trace their baptisms in the parish registers at Derby, but they do appear in various other documents, such as the 1881 census returns, where their age and place of birth is given. (see further on in biography). There is also an entry in *Pigot & Co's National Commercial Directory, 1828-29, Derby Section* which reads, 'Stanesby John, (portrait painter) 1 North Parade'.

Again referring to his time in Derby, Haslem continues, 'He usually painted miniatures on ivory,

or heads of a larger size on paper, and sometimes he executed life-size portraits in oil. In 1832 on occasion of his eldest son (John Tatum), whom it had been his delight to train up in a love of art, obtaining a medal from the Society of Arts he returned with his family to London, where for several years he devoted himself chiefly to portraiture. One after another of his children became a successful competitor for the prizes offered by the Society of Arts in various departments of drawing and engraving.'

Haslem also says of John Stanesby's return to London in 1832, 'For several years Stanesby devoted much time and labour to an attempt to introduce an ingenious process of relief-engraving of his own invention, as a substitute, under certain circumstances for wood-engraving. While, however, he brought the process itself to a considerable state of perfection, he was not the man to grapple successfully with the commercial difficulties, which stood in the way of such an innovation. Very few specimens of the art were published, the principal being a series of maps issued by the late Charles Knight, who took great interest in Stanesby's experiments'.

According to *Kelly's Commercial Directory* in 1848, John Stanesby was living at 8 Robert Terrace, Chelsea, and was described as an 'Artist'. In the last few years of his life he was still fond of his art and delighted in producing bookmarks and other trifles decorated with his favourite flower. In the 1861 census for Chelsea he is described as an 'Artist Portraiture' and was living at 8 Elizabeth Street, Chelsea, with his wife, Mary, and his son, Henry. At the time of his death, in his 79th year on 18th December 1864[2], he was described as an 'Artist and Portrait Painter', and was living at the same address.

As well as obtaining medals from the Society of Arts, three of his sons had paintings exhibited at the Royal Academy and went on to have enduring careers as painters.

Joshuah, then aged 20 and described as a 'Painter', had two paintings shown in 1848: 'A Chelsea Pensioner' and 'An aged Sempstress'. These were exhibited from 8 Robert Terrace, Chelsea. In 1849, from 86 Warwick Street, Pimlico, he exhibited 'Evening', described as a domestic scene. 'The sun's last ray smiles on the window, and prolongs the day' (Crabbe). The second was described as 'A Portrait'. Finally, in 1850, from 14 Charlwood Place, Pimlico he exhibited 'A student in the Royal Academy'. There are several paintings, exhibited at the Royal Academy, attributed to Joshua Stanesby in 1821, 1822 and 1823, before he was born. These however, are probably wrongly entered in his name and are either by another Joshuah Stanesby or more probably should be attributed to his father John, and could be the missing exhibits described by Haslem. More research into this is necessary. Later, in the 1881 census returns, he is described as an 'Artist, Figure Subjects Painter', aged 53, born in Derby, living with his wife, Arabella, and his three children at 3 Miranda Road, Islington[3].

Alexander, then aged 16 and described as a 'Miniature Painter', exhibited two paintings in 1848, both described as 'Portraits'. These were exhibited from 8 Robert Terrace, Chelsea. In 1849 he exhibited two paintings, which again were portraits. The first was described as 'Portrait of an associate of the Society of Painters in Water Colours'. The other was described as 'George Lance Esquire'. These were exhibited from 1 York Place, Denmark Hill. In 1850, from the same address, he exhibited two more portraits, 'Portrait of a child' and 'William Powell Frith, Esq., A.R.A'. His last two exhibits, in 1853 and 1854 were from 13 Tachbrook Street, Pimlico in 1853 a portrait of 'William Samuel Woodin, Esq.', and in 1854 'Charles, son of Richard Martin, Esq.'. Later, in the 1881 census returns, he is described as an 'Artist Portrait Painter' aged 49, born in Derby, living with his wife, Henrietta, and his seven children at The Mount, Accrington, Lancashire[4].

Samuel, then aged 22 and described as a 'Painter', exhibited in 1850, from 14 Charlwood Place, Pimlico, 'A Portrait' and in 1853, from the same address, 'Cochin-China fowls'. Later, in the 1881 census returns, he is described as an 'Artist Portrait Painter', aged 51, born in Derby, living with his wife, Elizabeth, and his seven children at 20 Gowrie Road, Battersea, London[5].

John Tatum, who, according to Haslem, was John Stanesby's eldest son, was in his early life a wood engraver and won a medal from the Society of Arts. Haslem states, 'Mr. John Tatam Stanesby (who now holds an important commercial position in London), after some years' practice as a wood engraver, quitted the pursuit of art for that of literature, to which he had equally received a bias from his father's character and training, and became a contributor to the *Penny Cyclopoedia, Companion to the Almanac, Pictorial History of England*, and other works, chiefly in connection with mechanical science and the history of the useful arts'. Evidence, which gives credence to Haslem's information, is in an entry in *Kelly's Commercial Directory*, which describes him as a 'Bookseller, of Murray and

Stanesby'. He also exhibited a watercolour copy of a portrait of Richard II and five pen drawings at the Society of Artists between 1833 and 1834. Later, in the 1881 census returns he is described as an 'Actuary, Accounts', which agrees with Haslem's description of 'an important commercial position'[6].

[1] *Painters and the Derby China Works*, John Murdock & John Twitchett, Trefoil, 1987.

[2] Civil Register, Deaths, December Quarter 1864, Chelsea, Volume 1a, Page 177.

[3] 1881 British census returns, RG11 0257/54 Page 24.

[4] 1881 British census returns, RG11 4145/114 Page 26.

[5] 1881 British census returns, RG11 0645/97 Page 21.

[6] 1881 British census returns, RG11 0646/62 Page 2.

Thomas Steel

Thomas Steel was born in 1771 and was a native of Staffordshire[1]. He was an apprentice in the Potteries, where he also seems to have worked as a journeyman, early in his career. Evidence for this comes from the Burslem register, where both his marriage to Susanna in 1806, and the christening of his two sons Horatio and Edwin, in 1807, are recorded. Godden and Lockett, in their book *Davenport, China, Earthenware & Glass 1794-1887*, state:

'Tradition has it that Thomas Steel was apprenticed to, or worked at, the Davenport factory. He can hardly have been apprenticed there for he was about 23 when the Davenport pottery was established. He could certainly have decorated Davenport porcelains in the early years of the nineteenth century up to his leaving for Derby c.1815.' Unfortunately there is no evidence available to support this tradition, except for the fact that the family were certainly living in the right place, as in the later 1851 Derby census returns, his son Horatio's birthplace is given as Longport.

There has been much discussion about the extra 'e' on the end of his name. The register records his name and the names of his children at baptism as 'Steel'. It appears that his children added an extra 'e' for whatever reason.

Haslem states that he came to Derby in 1815. No records are available to verify this, but the fact that both his sons were apprenticed at the Derby factory tends to place him at Derby around this date. The birth of his daughter Eliza on 28th June 1826, at St. Peter's, Derby, suggests that he was still at the Derby factory at this time, thus making his stay in

Derby of at least 11 years' duration.

Godden, in his book *Minton Pottery and Porcelain of the First Period 1793-1850* states that after he left Derby, Thomas Steel worked for a short time at the Rockingham factory, and goes on to say that there is a signed tray in the Rotherham museum, painted by Steel, which bears evidence to this statement. It bears an early mark not used after 1830, which indicates that Steel left Derby sometime before this date. There is now evidence that supersedes these remarks. As can be seen from Colour Plate 160, this plaque is dated 1830. In fact, the earliest known dated Rockingham plaque by Thomas Steel is 1828[2]. Taken together, it seems that, according to the above evidence, he left Derby sometime between 1826 and 1828. There is also other evidence, which suggests that his son, Edwin, also left Derby at this time to accompany his father to Swinton.

He then joined the Minton factory on 17th March 1832 and stayed until his death in 1850. An entry in the *Staffordshire Advertiser*, of 5th November 1850 notes, 'Thomas Steele, Broad Street, Shelton, 18 years china painter at Minton, died 25th October, age 78'. Also, the returns for the Stoke-on-Trent census for 1851 show his wife, Susanna Steele, 'widow', living with a John Steele (son), and daughter Eliza, in Broad Street.

An interesting anecdote concerning this painter comes from the book *Old Times in the Potteries*, by William Scarratt, who says, about Thomas Steele, 'At one time it is said that he lived at one of the four cottages next to the Red Lion, Shelton. He there, in spring, cultivated a small bed of tulips. These would be protected by a covering from dust &c., but he generally exposed them to sightseers on Sundays'.

[1] He was probably the Thomas Steel registered as christened 22nd March 1772 at Burslem, but this is not certain.

[2] Plaque painted with white grapes and a peach by Thomas Steel and signed and dated 1828. Painted inscription in puce on the reverse states: To. Steel[sr] Pinx 1828/ Drawn from a Bunch of Grapes in the Hot House of Earl Fitzwilliam Wentworth House/ Yorkshire. Lit: *Rockingham 1754-1842*, Alwyn and Angela Cox, page 371, figure 323.

Colour Plate 151. Circular porcelain plaque painted by Thomas Steel with a bird perched on a group of fruit, very much in the style of George Complin, a painter at the Derby factory in the 18th century. Plaque in view 9 in diameter. *Harry and Valerie Cordwent Collection.*

Colour Plate 152. Large circular Derby plaque painted with a flower and fruit group by Thomas Steel. Diameter: 15½ in across largest point. *William Allen Collection.*

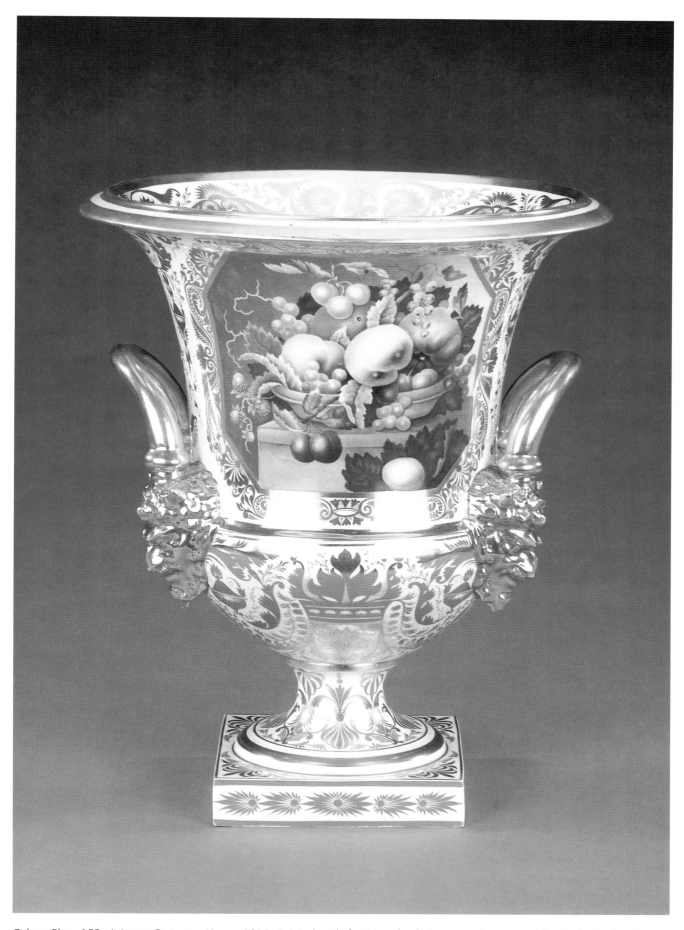

Colour Plate 153. A Large Campana Vase c.1815. Painted with fruit in a basket mounted on a marble plinth. Marks: Crown, crossed batons, dots, and D in red. Numeral 2 in red for the gilder James Clark.16½ in high, Diameter: 12½ in.
The Late Anthony Hoyte Collection. Photograph Courtesy Neales Auctioneers of Nottingham.

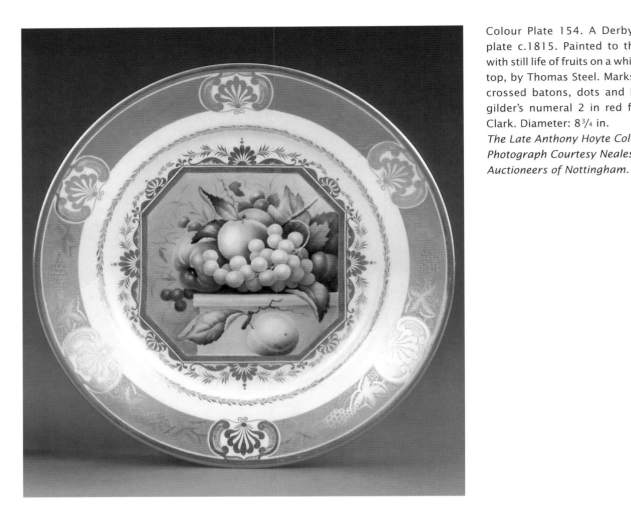

Colour Plate 154. A Derby dessert plate c.1815. Painted to the centre with still life of fruits on a white marble top, by Thomas Steel. Marks: Crown, crossed batons, dots and D in red, gilder's numeral 2 in red for James Clark. Diameter: 8³/₄ in.
The Late Anthony Hoyte Collection. Photograph Courtesy Neales Auctioneers of Nottingham.

Colour Plate 155. A Derby plate c.1815 painted overall with summer fruits by Thomas Steel. Marks: Crown, crossed batons, dots and D in red, gilder's numeral 2 in red for James Clarke. Diameter: 8³/₄ in.
The Late Anthony Hoyte Collection. Photograph Courtesy Neales Auctioneers of Nottingham.

Colour Plate 156. First of two rare Rockingham coffee cans side 1. Painted by Thomas Steel. Red griffin mark.
Bryan Bowden Antiques.

Colour Plate 156a. Rockingham coffee can side 2.
Bryan Bowden Antiques.

Colour Plate 157. Second Rockingham coffee can side 1. Painted by Thomas Steel. Red Griffin mark.
Bryan Bowden Antiques.

Colour Plate 157a. Rockingham coffee can side 2.
Bryan Bowden Antiques.

Colour Plate 158. Rockingham rectangular porcelain plaque painted by Thomas Steel with still life of various fruits and leaves on a shaded brown ground. This plaque was painted during his stay at the Rockingham works. *Bryan Bowden Antiques.*

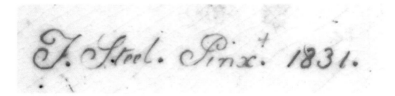

Colour Plate 158a. Reverse of previous plaque showing inscription.
Please note spelling of his name.

Colour Plate 159. Rockingham plaque painted with a bowl of fruit by Thomas Steel. Reverse of plaque has red griffin mark and inscription 'Steel Pinx: No 6.' *Bryan Bowden Antiques.*

Colour Plate 160. Rockingham porcelain plaque painted with flowers and fruit by Thomas Steel. Red griffin mark and inscription 'T Steel. Pinxt. 1830.' *Bryan Bowden Antiques.*

Colour Plate 161. Watercolour signed by Thomas Steel and dated 1837. Diameter: 9½ in This watercolour was painted during his time at the Minton factory. *Dr. John Freeman Collection.*

Colour Plate 162. Minton 'Dresden' Card Tray. Pattern 120 in the Minton pattern book, '16, 14 or 12 in. Scroll-edged oval tray with or without raised flowers'. Painted by Thomas Steel c.1840. Shown is the 12 in version. *Sam Collins collection.*

Colour Plate 163. Double handled Pembroke vase on plinth. Number 3 in the Minton Ornamental Design Book. Painted by Thomas Steel c.1835. Plinth 2³/₄ in wide, Height 10¹/₂ in. *Sam Collins Collection.*

Edwin Steele

Edwin Steele was the son of Thomas Steel, the Derby flower and fruit painter. He was born in 1805, and was christened at Burslem on 12th December 1807. He was apprenticed at the Derby factory around 1818 and would have completed his time by about 1825. According to Haslem, he was a clever flower painter and had inherited much of his father's talent.

He was married to Charlotte Laban at All Saints, Derby on 12th June 1826. At this time he is described as a 'China Painter', and was living at Morledge, Derby. It appears that he left the factory shortly after his marriage and accompanied his father, Thomas Steel, to Swinton in Yorkshire where he worked at the Rockingham factory.

Haslem states that after he left Derby, he worked at the Rockingham works at Swinton, and that in the Victoria and Albert museum there is a large vase, which was manufactured there and painted with flowers by Edwin Steele. Haslem further states that on leaving Swinton, he was employed at Mintons.

Recent evidence of his stay in Swinton comes from *The Rockingham Factory*, by Alwyn and Angela Cox, where Edwin Steele is found in the Militia Lists for 1827 and 1828. The precise length of his stay at Swinton is not clear. However, he was back in Derby by 1832, where his daughter, Sarah Anne, was christened at All Saints, Derby, on 4th November of that year, and at which time he is described as a 'China Painter'. As he is not in the list of workpeople at the factory in 1832, it is possible he was either not at the factory at the time the list was drawn up, or that although he returned to Derby, he failed to regain employment at the factory.

Soon after, he moved to the Potteries, where a son, Thomas, was christened at Stoke-on-Trent on 24th May 1835. There seems to be some doubt that it was the Minton factory that he moved to immediately, as Godden says that he is not in the 1831 to 1836 wages book, nor are there any documented examples of his work at Minton. On the other hand, Scarratt, in his book *Old Times in the Potteries,* says, when talking about his father, Thomas, 'Mr. Thomas Steele was employed at Minton. His son Edward *(sic)* was at Alcock's at the Hill Pottery, Burslem'.

He continued, however, to work in the Potteries and in May 1839, his son, Edwin, was born at Shelton. He is next found in the 1851 Stoke census, living at 50 Keelings Lane, with his wife Charlotte, and five children, and is described as an 'Artist'. He was still working in the Potteries in 1861 and is again mentioned in the 1861 census returns. He

Colour Plate 164. Porcelain plaque monogrammed 'E S'. *Derby Museums and Art Gallery.*

Colour Plate 165. Porcelain plaque Monogrammed 'E S'. *Derby Museums and Art Gallery.*

died on 25th August 1871, at the age of 66[1] (age given on certificate, 64). At his death his address was given as 26 Broom Street, Hanley, and his occupation as a 'Potters Painter'.

His son, **Edwin**, who was to follow his father's profession, was married to Elizabeth Walker on 8th September 1859[2]. At this time he was described as a 'China Flower Painter', living at High Street, Hanley. Subsequently, in the 1861 census for Staffordshire, and later, in the 1881 census returns he is described as an 'Artist (Painter)', living with his wife Elizabeth and six children at 57 Peel Street (late Regent Street), Stoke-on-Trent[3]. His son, **Edwin J**, is described as a 'China Painter'.

1. Civil Register, Deaths, Stoke-on-Trent, September Quarter 1871, Volume 6b, Page 110.
2. Civil Register, Marriages, Stoke-on-Trent, September Quarter 1859, Volume 6b, Page 295.
3. British Census 1881 RG11 2720/132 Page 28.

Colour Plate 166. Porcelain plaque painted with a fruit arrangement on a table by Edwin Steele senior. Dimensions: 8 in X 10 in.
Sam Collins Collection.

Colour Plate 167. Rockingham Vase of urn shape painted with a continuous band of strawberries by Edwin Steele. Red Griffin mark c.1826-32.
Rotherham Libraries, Museums and Arts Service.

Colour Plate 168. Rockingham leaf moulded comport painted by Edwin Steele c.1826-32. Red griffin mark. 10 in wide at top, height 6 3/4 in. *Sam Collins Collection*.

Colour Plate 168a. Close-up of one of four panels of above comport showing detail of flower painting.

158

Colour Plate 169a. Signature on bottom right of plaque.

Colour Plate 169. A finely enamelled floral study on a bone china plaque signed and dated E.Steele 1838. The back of this plaque remains unglazed and bears no manufacturers mark. 6½ in high, 7½ in wide. *Private collection.*

Colour Plate 170. Close up of centre of Primrose Leaf moulded Dessert Plate painted by Edwin Steele. 9½ in Diameter. Red Griffin mark. Note similar technique used on plaque and plate to place second rose into background by using a thin ivory wash. *Private collection.*

159

Colour Plate 171. Watercolour of flowers signed by Edwin Steele junior. Height 11 in, Width 7½ in. *Dr John Freeman Collection.*

Colour Plate 175. Spill vase c.1835-48. Painted with a flower group probably by Horatio Steele. Marks: Crown over Gothic D. height 4 in, diameter 2 in. *Dr. John Freeman Collection.*

the second Mr. William Duesbury of the Derby china works), in conjunction with a Mr. Tunnicliffe, commenced an earthenware (yellow ware) manufactory at the Hay, Burton-on-Trent. Later on the manufacture of china or "artificial marble" was commenced; **workmen having been brought from the Potteries and from Derby.**' The project was a failure and the works lasted only a few years.

He appears to have returned to the Derby factory sometime before 1841, as Haslem says that he painted the dessert service, which was made for Queen Victoria in 1841 and '42. He is found in the 1841 Derby census returns, where he was living in Sidalls Lane, with his wife, Mary, and daughter Susannah. At this time he was described as a 'China Painter'. He is later found in the 1851 Derby census returns, where he is again described as a 'China Painter', and was still living at Sidalls Lane. This raises the possibility that he painted at the King Street factory.

At sometime after this date he moved to the potteries, where he died at 21 Derby Street, Hanley, on 14th February 1874, at which time he was described as a 'Potters Painter'[1].

[1] Civil Register, Deaths, March Quarter 1874, Stoke-on-Trent, Volume 6b Page 106.

Thomas Till

Thomas Till was born in Darlaston, Warwickshire and was christened at St. Phillip's, Birmingham, on 8th January 1782. He was probably apprenticed, as an enameller, to one of the establishments in the Birmingham area, as he is described as a 'Painter and Enameller' in the register at his later marriage.

He was married to Hester Cheeseman at All Saints, Derby on 28th April 1819 and would therefore, presumably, have been in Derby for some time prior to this date. Haslem states that Till 'worked at the old factory for several years prior to 1820'. Since his gilder's number, 33, is given in the list, which Haslem says was produced in about 1820, he was probably working at Derby at least until this time.

By 1831, and probably earlier, Thomas Till was working at Mintons. According to Geoffrey Godden, in his book *Minton Pottery and Porcelain of the First Period*, his name is mentioned in the 1831-32 entries in the estimate book, which suggests that he was their leading gilder at that time and further suggests that he had been working for them for some time prior to 1831. Godden also says that his name occurs under the heading 'Painters and Gilders' in the Minton wages book, during the whole period covered by that book, i.e. from October 1831 to November 1836. He is also found in both the 1841 and 1851 Staffordshire census returns, where he is described as a 'Pottery Gilder' in the first and a 'China Gilder', aged 69, in the latter, where he was living at Sun Street, with his wife Esther *(sic)*.

He died on 1st April 1858, at the age of 75 years[1]. At this time he was living at 63 Sun Street, Shelton, and was described as a 'China Gilder'.

[1] Civil Register Deaths, June Quarter 1858, Stoke upon Trent, Volume 6b Page 99.

Colour Plate 176. A Derby shaped rectangular tureen and cover. Painting attributed to George Robertson, gilding by Thomas Till c.1818. Marks: Crown over D in red, gilder's numeral 33 in red for Thomas Till. 8½ in X 10 in, 6 in high.
The Late Anthony Hoyte Collection. Photograph courtesy Neales Auctioneers of Nottingham.

Colour Plate 177a. Reverse of vases showing the raised and tooled gilding by Thomas Till.

Colour Plate 178. Pair of Minton 'Rutland vases' on lion's paws feet with floral panels painted by Thomas Steel. Number 21 in Minton design book c.1835. Marks: + sign on a circle in gold. Height to top of handles 7½ in. *Sam Collins Collection.*

Colour Plate 178a. Reverse of vases showing raised and tooled gilding by Thomas Till.

William Timmis

William Timmis is first found in Derby in 1811, when he was married to Mary Bateman at Duffield on 25th May 1811.

The couple's first child, Marianne, was christened at St. Peter's, Derby, on 2nd March 1812. At the christening of their second child, a son, Francis, on 25th April 1814, he was described as a 'China Painter', and was living at Burton Road. The couple had four further children christened at St. Peter's, Derby, between the years 1816 and 1823, where he was described as a 'China Painter', and the family were living firstly at Spring Gardens and then at Eagle Street. As he is not in the list of workpeople at the factory, in 1832, he must have left before this time.

It is not known if this workman was a gilder or a painter, but as he worked at the factory for at least 12 years he must have decorated many articles, which are yet to be discovered.

Joseph Torkington

Joseph Torkington was born in Derbyshire in 1787, and was apprenticed at Derby as a gilder around 1799 and would have finished his time by 1806.

He married Elizabeth Saunders on 12th September 1808 at Duffield, and his first child, William, was christened at St. Alkmund's, Derby on 20th October 1811. Two further children were then christened at St. Peter's, and then on 19th February 1818, his fourth child, Thomas Joseph, was christened at St. Alkmund's, Derby. At this time he was described as a 'China Painter', and was residing at Bridge Street, where he remained until at least 1819. Between 1824 and 1827, two further children were christened at All Saints, Derby. All of the above suggests a long career (at least from 1806 to 1827) at Derby, which does not seem to have been recognised by previous research.

By 1831, Joseph Torkington had moved to Mintons, where he is found in the Summary of Staff

Colour Plate 179. Derby shell-shaped dish painted by Richard Dodson. Gilded by Joseph Torkington. Marks: Crown, crossed batons, dots and D in red, gilder's numeral 7 in red for Joseph Torkington c.1815. 9³/₄ in X 9¹/₄ in. *The Late Anthony Hoyte Collection. Photograph Courtesy Neales Auctioneers of Nottingham.*

in October of that year. He continues to appear in the wages book, under 'Painters and Gilders', until November 1836. As this is the only wages book preserved at Minton he could, of course, have stayed for a longer period.

He is later found in the 1851 census for Stoke, where he is described as a 'Gilder', aged 64, living at Broad Street, with his sons, Joseph and Arthur, who are both 'Potters'.

As he was employed at Derby at an early date (possibly in the eighteenth century), and remained until at least 1827, the gilder's number 7 (taken over from William Billingsley) will identify his work when found on items during this period.

William Walplate

William Walplate was baptised at St. Michael's, Derby, on 16th November 1784. He was almost certainly apprenticed at the Derby factory as a potter and turner. This would probably have been in about 1796, and he would have finished his time around 1801.

He was married to Anne Rayer at Duffield, Derbyshire, on 25th December 1803. He had several children baptised at both St. Michael's and All Saints churches in the years immediately after his marriage. However, it is not until the year 1822 that his occupation is partly revealed[1], as it was at the baptism of his daughter, Eliza, at St. Michael's, Derby, on 10th November 1822, that he was described as a 'China Man'. At this time he was living at Bag Lane. Later, at the baptism of his son, John, at St. Alkmund's, Derby, on 6th February 1825, he is described as a 'China Potter' and was then living at Darley Lane. At the baptism of a daughter, Elizabeth, on 8th June 1829, again at St. Alkmund's, he was described as a 'China Turner', and was still living at Darley Lane. He continued to work at Nottingham Road and is next found in the list of workpeople at the factory, in 1832.[2]

Further evidence, confirming his continued employment at the factory, is the entry in the 1841 census for Derby. In this he is again described as a 'China Turner', living with his wife Ann and four of their children at 22 Goodwin Street. He was still at the factory in 1845, when he is once again described as a 'China Turner' at the wedding of his son, John, at All Saints, Derby, on 12th January of that year.

He almost certainly carried on working at Derby until the closure of the factory, in 1848. He may also have worked at the King Street factory as, at the wedding of his daughter, Elizabeth, which took place at St. Alkmund's, Derby, on 20th May 1850, he is again described as a 'China Turner'.

From the evidence it seems that this workman had a long career at the Nottingham Road factory, and was probably responsible for the quality of the finished articles of turned 'useful ware', used by the painters and gilders as the canvas for their work.

[1] There were also two children, William, born 13th April 1815, and James, born 17th May 1817, that were not registered until 14th December 1828. Their baptisms took place on this latter date at St. Michael's, Derby, when he is described as a 'China 'Potter'.

[2] The entry actually states 'William Walklate', but this is consistent with the difficulties encountered when tracing this man's family and career. The spelling of his name has many versions in the registers at the baptisms of his children, his marriage and the entry in the census returns. However, I am confident that the information reproduced here is correct.

Moses Webster

Moses Webster was the son of Robert Webster and Elizabeth (née Bentley) and was born in Derby, and baptised at St. Werburgh's Church on 10th October 1792. He was apprenticed at Derby sometime around 1804, and would have completed his time by 1811.

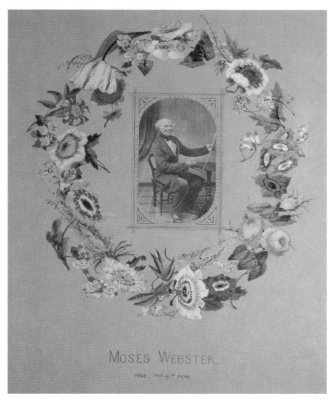

Colour Plate 180. Carte-de-visite of Moses Webster. *Royal Crown Derby Museum.*

Colour Plate 181.
Pencil sketch by
Moses Webster of
Darley Grove.
Dimensions:
Height 5 in.
Length 5 ½ in On
the reverse is a
poem lamenting
the 'Fall of Darley
Grove November
27th 1820'.
*Dr. John Freeman
Collection.*

Colour Plate 182.
Derby from
Darley Grove.
Transparent
watercolour.
Signed verso and
inscribed 'Darley
Grove by Moses
Webster, Derby'.
Dimensions: 7 in
X 7 in. This view
of Darley Dale
was painted later
than the previous
example, as can
be seen from the
absence of many
of the trees.
*Royal Crown
Derby Museum.*

Haslem states that 'in early life he was away from Derby for a few years, during which he worked in London and Worcester. While in the latter city he received instruction in drawing from Baxter, who, Mr. Binns says, had a School of Art there from 1814 to 1816.'

As Moses Webster's wife, Jane, was born in Derbyshire[1], and his first child, Jane, was baptised at All Saints, Derby, on 16th July 1816, it is possible that he was away from Derby in two separate periods. The most likely period that he was in London was between 1817 and 1820, when he is said to have worked for Robins and Randall, and painted on Nantgarw porcelain. During this time, no children were baptised in Derby between 16th July 1816, when he was living at Bold Lane, and 31st May 1820, when, at this latter date, the baptism of his son Frederick Thomas, he was registered as living at Kensington Street, Derby. Possible supporting evidence for his time in London during this period, is an entry in Graves, *A Dictionary of Artists 1760-1893*, where a "Webster M" exhibited 3 watercolours of flowers at the Old Water Colour Society in 1818, from an address in London. This, taken together with the fact that he was a member of a London watercolour association, (see following advertisement), seems to support Haslem's assertion.

His next child, a son, Frederick (Frederick Thomas must have died shortly after birth), was baptised at St. Werburgh's on 1st June 1822, at which time he was described as a 'China Painter', still residing in Kensington Street.

Haslem also states that on Webster's return to the Derby works, he painted flowers and occasionally birds, until 1826. A slightly earlier date is indicated by an advertisement in the *Derby Mercury* dated 13th July 1825:

Mr. Webster,
Flower Painter,
Castle Street, Derby.
Member of the Spring Gardens Association of
Water Color Painters London.

Respectfully informs the Nobility and Gentry of Derby and its Vicinity, that he has commenced Teaching the Art of Flower Painting, of which he flatters himself that he has a perfect knowledge, and begs to refer them to specimens of his abilities, which are close copies of nature, and may be seen at the Mercury and Reporter Offices; and Mr. Moseley's, Corn Market.

The most sedulous attention, joined to a practical and intimate Knowledge of the above Art, will, he hopes, secure to him the favor and Patronage of all who may honor him with their commands.

Colour Plate 183. Marvel of Peru *(Mirabilis Jalapa)* Transparent watercolour painted by Moses Webster. Signed lower left.
10¾ in X 9 in.
Royal Crown Derby Museum.

Colour Plate 184. Morning Glory *(Ipomoea Caerulea)*. Transparent watercolour. Signed verso by Moses Webster. 9 in X 6¾ in. *Royal Crown Derby Museum.*

Colour Plate 185. Fruit basket c.1820-25. 'Trotter' pattern. Painted by Moses Webster. Dimensions: 11 3/4 in x 9 1/4 in x 4 in height. Marks: Crown, crossed batons, dots, and D in red, 90 in red to footrim. The Late Anthony Hoyte Collection.
Photograph Courtesy Neales Auctioneers of Nottingham.

There is also the evidence from the baptismal register, where on 1st June 1823 a son, Charles, was baptised at St. Werburgh's, and at that time Moses Webster was described as a 'China Painter'. However, when his next son, Henry, was baptised on 3rd May 1826 he was described as a 'Portrait Painter', now living at Castle Street. When subsequent children were baptised between the years 1828 and 1833 he was described as an 'Artist', and had moved firstly to George Street and then to Wilmot Street. He appears in *Pigot & Co's Directory of Cheshire, Cumberland, Derbyshire, etc 1828-29* under a section entitled 'Professors and Teachers' as 'Webster Moses (Drawing) 7 George Street' and again in the *Directory of the County of Derby 1829* under two sections, 'Artists' and 'Drawing Masters' as 'Webster Moses, fruit and flower painter, George Street'. In the 1835 *Pigot's Directory of Derbyshire*, he is listed under 'Artists' as 'Webster Moses (painter) 6 Wilmot Street'.

He is next found in the 1841 census returns for Derby, living at number 4 Derwent Row with his wife, Jane, and his seven children. In these returns he is described as a 'Drawing Master'. Both he and his wife, Jane, are shown as having been born in Derbyshire. As he is listed in both *Pigot's Directory of Derbyshire, Dorset, etc 1842* and *Slater's Directories of Important English Towns, 1847*, under 'Artists' at 6 Wilmot Street, he must either have moved back to this address or the address was now just an artists studio.

By 1858 he had moved to Nottingham and is listed in *Wright's Nottingham Directory, 1858*, where the entry reads 'Webster Moses teacher of drawing and Miss Sophia, school, Derby Road'. Sophia was his youngest daughter, and was born in 1831.

He died on 20th October 1870, aged 78, at his home, Liversage Alms Houses, London Road, Derby[1].

[1] Information taken from 1841 census returns for Derby. "Yes" in column for 'Born in County'.

[2] Civil Register, Deaths, December Quarter 1870, Derby, Volume 7b Page 274.

Samuel Webster

Samuel Webster was the elder brother of Moses Webster, the well-known Derby painter. He was christened at St. Werburgh's, Derby on 4th March 1789, and was apprenticed to the Derby manufactory as a potter, in about 1801. He would have finished his apprenticeship by about 1808.

He was married to Elizabeth Yeomans at Duffield on 17th June 1810. At the christening of the couple's second child, Ruth, at St. Michael's, Derby, he was described as a 'China manufacturer', living at Walker Lane. The couple had a further four children between the years 1816 and 1825, when he was described variously as a 'China manufacturer', a 'Turner in the Porcelain' *(sic)* and a 'Potter'. He continued to live in Walker Lane, until, in 1825, he is found in Bridge Gate.

He continued to work at the Derby factory and is in the list of workpeople at the factory, in 1832, under 'Potters'.

William Wheeldon

William Wheeldon was born on 19th December 1789, and was the nephew of William Billingsley. His mother, Anne (Rigley), was the sister of Sarah Rigley, who was married to Billingsley. In January 1801, at the age of eleven years, he went to Mansfield, where his uncle had a decorating establishment, to learn the art of flower painting. He stayed with him for only a short time, until the end of the year. He then returned to Derby, where he was apprenticed as a flower painter at the china factory.

Haslem, in his book *The Old Derby China Factory* says, 'He continued to work at the factory until 1823 and on leaving, he succeeded to a business in Bridge Gate, in the premises formerly occupied by Billingsley'.

This statement is interesting, as amongst the documentation that Haslem had in his possession were five mortgages, previously held by Billingsley, but sold by him between 1796 and 1805. It seems that Billingsley gradually sold all the property he held in Derby to his brother-in-law, William Wheeldon senior. In 1823, his son, who then left his employment at the factory, inherited these. The explanation as to why Haslem had access to so many of the letters and documents relating to William Billingsley is that he was the executor of William Wheeldon's will, when he died on his 85th birthday, on 19th December 1874.

He never married, and at his death his property and effects were shared amongst his nephews and nieces. One of the branches of the family was the Fletchers and in 1970, at a sale at Sotheby's, a Mr. Fletcher sold a garniture, made at the Pinxton factory.

In the week following his death a short obituary appeared in the *Derby Mercury*:

'In Mr. William Wheeldon, who sank quietly to rest on Saturday last, the 19th inst. (his 85th birthday), has passed away, with one exception, the oldest relic of the old Derby China Factory. As boy and man he worked there a little over twenty years, leaving about 1823, when he succeeded to a small retail business in the town. Several specimens of his work on Derby China, which were in the Fine Arts Exhibition in this town in 1870, proved that he possessed considerable merit as a painter of flowers, and in early life he had the advantage of receiving instruction in that branch of art from his uncle, William Billingsley, the most eminent of the Derby painters. Mr. William Wheeldon was much esteemed for his genial disposition; and to his temperate and regular habits, and his uniform moderation in all things, he was doubtless indebted for a long life and a painless death. He only kept his bed on the day he passed away. At the banquet given little more than a month ago to our late worthy Mayor, might have been seen the tall and manly form, military in its bearing, and unbent in the least by age, of the subject of this brief sketch, and it was not without enjoyment and a degree of justifiable pride that he mingled among those who were assembled to do honour to his nephew on the completion of his year of office.'

John Whitaker (Modeller)

John Whitaker was christened at All Saints, Derby on 20th March 1808, and was the grandson of Richard Whitaker, one of William Duesbury's first apprentices. He is entered at birth in the register as 'John Whitacre', and is the son of William Whitacre and Mary.

Haslem says that he started to work at Derby in 1818, at the age of eight, although he did not start his apprenticeship until 23rd February 1821. His apprenticeship was for 8 years and one month (bringing him to the age of twenty-one), and he was to learn the art of repairing porcelain.

He was married to Edna Mountford, the daughter of Thomas Mountford, the Derby enamel kilnman, at All Saints, Derby, on 2nd February 1829. Five children were born to the couple between the years 1829 and 1840, all christened in Derby (the entries in the register at these times state 'John Whitaker'). At the baptism of their first child, Eliza, at St.

Werburgh's, on 18th May 1829, the entry in the register records him as a 'China Modeller', living at Cross Lane.

In 1830 he succeeded Samuel Keys as the manager of the ornamental department, and in the 1832 list of workpeople at the factory, he is recorded as Overlooker of the Figure Makers, called ornamental repairers. He is next found in the 1841 Derby census, listed as a china modeller, living at 26 Erasmus Street. After the death of James Barlow, in 1842, he became the foreman of the whole potting department until the factory closed in 1848.

In a Memorial to John Whitaker, written by John Haslem (see Colour Plate 185), he says, 'On the close of the old works he remained in Derby some years, and will still be remembered by many as the keeper of a shop for the sale of china and earthenware, in Victoria Street. About fifteen years ago, he went into the Staffordshire Potteries, where he was employed as a figure maker at Messrs. Mintons celebrated establishment at Stoke upon Trent, until the Christmas of 1872, when he was compelled, from failing health to relinquish his employment'.

Evidence, which supports these statements, is found in the 1849 *Glovers Directory for Derby*, where he is listed as a 'China, Earthenware and Glass Dealer', with a warehouse (shop) in Victoria Street. He does not appear in the 1851 census for Derby in Victoria Street. There is, however, an entry for his wife, so it would appear that he was elsewhere the evening of the census. The entry records that Edna Whitaker, aged 42, was born in Burslem, Stafford-

Colour Plate 186. A Peacock modelled by John Whitaker c.1830. Length 6 1/2 in, Width 4 in, Height 6 1/4 in. *William Allen Collection.*

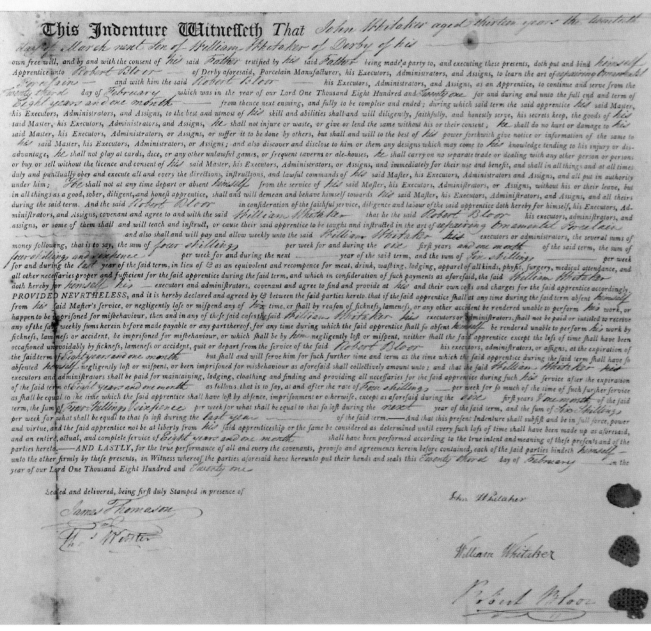

Colour Plate 187. Composite containing the indenture of John Whitaker, a likeness, presumed to be Whitaker, and a Memorial by John Haslem. *Royal Crown Derby Museum.*

shire, and was a 'China Dealer', living in Victoria Street with her eight children, all of whom were born in Derby. He next appears in the *1857 Whites Directory for Derby*, and the entry reads 'John Whitaker, Glass China and Earthenware Dealer, 29 Victoria Street'. However, the family doesn't appear in the 1861 census returns for Derby, at the Victoria address, so it is surmised that they had left for the Potteries by this time.

After leaving Derby, he was employed by Messrs. Mintons at Stoke-on-Trent for about eleven years. He died, two years after his retirement, at Fenton on 2nd October 1874. At this time he was described as a 'Potter (figure maker)' aged 67, and his address was given as 6 Bridge Street, New Basin, Fenton.

John Whitaker (Gilder)

John Whitaker was christened at St. Werburgh's, Derby, in 1784. This probably means that he started his apprenticeship around 1796, and had finished his time by 1803. Haslem says that he served his apprenticeship at the Derby works, and states that

he worked there until 1826, at which time there was a 'turnout' of the gilders and Japan painters. According to Haslem, 'He then joined George Cocker, and they had a small establishment in Friar Gate, Cocker making small figures, and Whitaker gilding and decorating china of a useful character, which was bought in the white for the purpose. This partnership lasted little more than a year'.

John Whitaker was married to Ann Stanesby on 11th December 1809 at St. Werburgh's, Derby. Six children were christened at Brook Street Chapel Independent, between 1810 and 1830, the last, Salome, being christened on 9th April 1830. This information seems to extend his stay in Derby by about 3 years. The gilder's numeral, used by him during his stay at Derby was 37.

He is stated by Godden to have worked at Mintons, from 1853 to 1855, as a figure maker. He says, correctly, that Whitaker was originally a gilder but that after his partnership with Cocker he turned his attention to figures. After leaving Mintons he is said to have modelled for several Staffordshire firms, including that of John Mountford.

Colour Plate 188. Derby Vase c.1813 gilded by John Whitaker. Marks: Crown, crossed batons, dots and D in red. 37 in red for the gilder John Whitaker. Height 13 in, Diameter 8³/₄ in. *Derby Museums and Art Gallery.*

Colour Plate 189. A Derby two handled chocolate cup painted by William Corden c.1815. Marks: Crown, crossed batons, dots and D in red, pattern 216 in red, gilder's numeral 37 in red for John Whitaker. Height 3 in. *Late Anthony Hoyte Collection. Photograph courtesy Neales Auctioneers of Nottingham.*

Colour Plate 189a. Reverse of chocolate cup.

John Whitaker (junior)

John Whitaker junior was the son of John Whitaker senior, who was a gilder at the Derby factory, and was baptised at Brookside Chapel Independent, Derby, on 9th May 1813. He was apprenticed at the Derby factory about 1825, and would have finished his time by about 1832.

Haslem, in his book *The Old Derby China Factory*, states, 'A son of Whitaker, also named John, when a youth painted at the old works, and on leaving was under Moses Webster for a short time. He afterwards went to London, but eventually removed to Manchester, where he resided for many years as a designer of patterns for muslin-de-laines and other similar fabrics. Many of his designs commanded a large sale. He died, somewhat suddenly, in Manchester in 1871.'

He is first found in the Manchester area on the occasion of his marriage. This took place on 9th July 1844 at the Independent Chapel, Rusholme Road, Chorlton upon Medlock, where he was married to Sarah Pegg[1]. On the marriage certificate he is described as a 'Pattern Designer', and was living at Welcombe Street, Hulme. His father's occupation was recorded as 'China Manufacturer'. His wife appears to be the daughter of William Pegg the Younger, as he is described in the document as 'William Pegg, Calico Printer'. Also the witnesses who attended the wedding were William Pegg and Mary Ann Pegg.

The couple's first child, a son, John William, was born in 1845[2]. Another child, a daughter, Sarah Ann, was born on 20th October 1847[3], at which time he was described as a 'Pattern Designer', and was living at 3 Blanchard Street, Chorlton upon Medlock. In the *1851 Slaters Directory for Manchester and Salford*, he is again listed as a 'Pattern Designer', living at Droylsden Road, Newton Heath. In the 1861 census returns for Chorlton and Medlock, he is described as a 'Calico Printer Designer', born in Darley, Derbyshire, living at 4 Arnott Street with his wife Sarah and his two children, John William, and Sarah Ann. He died in 1871.

[1] Civil Register, Marriages, September 1844, Chorlton, Vol 20 Page 165.

[2] Civil Register, Births, December 1845, Chorlton, Vol 20 Page 225.

[3] Civil Register, Births, December 1847, Chorlton, Vol 20 Page 223.

John Winfield (junior)

John Winfield was the son of John Winfield senior, a labourer at the Derby factory. He was christened at St. Werburgh's, Derby on 30th December 1812. He was apprenticed, as a gilder, at the Derby factory, in about 1824 and would have finished his time by about 1831.

He was married to Louisa Bircher at St. Alkmund's, Derby on 27th December 1834. The couple's first child, Sarah, was christened at St. Alkmund's, Derby on 10th May 1835. At this time he was described as a 'China Painter', living at William Street.

He is found in the list of workpeople at the factory, in 1832, under the 'gilders' department. He continued to work at Derby until at least 1842, as a daughter, Jane, was christened at St. Alkmund's, Derby on 15th December 1842. At this time he was described as a 'China Painter', then living at Erasmus Street. He almost certainly continued until the closure of the factory in 1848.

After the closure of the factory he moved to the Potteries, and is found there in 1855, where on 2nd December of that year his son, John, was born to his second wife, Elizabeth (née Mellor). At this time he was living at 12 Hanover Street, Shelton, and was described as a 'China Painter'.

He is found still living in the Potteries in the 1881 census returns for Stoke-on-Trent. He is described as a 'Potters Gilder', aged 68, and was living with his second wife, Elizabeth, at 42 Hope Street, Stoke-on-Trent.

He then appears to have moved back to Derby between 1881 and the time of the 1891 census. He is found in the Derby census returns, living at number 8 Sacheverell Street, with his wife Elizabeth. He returned to Derby to work at the Royal Crown Derby works at Osmaston Road, where his initials are often found on articles painted by Edwin Prince. There is also a gilded jug, illustrated in the recent book *Old Crown Derby China Works – The King Street Factory 1849-1935*, (page 197), indicating that these initials refer to a gilder. All of which evidence points to this being John Winfield.

He died on 12th October 1899, aged 87 years, at 146 Gerard Street, Derby, at which time he was described as a 'Gilder'.

Colour Plate 190. King Street saucer painted and signed by Edwin Prince with a view of Netherby Hall. Diameter 5½ in. *Dr. John Freeman Collection.*

Colour Plate 190a. Reverse of saucer showing monogram of the gilder John Winfield.

William Winfield

William Winfield was born in 1796, in Derbyshire. He was apprenticed at Derby as a figure maker in about 1807, and would have finished his time by 1814.

He was married to Sarah Jones at All Saints, Derby, on 14th August 1815. The couple's first child, James, was christened at All Saints, Derby, on 2nd October 1815. At this time he is described as a 'China Repairer', and was living at Walker Lane. A further four children were christened at All Saints between the years 1816 and 1825. During this time he was variously described as a 'China man' and 'China Repairer' and was still living at Walker Lane.

He died in March 1825. The *Derby Reporter* announced his death and spoke highly of his talent as a modeller, and stated that he left many specimens of his ability.

He left a young family, and indeed his last child, Frances, was born several months after his death. It is difficult to know how the family could have survived the loss of the main breadwinner, but seven years later, Sarah Winfield is found in the list of workpeople at the factory, where she is employed as a paintress.

John Wright

John Wright was born in Pinxton in 1778. Haslem says that he was on board a ship called the *Spitfire* at the battle of the Nile, on August 1st 1798. This, of course, means that his earlier career was spent in the Navy.

Although subsequent research has revealed that the *Spitfire* was not at the Nile, there was a ship with a similar sounding name, the *Swiftsure*, at that battle.

He returned to Pinxton sometime between 1798 and 1803, and was married to Mary Barras at Pinxton Parish Church on 8th February 1803. Three children were born to the couple, between the years 1805 and 1809, at which time he was working at the Pinxton China Factory. A document relating to the marriage of Samuel Blythe and Amy Barrows (sister to Mary Barras, Barras being a corruption of Barrows), where John was a witness to his sister-in-law's wedding, states that he was 'a workman at the Pinxton China Manufactory in the County of Derbyshire'.

His next child, Arthur, was christened at St. Alkmund's, Derby on 2nd November 1812. At the christening of his daughter, Mary, at St. Alkmund's, on 4th May 1815, he was described as a 'China facturer', living at Nottingham Road, Derby. An advertisement, which appeared in the *Staffordshire Advertiser* of Saturday 6th June 1812, may be the reason that John Wright moved to Derby from Pinxton at this time:

WANTED

A man who completely understands burning China in an earth kiln and muffle – A person of the above description will meet with constant employment and liberal treatment by application to Messrs. Robert Bloor & Co, Derby.

A good Figure and Flower painter wanted.

N.B. None need apply but such as can bring the work satisfactory references to character.

Although this advertisement appeared in Staffordshire, no doubt it also appeared in the *Derby Mercury* at the same time.

Haslem states 'John, the father of Arthur Wright, had been one of the Pinxton hands, and up to the time of his death, in 1819, was biscuit fireman at Derby. He had been on board the *Spitfire* at the battle of the Nile, for which he received a medal. On one occasion Sir Sidney Smith, under whom Wright served, visited the Derby works, when Wright, meeting his old Admiral in the factory yard, saluted him in such a manner that Sir Sidney knew he had been one of his men, and after asking to what ship he had belonged, gave him a guinea.'

The rather sad end to the tale was that John Wright, his wife, Mary, and their four-year-old daughter, Mary, all died within a few months of each other, in 1819.

Arthur Wright

Arthur Wright was christened at St. Alkmund's, Derby, on 2nd November 1812. He was the son of John Wright, the Derby biscuit fireman from 1812 to 1819. He was apprenticed at the Derby factory as a gilder, in about 1824. This date may actually be earlier as both his mother and father had died in 1819, when he was only seven years old, and he would have been brought up either under guardianship, or 'on the Parish'. By any account, he would have finished his apprenticeship by about 1831.

He was married to Priscilla Underwood at Duffield on 22nd January 1832. At this time he was working at the factory and is in the list of workpeople at the factory, in the gilders section. The couple's first child, John, was christened at All Saints, Derby, on 18ᵗʰ June 1832, where he is described in the register as a 'China Painter'.

He continued to work at the factory until at least 1836, as a son, Jesse, was baptised at All Saints, Derby on 29ᵗʰ December of that year. However, as he is not in the 1841 census for Derby, he must have left the factory before this date.

Haslem, in his book *The Old Derby China Factory*, states, 'Arthur Wright was a gilder, and also a painter of insects. He left Derby some years before the close of the works, and is now (1876) superintending the Encaustic Tile Works, at Messrs. Hollins (Minton and Hollins), Stoke-upon-Trent; he also makes colours for that establishment'. Some evidence which supports this statement comes from the 1881 census returns for Stoke-on-Trent, where he is listed as a 'Potters Manager', and was living with his daughter, Priscilla, and his granddaughter, Ann, at 12 Bath Street, Stoke upon Trent. From the date of his daughter's birth it is evident that he was in the Potteries by at least 1851.

His son Jesse obviously followed his father's profession, as when he is found in the 1881 census returns for Stoke-on-Trent, Jesse is described as a 'Manager Earthenware Decorative', and was living with his wife, Mary, and eight children at 5 Penkhull New Road, Stoke upon Trent.

APPENDIX A

Derby Painters Timeline

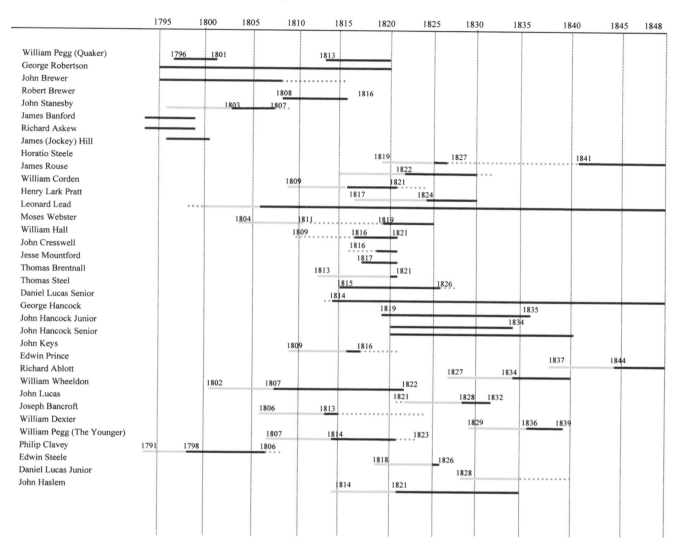

KEY

▬▬▬ At Derby

● ● ● Area of Uncertainty

▬▬▬ Apprentice

● ● ● Possibly working for Derby
& Outside interests

Derby Gilders Timeline

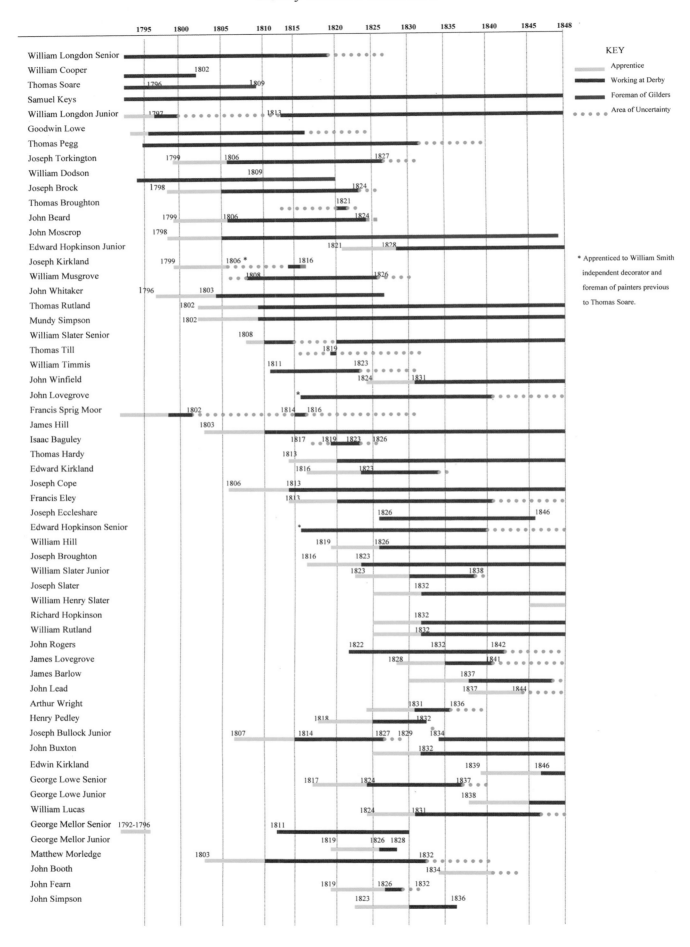

KEY
- Apprentice
- Working at Derby
- Foreman of Gilders
- Area of Uncertainty

* Apprenticed to William Smith
independent decorator and
foreman of painters previous
to Thomas Soare.

Derby Potters, Modellers and Kilnmen Timeline

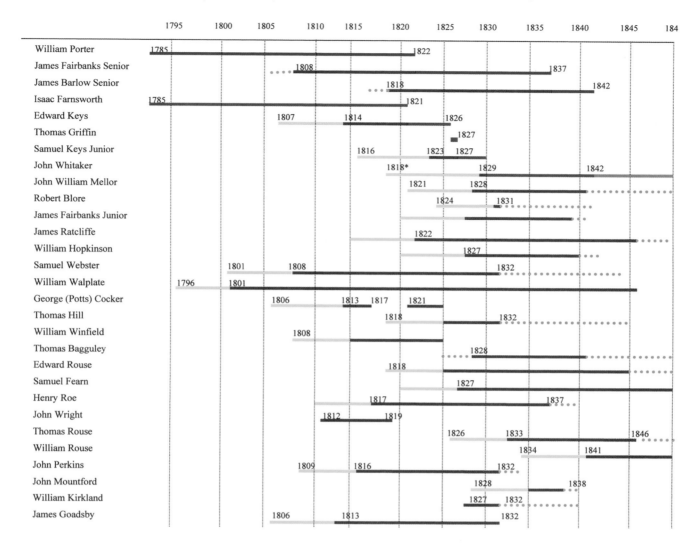

	1795	1800	1805	1810	1815	1820	1825	1830	1835	1840	1845	184
William Porter	1785					1822						
James Fairbanks Senior			1808						1837			
James Barlow Senior						1818				1842		
Isaac Farnsworth	1785					1821						
Edward Keys			1807		1814		1826					
Thomas Griffin							1827					
Samuel Keys Junior					1816		1823 1827					
John Whitaker						1818*		1829		1842		
John William Mellor						1821		1828				
Robert Blore							1824	1831				
James Fairbanks Junior							1822					
James Ratcliffe						1822					1845	
William Hopkinson							1827					
Samuel Webster		1801		1808				1832				
William Walplate	1796	1801										
George (Potts) Cocker			1806		1813 1817	1821						
Thomas Hill						1818		1832				
William Winfield			1808									
Thomas Bagguley							1828					
Edward Rouse						1818						
Samuel Fearn							1827					
Henry Roe					1817				1837			
John Wright				1812	1819							
Thomas Rouse							1826	1833			1846	
William Rouse									1834	1841		
John Perkins			1809		1816			1832				
John Mountford							1828		1838			
William Kirkland							1827	1832				
James Goadsby			1806		1813			1832				

* Worked at factory
at age 8 but did not start
apprenticeship until 1821.

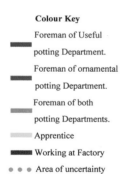

Colour Key

▬▬ Foreman of Useful
potting Department.

▬▬ Foreman of ornamental
potting Department.

▬▬ Foreman of both
potting Departments.

▬▬ Apprentice

▬▬ Working at Factory

● ● ● Area of uncertainty

APPENDIX B

Record Offices

All Births, Marriages and Deaths for Derbyshire, can be found at Derby Record Office, Matlock, Derbyshire DE4 3AG.

All Births, Marriages and Deaths for Staffordshire, can be found at Lichfield Joint Record Office, The Friary, Lichfield WS13 6QG.

All Births, Marriages and Deaths for Shropshire, can be found at Shropshire Records and Research Centre, Castle Gates, Shrewsbury SY1 2AQ.

All Births, Marriages and Deaths for Swinton by Sheffield can be found at Doncaster Archives, King Edward Road, Balby, Doncaster DN4 0NA.

All Births, Marriages and Deaths for Birmingham can be found at Birmingham City Archives, Chamberlain Square, Birmingham B3 3HQ.

All Births, Marriages and Deaths for Middlesbrough can be found at Teeside Archives, Exchange House, 6 Marton Road, Middlesbrough TS1 1DB.

All Births, Marriages and Deaths for Worcestershire can be found at Worcestershire Record Office, County Hall, Spetchley Road, Worcester WR5 2NP.

All Births, Marriages and Deaths for City of Westminster, Middlesex can be found at Westminster City Archives, 10 St. Annes Street, London.

Some initial tracing of Births, Marriages and Deaths can be done on-line at www.familysearch.org (The Church of Jesus Christ of Latter-Day Saints, but must always be checked at the relevant record office).

Civil Register Offices

Stoke-on-Trent Register Office, Town Hall, Hanley, Stoke-on-Trent ST1 1QQ. Tel: 01782-235260.

Derby Register Office, 9 Traffic Street, Derby DE1 2NL Tel: 01332-716020.

Nottingham Register Office, 50 Shakespeare Street, Nottingham NG1 4FP. Tel: 01159-475665 Ext. 21/23.

Newcastle-under-Lyme Register Office, 20 Sidmouth Avenue, The Brampton, Newcastle-under-Lyme, Staffordshire ST5 0QN Tel: 01782-297580.

Birmingham Register Office, 300 Broad Street, Birmingham B1 2DE Tel: 0121-2123421.

Wolverhampton Register Office, Civic Centre, St. Peter's Square, Wolverhampton WV1 1RU Tel: 01902-554989.

Middlesbrough Register Office, Corporation Road, Middlesbrough TS1 2DA. email: register@middlesbrough.gov.uk. Direct access to indexes: www.middlesbrough-indexes.co.uk.

Manchester Register Office, Heron House, 47 Lloyd Street, Manchester M2 5LE. Tel: 0161-2347878.

Worcester Registration District 29-30 Foregate Street, Worcester WR1 1DS. Tel: 01905-765350.

Shrewsbury Register Office The Shirehall, Abbey Foregate, Shrewsbury SY2 6ND. Tel: 01743-252925.

Borough of Telford & Wrekin Registration District, The Beeches, 29 Vineyard Road, Wellington, Telford TF1 1HB. Tel: 01952-248292. email: register.office@wrekin.gov.uk.

Bridgnorth Registration District, 12 West Castle Street, Bridgnorth, Shropshire WV16 4AB. Tel: 01746-762589.

Newcastle Register Office, Civic Centre, Newcastle upon Tyne NE1 8PS. Tel: 0191-2328520 Ext. 25089.

South Staffordshire, Civic Centre, Gravel Hill, Wolverhampton WV5 9HB, Tel: 01902-895829.

Stockton-on-Tees, Nightingale House, Balaclava Street, Stockton-on-Tees. TS18 2AL. Registration District & Census District 1852-1946 10a Tel: 01642-393939.

Kensington and Chelsea, Chelsea Old Town Hall, Kings Road, London. SW3 5EE, Tel: 0207 361 4100

Bury Register Office, Town Hall, Manchester Road, Bury, Lancashire BL9 0SW. Tel: 0161-2536026.

Burton upon Trent (East Staffordshire Register Office), Rangemore House, 22 Rangemoor Street, Burton upon Trent Staffordshire DE14 2ED. Tel: 01283-538701.

Leicester City Register Office, 5 Pocklingtons Walk, Leicester LE1 6BQ, Tel: 0116-2536326.

Hammersmith & Fulham Registration District, Fulham Town Hall, Harwood Road, London SW6 1ET. Tel: 0208-7532140.

Ramsgate Area, Register Office, Aberdeen House, 68 Ellington Road, Ramsgate, Kent CT11 9ST. Tel: 01622-772705.

Census Locations

Census returns for Stoke-on-Trent: Hanley Library, Bethesda Street, Hanley, Stoke-on-Trent.

Census returns for Worcestershire: Worcester Library and History Centre, Trinity Street, Worcester WR1 2PW.

Census returns for Derbyshire: County Hall, Matlock, Derbyshire DE4 3AG. Tel: 01629-580000.

Census returns for Shropshire: Shropshire Records and Research Centre, Castle Gates, Shrewsbury, SY1 2AQ.

Census returns for Middlesex (London area): Westminster City Archives, 10 St. Annes Street, London.

Census returns for Chelsea: Chelsea Local Studies, Chelsea Library, Old Town Hall, King's Road, London SW3 5EZ. Tel: 0207-3526056.

Census returns for Swinton by Sheffield: Archives and Local Studies Service, Central Library, Walker Place, Rotherham S65 1JH.

1881 census returns for England and Wales: On-line via www.familysearch.org

BIBLIOGRAPHY

1. *The Old Derby China Factory*, Haslem J., George Bell, 1876.

2. *Derby Porcelain 1748-1848 An Illustrated Guide*, Twichett, J., Antique Collectors Club, 2002.

3. *Minton Pottery and Porcelain of the First Period*, Godden, G., Herbert Jenkins, 1968.

4. *Coalport and Coalbrookdale Porcelains*, Godden, G., Herbert Jenkins, first published 1970, 1981 edition.

5. *Painters and the Derby China Works*, Murdock, J & Twitchett, J., Trefoil, 1987.

6. *Davenport Pottery and Porcelain 1794-1887*, Lockett, T.A., David & Charles, Newton Abbott, 1972.

7. *Rockingham 1745-1842*, Alwyn & Angela Cox, Antique Collectors Club, 2001.

8. *Ceramic Art of Great Britain*, Jewitt, Llewellyn, Virtue & Co, 1878.

9. *Coalport 1795-1926*, Michael Messenger, Antique Collectors Club, 1995.

10. *Old Times in the Potteries*, William Scarratt, first published 1906, and republished by S.R. Publishers Ltd, 1969.

11. *When I was a Child*, Charles Shaw, first published 1903 and republished by Caliban Books, 1977.

12. *Davenport China, Earthenware & Glass 1794-1887*, T.A. Lockett and G.A.Godden, Barrie & Jenkins, 1989.

13. *Royal Crown Derby*, John Twitchett and Betty Bailey, Antique Collectors Club, 3rd Edition 1989.

14. *Victorian Porcelain*, Geoffrey A. Godden, Herbert Jenkins Ltd, London 1961.

15. *The Doulton Burslem Wares*, Desmond Eyles, Barrie and Jenkins Ltd, 1980.

16. *Shelley Potteries – The History and Production of a Staffordshire Family of Potters*, Chris Watkins, William Harvey and Robert Senft, Barrie and Jenkins Ltd, 1980.

17. *The Pottery That Began Middlesbrough*, Mary Williams, C Books, 1985.

18. *Wedgwood Ceramics 1846-1959. A new Appraisal*, Maureen Batkin, Richard Dennis, London, 1982.

19. *Old Crown Derby China Works – The King Street Factory 1849-1935*. Robin Blackwood & Cherryl Head, Landmark Publishing Ltd, Ashbourne, Derbyshire, 2003.

20. *Victorian Stained Glass*, Martin Harrison., Barrie and Jenkins, London, 1980.

21. *Ceramics of Derbyshire 1750-1975*, H.G. Bradley, Bradley, 1978.

22. *Crown Derby Porcelain*, F.B. Gilhespy, Lewis, 1952.

23. *Derby Porcelain*, F.B. Gilhespy, MacGibbon & Kee, 1961.

24. *Spode – Copeland – Spode; The Works and its People 1770-1970*, Vega Wilkinson, Antique Collectors Club, 2002.

25. *A Dictionary of Artists 1760-1893*, Algernon Graves, F.S.A., 3rd Edition 1901, republished by Kingsmead Reprints, Bath, 1973.

INDEX TO ILLUSTRATIONS

INDEX